SMUG PUN

More short tales about long odds

David Atkinson

PREFACE

Picking up the dysfunctional threads of the original Mug Punting opus, this second collection of real-life racing and sporting yarns meanders haphazardly through ten more years of furiously celebrated small time gambling adventures.

Since that first volume, the blog site *Mug Punting* has become established as an outlet for racing, sport and betting rambles, together with a ridiculous array of general escapist nonsense, bellyaching and disturbing trend towards telltale middle-aged grumpiness. Time marches on…

The blog has implausibly gathered a loyal troupe of curious visitors, to whom I am massively grateful. Many of those posts provide the source for the stories here, and have been expanded and edited into new tales that are set against the backdrop of a decade of horse racing and other iconic sporting moments.

ABOUT THE AUTHOR

David was born in Yorkshire in the mid-60's and developed a passion for racing in his formative years around some of the finest tracks in England.

He moved to London after graduating, primarily to see more of the bands he loved whilst harbouring a quiet ambition to become a heavy-metal lead guitarist. Cursed with no musical ability whatsoever, he instead pursued a half-hearted career in the Civil Service.

Mug Punting: Short tales about long odds was published in 2012. Smug Punting is the follow up.

David now lives in Hertfordshire with his wife and two daughters.

CONTENTS

1. SILENT AUCTION

The profession of book writing makes
horse racing seem like a solid, stable business.
John Steinbeck, Newsweek, 1962

My mate Nick was to blame. Nick and a school Summer fair. Such events tend to follow a tried and tested formula: parents donate wine, beer, food, chocolates and toiletries to the school and then pay exorbitant raffle ticket prices to win them back. They help their offspring create variations of throw/guess/dip games to win sweets/stickers/cakes. If they are lucky, amongst the tat, broken toy and homemade gift stalls, parents will stumble upon a bar and a hot-dog stand. This isn't criticism. School associations need to raise cash and parents rise to their responsibilities with a mixture of resigned stoicism and secret pleasure.

Nick pitched up at just such an event to support his son's school one boiling Saturday afternoon. Amongst the 'find the lolly in the frogspawn' tables and the 'guess the combined weight of the teaching assistants' games, Nick spotted a stall proclaiming a silent auction. A quick shuftie at the prize list sent Nick's eyebrows into overdrive: hidden between the cut and blow dry at Mario's and a family meal at Wong Kei's was a very plainly stated voucher for two in the Queens Stand at any weekday evening meeting at Epsom Downs. Nick's inquisitive looks prompted a conversation with the stall minder.

"That's Epsom the racecourse?"

He checked, just to be clear. It was confirmed that the prize was neither an evening of salt related medicinal pleasures nor a rare duck-related pillow stuffing material. In fact someone on the parent's committee was well connected at the track. The tickets had generously been blagged as a school fundraising opportunity.

So Nick enthusiastically scribbled his bid on the proffered slip and carefully placed it in an envelope. Whether he furtively snuck glances to either side before sealing it went unrecorded. The rules were simple: the highest blind bid won each of the prizes. After some lubrication in the beer tent and, clearly some mulling of the options, Nick returned to the silent auction table and engaged the host in conversation again. The crafty one pondered out loud his view that he might submit another, slightly higher bid for the racing tickets. Yes, this was a silent auction….but not necessarily uncommunicative. Some well-placed body language intimated that another bid might now be necessary; and as Nick's pen hovered over a figure on the paper, a quick exchange of glances and a barely perceptible shimmy of the hand suggested that a fractionally higher value might just do the job.

And sure enough, half an hour later, our hero was pronounced the winner of the auction, having secured the pair of tickets for the princely sum of £20! I'd hate to play him at poker.

A couple of days later, Nick and I were having a conversation about this unmitigated success in the pub. I was roaring with laughter! What a coup. Top price tickets for the best end at the home of the Derby cost easily 50 notes each. Just how far the mug punters have come in only a few years. Such a scenario would not have been on the radar before that first trip to Cheltenham at the turn of the century.

As the conversation unfolded, Nick set out the range of dates available to him.

"So anyway, Den doesn't fancy going, so if you can manage one of the fixtures, do you fancy a ticket?"

"Do I?" I yelped, close to the top of my register.

"Ahem. Do I?" I repeated, with a fraction more considered baritone. "No, come on. Den must want this, I couldn't possibly…"

"Look, I'll check again, but she's really not that bothered. And have you seen the new promotion they've brought in? Rock and racing! There's gigs after some of the fixtures."

We had a look at the flyer. Status Quo were booked for one of the July meetings. That was too much. It would be rude not to.

So on a balmy late Summer's afternoon we bunked off work early and landed at Tattenham Corner attired in the appropriate smart casual. As we approached the turnstiles for the Queen's Stand my mind rolled back to my first visit here on Oaks Day a couple of years before when we were waved away from that entrance by a snooty red-coated steward who scoffed at our tickets and sent us across the car park to the cheap seats. Not today, I thought, before I chucked Nick a sidelong look.

"Is this where you tell me it's a windup?"

"If it is, I'm being wound up too!"

No alarms though. We gained admission with a polite welcome and were soon knocking back pints of Guinness in the Mezzanine bar, checking out the view down the track from the outside balcony.

To be honest, the racing was fairly average fodder. There was a couple of interesting maiden events and a handicap or so to get stuck into. But that was hardly the point of this delicious jolly on such a gorgeous evening. We did actually have a couple of short-priced winners each to keep the sense of righteousness intact. Though I was aggrieved to see that a few Quo fans had breached the security to blatantly flaunt their patchwork denim jackets in our stand. I briefly considered dobbing them in, but that would be churlish. How easily I am seduced by my own false status (quo).

The seasoned rockers were comfortably entertaining. I had seen them on two occasions previously. Both times I had gone to see someone else. The first experience was at Knebworth when the majestic Queen were in full cry on the Live Magic tour. Quo were supporting. The next time was at the NEC in Birmingham where one of my favourite bands, classic Brit rockers Waysted were filling the undercard for Rossi's lads. Waysted's riff-heavy, balls out, hard rocking sound echoed around the third-full hanger of a venue and bounced off plastic bucket seats before crawling, shell-shocked and broken, into the indifferent ears of the Quo army supping gassy lager in the bars.

At Epsom, however, I had no divided loyalties. The band ripped through back-catalogue crowd-pleasers like the 80's never happened. Even though these perpetual boogie merchants churned out big selling albums every 18 months or so, the most recent track they played was a solitary cut from 1988, 'Burning Bridges'. Apart from that it was unadulterated 25 year-old three chord boogie pumped out with cheeky charm and easy confidence: 'Down Down', 'Mystery Song', 'Roadhouse Blues', 'Caroline'… Assured.

Our self-congratulatory mood in the Tattenham Corner boozer over a couple pints of IPA was soon burst. We were in understandably good spirits: a couple of winners, a top gig and bargain-bagging in the name of charity to boot. Winners all round. Until we tried to get home, at least.

We had missed the last train back to town. It didn't feel that late. Indeed, by central London standards, it wasn't. I hadn't event thought to check. But the timetable couldn't have been clearer. We stood around scratching our heads and squinting at the information boards as if prolonged staring would change its contents. Just then, a Southern Railways eight-car train pulled in. We breathed a sigh of relief and hopped on. The guard clocked us as he walked from the cab to the exit and stuck his head into the carriage.

"You'll have a long wait there lads. This one doesn't pull out until 6.05 tomorrow morning".

He waited for us to haul our reluctant arses off the train before chuckling and manually closing the doors behind us.

We made a few inquiries. The mini-cab office was long closed. The nearest alternative station in Epsom proper was a 45-minute walk -

and no guarantee of trains from there by then. The weekly bus had departed days ago… Nick concluded there was only one option.

"I'll call Den. She'll come and get us."

I was distraught. "You can't do that. It's miles! And it's late now".

"Well do you want to walk to Epsom? And than have to cab it from there anyway?"

I relented. Nick found a public phone box (mobiles were pretty common by then, but far from indispensible - neither of us had brought ours), one of the few public services still available in this leafy part of Surrey at that hour. I didn't hear the conversation, but there was a lot of shrugging shoulder action and holding upwards of palms in supplication.

"She's on her way", he said, poking his head out of the booth.

"I don't think Mrs A would have come".

Den turned up a while later, the two children fast asleep in the back seats. She'd had to wake them up and pile them into the Mondeo before setting off on the rescue mission. To assuage my guilt I sat in the front seat, telling Den how sorry we were and regaling her with stories of the night. I don't think it helped.

Nick was cuddling his kids in the back. At Worcester Park I jumped out and checked my trains. As expected, the last one had gone and I was to be the guest of Nick and Den for the night. I climbed back into the car.

"No joy. But the kebab shop over there is still open…"

I felt, rather than saw, Nick's grimace.

"Is it?"

Den shot the car shot forward and we spat gravel, leaving the kebab shop well in our wake. I could just about detect the aroma of doner meat competing with the thick stench of burning rubber. A request too far maybe. I rang Mrs A from Nick and Den's.

"You're bloody lucky", she declared. "I wouldn't have come for you!"

2. THE TIPPING SERVICE

I can't imagine anything better than coming third in a sweepstake...

PG Wodehouse, in 'Ukridge', 1924

It wasn't much longer before I was picking up the hot trail laid down by Nick in his school silent auction. I had been so very impressed by his stunning precedent-setting blend of altruistic education support and hedonistic gambling pursuits. A little later that year, I got my own chance.

The Greenway First School Promises Auction was from much the same mould as Nick's silent auction. It was a fundraiser designed to fleece parents of their cash whilst convincing them that they were having a good time. In this case, the committee had put together a brochure of eclectic activities, products and offers on which we could bid during the course of the evening. Mixed bag could have been coined for this collection. At one end of the scale a well-heeled couple put up a week's holiday in a downtown Singapore one-bed apartment, whilst another family offered a New Year's Eve break in their hideaway Norfolk cottage. At the more modest end of the auction we had promises of babysitting, photo framing and mince pie baking.

In a weak moment, I had tentatively suggested to Sue, the no-nonsense chair of the school association, that I might offer up a betting deal: I would fund a two-quid bet of my selection every day for the month of November. The winning bidder would keep any winnings and I would swallow the losses. A very generous potential contribution to the cause worth £60, I reckoned. Although I knew that I would want to double up all my selections. There was no way I could bear to tip up winners (thinking optimistically, as ever) without collecting on them personally. So on that basis, my adjusted maximum potential wipe-out could be £120. At that price, I felt comfortable batting away cheeky allegations of dipping into long pockets with short arms. We can't all offer up swanky apartments overlooking former Colonial outposts. On the other hand, who else was laying down such obvious trading profit potential? (Investments can go down as well as up…)

I didn't hear anything further for a while and was quietly hoping that the offer had been dropped: perhaps it was not quite the thing to be promoting at a respectable middle class school, or maybe the concept was too convoluted compared to, say, '24 fairy cakes, choose your own icing'.

But then Mrs A brought home the catalogue shortly before the auction and there was my promise, sitting mid-brochure, Lot 28, 'Horse Race Tipping Service'. My offer had made the cut. I immediately had doubts. Who was I to put up something so audacious? What sort of track record did I really have? Smug punting (© Bacchy, 2010) indeed!

The evening was a riot. The school hall had been transformed into the sort of hot-headed auction ring more reminiscent of the Doncaster Breeze Up Sales. The floor was heaving with twenty or so octagonal tables, each crammed with high-spirited parents filling the space where children usually gathered for assembly. A commercial property auctioneer, thickly coiffed grey hair and sharp, laughing eyes set in a face suspiciously well tanned for October, surveyed the scene from the stage. Brian had been recruited to sell promises the hard way. He did a fine job of cajoling, motivating and shaming the packed school hall into a frenzy of generous bidding.

The bring-your-own booze probably helped too. Our group was getting merrily plastered on vats of cheap vin rouge that loosened the tongue nearly as quickly as the wallet. Andy, opposite me, was shouting up for anything going: tree trimming services, photography portrait sessions, haircuts... He finally won an over-priced meal for two at the local gastro pub and collected a few vicious digs in the ribs from his missus to boot.

Brian the auctioneer was bigging up everything. Enthusiasm increasingly gripped the room with every passing lot. The cottage in

Norfolk went for £200 more than the Singapore apartment half an hour previously.

It came to my promise. "I've been looking forward to this one," said Brian. "Betting tips. I'm not even sure this one is legal!" The bidding started modestly and smoothly rose to an unsustainable level. I was pulling faces flitting between incredulity, pride and fear. Mrs A was just laughing. Andy considered a bid until I added to his collection of rib ticklers. The hammer finally fell at 120 quid. Much too high.

I did permit a little satisfaction at having boosted the school library fund by scamming some unsuspecting parent of a good few quid. But the fleeting delight was quickly overshadowed by the looming vertiginous challenge in front of me.

"Shit!" I mouthed. "I'll never win that back!"

The evening ended with a fish and chip supper during which the over-exuberant winning bidders were relieved of their cash and then hooked up with their donors to arrange delivery of the promise. I scanned the list pinned to Brian's impressive rostrum and went in search of 'Tim, Table 12'.

"Hello", I introduced myself to a well-groomed, smart-casually attired bloke of about the same age, stature and level of inebriation as me.

"I'm the amateur tipster. I think you've purchased my promise".

There was good-natured backslapping and licking of lips. He introduced me to his brother who had put up half the stake, and to his wife whom I vaguely recognised from the school run.

"We assumed you were a bookie? Or maybe a professional gambler? This is money for old rope isn't it?"

I wiped some errant ketchup off my chin and looked at the smear of red on the end of my finger. Was that the time to tell them that I was a mug punter and that they would never see their money again? Maybe they had begun to realise this for themselves.

But I was undeterred. The betting bonanza kicked off at the Cheltenham Paddy Power meeting the very next day. The Gold Cup is one of the crown jewels of the jumping calendar and I already had a horse in mind.

14th November

Hi Tim
Well, we got off to an absolute flyer yesterday. Celestial Gold showed all the fortitude of a gilded heavenly body to win the Paddy Power Gold Cup at Cheltenham, landing the odds at 12-1. That will do nicely. Jockey Timmy Murphy gave the horse a peach of a ride, holding him up out the back and letting the strong pace bring Celestial Gold's stamina into play. Murphy had him jumping like a dream and produced the gelding with his trademark exquisite timing to repel the challenge of Thisthatandtother. Masterful riding. We can do with a few more like this if we are turn ourselves a tidy profit.

Today's principal meetings at Cheltenham and Haydock do not offer as much obvious value. Nevertheless, there are some good races and I've plumped for the Greatwood Handicap Hurdle, 2.40pm at Cheltenham. This is an excellent race with some of the best hurdlers making their seasonal reappearance. The selected horse is TROUBLE AT BAY who is a young horse (4), improving all the time. This is a tough race and he is up against older and more experienced horses here, notably in the shape of former Champion Hurdle winner Rooster Booster, and Accordion Etoile an Irish raider with strong credentials. These two will likely vie for favouritism. But Trouble is well weighted at the bottom of the handicap, has won four of his last six races and has had the benefit of a good 2nd last month which should put him spot on for this race. I've backed him this morning at 6-1.

I could hardly believe my luck! What a way to start. On a personal level it was even better as another of Martin Pipe's runners Stormez had also won in the 3 mile handicap chase at the end of the card, despite hitting every single fence down the back straight. I was delirious. Breathless. Our neighbours popped over to see how our loft conversion was progressing.

"Come in, come Fay, Adrian. Come in. Lovely to see you. Sorry, bit all over the place. Stormez just won me a packet at Cheltenham. Ha! And I'm running this tipping service and the first one has come in! Ha! Would you believe it? A tipping service? Me? Right just going out for some air. Need to breath. Helen's in the loft. See you later."

Fay was nodding and smiling politely, trying to comprehend the merest sliver of the molten garbage I was Lewis-gunning her way. Her eyes betrayed mirth and pity in equal doses. Once outside I marched up the hill, grinned, breathed deeply and finally began to feel the adrenaline subside.

15th November

Dave
I have to say I'm most impressed and I wish that I had been able to watch the Gold Cup to share a bit of the excitement. I should of course have placed a side bet on that one! Perhaps we can see what's on next weekend.

The level of info you're giving is brilliant, although I hope you don't feel obliged to produce race reports like this everyday!

Onwards and upwards.

He didn't even have a bet! Unbelievable! There I was, busting my nuts…

15th November

Tim

*Shame yesterday's selection didn't quite do the business.
Trouble At Bay ran with credit and was with the leaders
until 2 hurdles out when he weakened to finish a game
5th. But I guess the conclusion is that he hasn't quite
made the jump to join the top class hurdlers yet. One to
keep an eye on. Today's selection - and apologies for the
lateness of this tip – emerges after casting around some
very thin cards at a couple of pokey little tracks around
the country. They provide a shocking antidote to last
weekend's stellar meetings.*

*So we head to the East Midlands in search of inspiration.
There are not many who can say that! The 2.20 at
Leicester is admittedly a long way from inspiration.
However, the Ladbrokes.com Novices Chase (Class D)
looks like the best we will get! The tip is JODANTE at
13-2 in a race where all the money is for a horse called
Raw Silk. I think the favourite can be opposed on the
basis that Jodante was beaten only a length last time
they met and our horse gets his favoured good ground
today. Jodante's form is solid and I'm hopeful of a good
run.*

Stay lucky!

16th November

*Dave,
How do you follow the races? Internet? Do you place
your bets over the net or do you live above Corals?!*

*Could you please also copy emails to my work address,
where I spend a lot of time during the day?*

So a couple of losers to follow up the winning start. But at least Tim
was getting into the swing of things.

17th November

Tim
We had a non-runner yesterday. Monger Lane was withdrawn well before the off. The stake is returned so I'll put up two selections on Saturday to keep us on course for the month. There are plenty of good fixtures over the weekend.
The best fixture today is at Kempton, but the fields are small and there are too many poor value odds-on runners.

So we head north to Hexham. Bandit Country. The 1.55pm is a decent handicap hurdle with a field of 16. The race is wide open, offering value opportunities. The key here will be the going conditions. The ground is heavy and so we are looking for mudlarks. Horses that like it hock deep. I've backed FLORRIES SON at 14-1. He has won on soft and heavy going, loves it round this track and comes from a stable in good form just now. He has been chasing most recently and so he reverts to his hurdles handicap mark where he has been placed in every one of his seven runs and has won 4 of them. He has been off the track for over 200 days, which is reflected in the price. But the trainer is adept at getting them fit first time out and I think he could go well.

17th November

Dave
Fascinating stuff. "Mudlarks in bandit country" raised a chuckle. When do you have time to work?!

Florries Son was another non-runner and reappeared in the strategy later on. More evidence here that Tim was at least enjoying the ride. The old clichés were suckering him in.

19th November

Tim
We really came off the rails yesterday. Barrow Drive ran an absolute shocker. Rain came and turned the ground soft, but even so this ultra-consistent gelding should at least have been competitive. He was pulled up with about 3 fences to go. I was quite confident about his chances before the race. I mentioned him to the bloke who sells me the Racing Post at the station. So that's another newsagent's I can't go back to.

Belting action today. Three-time Gold Cup winner and all-round superstar Best Mate returns to action in a four-runner race at Exeter. He lines up against at least one genuine pretender to his Crown, Sir Rembrandt who ran him a very close 2nd in last season's Gold Cup. Sir R is a horse I love (in a platonic way, naturally), but can't see him winning today. Although the race will be a cracker, then, it's actually a non-betting race.

'So where's the value?' I hear you utter. Well I'm suggesting a win double today. SAY WHAT YOU SEE from the Martin Price stable in the 1.20 at Exeter, who should go off at about 3-1 and ATAHUELPA in the 3.45 at Windsor at about 7-4. Both selections are skinny prices - too short by my value principles to stick a mere £2 on - but hold very strong chances on earlier form this season and so it's worth chancing a double.

19th November

Dave
Second, last or a non-finisher, I guess it matters not (almost philosophical!), although your pride is clearly at stake!!

Why don't you call me at home on Saturday morning with selections for tomorrow and we can have a chat. We might not yet be ready to retire, but I am really enjoying all this!

This was rank bad form. Half a dozen bets in and I was already putting up ridiculous win doubles. Absolute mug punting territory and a simple product of self-inflicted pressure. No good could ever have come of such shambolic tactics and sure enough none did. Both were unsighted.

21st November

Tim,
A couple of shockers today. Turgeonev ran a stinker in the handicap hurdle and Native Emperor, whilst running well for most of the race, never landed a blow in the Becher Chase.

Tomorrow's selection comes from Ludlow. In the 2.20 handicap chase for amateur riders, I've backed CARRYONHARRY at 11-2. This horse has decent form, but has been carrying too much weight in recent outings to trouble the judge. The handicapper has relented by dropping him a few pounds and on this mark; he should go well in a tight little race.

Celestial Gold is starting to feel like a long time ago!

22nd November

Tim
Another winner! Carryonharry absolutely hacked up at Ludlow. Won by 27 lengths, virtually unopposed. I took 11-2 last night, which is just as well. Stable confidence behind the horse saw him backed in to 7-2. So much the better for us. Not that eleven quid will break the bank, of course.

Tomorrow, we are back in the frozen North. Sedgefield. Grim as they come. The race is grimmer still. 3pm, Ken Bright Memorial Chase, 3m3f, Class F. Why Ken Bright's folks would choose to commemorate him with this bilge is hard to fathom. We can't go much further down the grading alphabet without backing Blackpool Beach donkeys. It's an open race though, which tempts us in. TROOPER, at 8-1 is burdened with our wedge in this sterling encounter. Down in the weights, soft ground performer, course and distance winner, top jockey booking. Must go close.

23rd November

Dave
RESULT!! Well done.

I didn't ask you what you do for a living, although judging by the jargon-loaded reports, I now assume you must be a sports journalist, aspiring to be a racing commentator!

That winner was a long time coming. Slowly I was convincing Tim that I was not a mug punter at all, but a seasoned tipster who knows what he's talking about. Who says jargon is a bad thing? Or clichés for that matter. And a bit of bullshit never did any harm either. Take that away and there's not a lot left.

25th November

Dave
All good stuff. Tell me, when you go into Corals, are the odds printed in the papers on the walls the ones they give or am I misunderstanding how they operate. When I popped in on Saturday and checked the odds following our conversation, I found that they were a lot shorter than you had got i.e. 11-1 was printed up at 11-5?

28th November

Tim
Yeah, the forecast prices on the eve of racing are called 'tissues' and are often wayward. Some bookies will offer prices for the Saturday cards and the big races on the previous evening and that's what I try to plough into. The other factor is that the prices can massively see-saw on the day, in response to the weight of money. Mind you, 11-1 in to 11-5 is pretty extreme. Clearly a plot horse lined up for an imponderable handicap! Good to see you are venturing into the local bookies now!

As regards the most recent raft of bets, no amount of cool analysis and dispassionate observation can swerve me from the view that on Saturday at Newbury we was robbed. Fleeced. Shafted. You probably feel the same about events at Twickenham. Two runners-up. Albahuera and Claymore. Each beaten by less than a length. I was gutted.

Puntal ran well for 6th in the big chase. You may have noticed our old mate Celestial Gold trotted up in that race. I passed over him on the basis that the price was too short. It didn't look too bad when he crossed the line in front though! The horse is in the form of his life. Royal Shakespeare also ran well for 3rd at Newcastle. Though the winner, Harchibald, looks something special. A real Champion Hurdle prospect. The bookies have already slashed his odds for that race next March.

No point moaning about near misses though. We need winners. We are now over half way through the bets. Only two victories in the bag at this stage is a touch below par. This is where the gloves come off.

Back to Newcastle tomorrow. FLORRIES SON runs in the 3m handicap hurdle at 2.20. I've backed him at 10-1.

This formerly useful chaser reverts to the hurdles on a handy enough mark. He goes well fresh, is a dour stayer and holds a strong chance in this very open race.

29th November

Dave
You were gutted and so were we! My brother-in-law and I placed £5 side bets on all Saturday's runners and watched the races on video, without knowing the results, after the rugby. I persuaded myself that the law of averages had to apply after an empty week and that one of the four would come in. WRONG! Found the races exciting all the same.

Just to compound matters, we then tried to recoup our losses by getting stuck into the 6 - 15 point winning margin in the France - New Zealand game. We backed both teams at 11-1. How could we lose? As you must know, the All-Blacks went on to stuff Les Bleus 45 - 6!!!!!!!!

My wife is very concerned that you're a bad influence on me…

Nice to see the gambling seed sown at the start of the month was beginning to flourish with such vigour (paving the way for inevitable disappointment…)

1st December

Hi Tim
I hope it comes as a pleasant surprise to you to learn that we bagged a winner today. MIOCHE D'ESTRUVAL landed odds of 12-1 in a handicap hurdle at Newton Abbot, 2.50pm.

I couldn't place the bet on-line at work. Damn, they must be catching up with me! So I left the bet cooking nicely in my addled brain til I could watch the race in the bookies. I couldn't believe that the horse had drifted out to 12s! I was expected 8-1 and no better when I plotted this one up. Our talismanic jockey, Timmy Murphy delivered the beast on a beautifully timed run out wide to pouch the race on the line. Spectacular stuff.

We've had three positive returns now, all from the Martin Pipe stable. I'm not usually a big fan of his – the prices are often too short - but I can't complain at this return. We've backed four of his, three have delivered and the other was 2nd! This brings us to £59 profit. I may not win you back all your £120 auction wedge, but I'd hope to land at least another two winners or so from the remaining 12 bets.

Tomorrow, the action comes from Plumpton and Catterick. The cards are more threadbare than a hooker's panties though, and I'm not putting up a selection. I'll double up on Saturday when there is an outstanding meeting at Sandown and you can sit in front of the box and watch the money roll in. I'm at the track for the first day of the meeting on Friday. It's a belter and I can't wait.

We did indeed have a good day at Sandown. The Friday of the wonderful Tingle Creek meeting has been a regular fixture in our diary for many years. Whilst it does not offer the same glitter and glory as the following day's main event, that dank day we saw both the future winner and runner up of the Festival's RSA Hurdle which would be run a few months later. We also saw my mate Bacchy snaffle the winner of the lucky last at 25-1 and polish off his hip flask in the Albert Arms on Esher High Street a brief moment before being invited to leave by the management.

I rang Tim on Saturday morning with that day's tips, speaking slowly and quietly so as not to unduly disturb my fragile state of being. Atahuelpa at 9-1 and Historic at 11-2 were the selections.

5th December

Hi Tim
Don't know if you caught Saturday's racing. Atahuelpa never landed a blow in that massive handicap hurdle, but Historic was simply magnificent in the marathon chase. Jumped his rivals ragged. His nearest pursuer coming a cropper four out was a handy outcome for us. I'd expected odds of 11-2, but as the price was drifting all morning, I waited till nearer the off and we landed 8-1. Bit of a bonus. So 75 quid in the bank and 8 selections to come.

Tomorrow we head north of the border to Ayr for a 2m5f handicap chase. JALASTEP is the selection - assuming I can get better than 6-1 tomorrow morning. This is a tricky little handicap, but this horse loves the track and his best form has come on good ground. The market is made by Huka Lodge on whom I have collected before, but tomorrow's distance is likely to be too short and he seems to like bottomless ground. The race is due off at 1.30pm.

I'll double up on Saturday so that the last bets of this series come at the very decent Cheltenham Bonusprint meeting this weekend.

Tim rang, ecstatic that he'd finally managed to cheer home a winner on a big Saturday afternoon. Unfortunately, Jalastep received a huge bump approaching the 1st fence at Ayr, knocking the jockey clean out of the saddle.

9th December

Tim

Bridesmaid again yesterday. We are getting too many of these. Lou Du Moulin Mas had every chance chasing the leader at the last fence, but he couldn't quicken and was beaten by three lengths. Cosy enough for the winner.

Today we venture to sleepy Huntingdon: land of animal research, former Prime Ministers and Martin Pipe hurdlers. HENRIETTA is the girl for us in the 2.20pm 3m handicap hurdle; part of Pipe's carefully assembled raiding party. This mare landed a three-timer over timber last season before being found out in a listed event at Aintree. Back to her level here in a Class D race I'm hopeful that she can land odds of 7-1.

I've been passed a tip today too. TOULON ROUGE runs in the 1pm Huntingdon novice chase. Currently trading at 10-1 I find it hard to believe that this beast is nailed on to win; but the source is adamant that the tip is 'red hot'. I don't know the source personally so can't vouch for his credentials. But I do know that the horse is trained by Ferdy Murphy who is a right old rogue and well capable of plotting up something like this. There's a chance that the info might have come from the stable, in which case the price should tumble. I've had a couple of quid on. Just for interest you know.....

Henrietta was a well beaten 3rd and Toulon Rouge went down by a mere three parts of a length at 12-1. I never found out whether Tim had got on at that price, but it was clear each-way territory and I satisfied myself with a small consolation collect.

10th December

Last three bets Tim, on this, your roller-coasting™ charity auction purchase. Unless we land all three races, I can't see this adventure turning into any real profit on your initial outlay, but we'll go down all guns blazing at any rate.

Today is a good-quality opening day of the Bonusprint meeting at HQ. We find our eyes drawn yet again to the winning machine master of Pond House for our first selection in the last race of the day. Martin Pipe's THEREALBANDIT is just that.

A horse known to criminally waste his prodigious talent and thieve the hard earned wedge of honest punters. A bandit indeed. But we can't let him go off at 6-1. If he recaptures a smidgeon of his novice form last year he will be bang there at a track he would like to roll up and take home.

Tomorrow, GAZUMP has the look of an improver about him in the novice chase. He has winning track and distance form and looks very solid at 11-2. And in the novice hurdle at 3.45, there should be more to come from JACKSON over hurdles and this extra 2 furlongs should play to his stamina strengths.

Here's hoping we go out with a scream!

13th December

Hi Dave
Therealbandit seemed to win very nicely on Friday. Well done.

Although having placed some modest each way side bets on Saturday and watched races on video on Sunday, I cannot help but think that this business is a bit of a lottery!! Gazump got us off to a particularly bad start!!

I managed to derive some satisfaction from Jackson edging a second place in the 3.45, but I only got 7-1 odds with Ladbrokes on Saturday. Hey Ho!

Notwithstanding that this has not proved to be a positive investment, the money went to a good cause. I've really been won over by the experience and have enjoyed the winners. And your commentaries have been excellent, so thanks for all your hard work.

It would be nice if you and the family could make it round for a pre-Christmas drink, either next weekend, or one evening next week when kids are off school.

How are you fixed?

So in the final analysis, I didn't win back Tim his £120 promises auction outlay. Indeed I was left with a lingering sense that he felt I should have done better. And yet by any standards the statistics during this period were solid. I landed 5 wins from 30 bets, which is a very respectable strike rate of 16%. The winners were big fat prices that you can properly scream home. None of that odds-on thievery: 12-1, 11-2, 12-1, 8-1 and 13-2, netting a profit of £28 on top of £60 staking (30 bets). This gives profit on turnover – the Daddy of punting performance indicators, so I'm told – of 46%. Four of the winners were trained by Martin Pipe. Never before had I had such a healthy return from his barn.

Mrs A and I, together with the girls gathered at Tim's for a lovely evening with him and his family just before Christmas. I thought I had detected the merest levelling off of Tim's enthusiasm for the project by the end. I projected onto his conversations his realization that there was no easy route to glory. In hindsight this is something I should have stressed to him at the outset, rather than inflating the operation. Though who would have bought a promise that said "you may lose all your money"! Expectation management is a tricky beast.

But over a few glasses of deep red claret, Tim was incredibly generous in his praise of my pimped up racing reports and was a tad disappointed to discover that I was just another desk-bound fantasist rather than an insider from the racing industry. If only he knew how

I had ploughed every avenue of hackneyed Racing Post one-liners I could muster. Another day would have sent me over the edge.

Tim's wife Hilary had equally become fascinated by the murky world of tipping and feared for the very moral soul of her hubby on a couple of occasions.

I wrote out a cheque for £88, which was the gross profit on the winners. I'd said in the auction that I would swallow the losing stakes. But to my client this was still a loss of £32, plus his own side bets, (for which I naturally could not take responsibility). So friends made, entertainment consumed and charities supported. Not quite everyone a winner, but this was good enough.

That said, Tim has never asked me for a tip since…

3. BIGGER THAN THE POPE

Rod Marsh: *How's your wife and my kids?*

Ian Botham: *The wife's fine but the kids are retarded.*
An Ashes exchange, 1981

One of the biggest changes to sport - and indeed every other aspect of life – since the first volume of Mug Punting is the emergence of social media as a platform to fizz news and views around cyberspace.

When Freddie Flintoff announced one of his many retirements from cricket in 2010, the Metro newspaper declared it to be more significant than the Pope's arrival in Edinburgh the same day. Based on trend analysis of tweets during the day, Freddie knocked the Pope into a cocked mitre. Freddie Flintoff was bigger than the Pope. Official.

Well, in the Twittersphere at least.

There can be no doubting Flintoff's hero credentials, though. The epic Ashes series of 2005 produced, without doubt, the most sustained high quality drama I've witnessed anywhere on a cricket pitch. Good test matches have their ebbs and flows, their moments of glory, skill and passion. But that series had enough adrenaline and emotion to fuel a manned mission to Mars and more u-turns, plot twists and shimmies than a week of back-to-back Eastenders. Not to mention enough comparisons with greatness to exhaust a hackneyed purveyor of similes (that's me).

Just one more simile, then: that of a heavyweight boxing match where two world-class fighters at the peak of their powers slug it out, toe-to-toe over the maximum distance, neither knowing when they were beaten and both conjuring up more big shots when each looked floored.

This prompts to me relive right now, in unapologetic partiality, that golden Summer of triumph. Duck out here anyone who is wincing at the prospect of overblown sentiment and nostalgia.

That clash was long anticipated, of course. Many are the nights that the lads spent down the boozer weighing up the pros and cons of England reclaiming the Ashes. This was in the Spring of 2005 as the dust was settling on a very successful tour of South Africa that had seen England prevail by two tests to one.

They were deep and subtle debates, too. Squads were dissected layer by layer with a scalpel-sharp precision and ruthless analysis that would not have been misplaced in the bleached walls of a research lab. Perhaps the standards of scientific debate fell away a little as the ale soaked discussions lurched into the deeper night, but nevertheless, the general pros and cons were intelligently argued and knowledgeably discussed.

The collective view was that, as sure as RightGuard, England would need to play at their very best to beat the Aussies. We had moved on from the role of perennial runner's up, that much was clear; we had developed a ruthless streak and a steel edge; a team spirit with a consistent approach and a strong fitness regime; and perhaps most crucially, a smattering of world class players – Flintoff, Harmison and Vaughan most obviously - that could turn games. We all seemed to think that Harmison's destructive potential would be needed. If he could fire on all cylinders, roar in like a Harley and make the Aussies jump like jiggy things on a vibro plate, we could in business. We would have an edge in the bowling department we hadn't seen since the likes of Willis and Botham.

Ultimately, we echoed the language of the cricket media in building up the confrontation. We all yearned for a close and competitive series. We believed that this time, at last, we had a chance. No more than that. Anything more would be dreamland.

Ben had applied speculatively and multiply for tickets for the Oval test in the public ballot earlier that Spring. Demand was high. No surprise there then, for the most anticipated series in a decade. And he got tickets for a bunch of us. Good news. And bad news. They were for Sunday 11th September. Day four of the final test. That didn't seem like a great result to be honest. Let's face it, we said, (betraying that pre-season analysis of our chances with knee-jerk early Summer signs of the crushing defeatism that had eaten away at the core of English cricket for a decade or more) the Ashes could be long gone by then, the fifth test. And that test itself could be over by Sunday. Nick declined the chance of a ticket. Too far off to think about, he said. Steve wasn't overly fussed either. He didn't commit. Never mind, Bryn and I were in there like rats up drainpipes. I wanted to be there somewhere, somehow for this showdown. I bagged my ticket from Ben.

The Summer's main event seemed to take an eternity to arrive. The Aussies landed and sparked the outbreak of media feast. The tourists stepped off the plane looking alarmingly blonde, bronzed and athletic. And that was just the craggy Stuart MacGill…. There was an aura about the side that closeness to invincibility brings. Ponting's first public comments struck the right tone about wanting a close series and respecting England's improvement. But every visiting Aussie captain since the 80's has paid lip service to those niceties without blinking and yet behind closed doors they were savouring the prospect of dishing out another proper spanking to the hapless Poms. Meanwhile Warney, Hussey, Watson and other squad members were already serving it up to our boys on the County circuit.

The first chance the two teams got to square up to each other was a Twenty20 match at The Rose Bowl. On the face of it, this would present a competitive warm up match for the Aussies whilst not putting too much at stake. Twenty20 had become cricket's saviour; a populist, thrill-a-ball instant hit. And we had invented it. The Aussies had played only one game so far – in which they had set the World's highest score. So there were no illusions about their ability to pick up the subtleties quickly.

The Phoenix was packed. It was one of the few pubs round Victoria that could be guaranteed to show cricket on big screen, wall-to-wall TVs. They showed other sports too, but the landlord was a cricket fan and was pulling in plenty of punters by showing live Twenty20 and test match cricket.

If this was a sign of things to come, Me, Nick, Ben and Bryn would have to start reserving tables. As it was we had bagged front row seats for this opening encounter.

In a fashion we had quickly come to expect in that still fledging format, runs piled up faster than haymaking on cider time. Trescothick played like he was born to the game and Collingwood smashed a lighting 46 off only 26 balls. The total of 179 at 8.95 runs per over is commonplace, even on the tardy side by today's standards. But those were heady days in the new format and it's hard to under-estimate the excitement this form of cricket played at the highest level was generating.

The total was a reasonable ask, we mused as we settled in to another round, but not out of sight. Indeed Australia raced out of the blocks. Adam Gilchrist and Matthew Hayden clipped and cuffed the England opening bowlers in dismissive fashion. The new ball was propelled by Darren Gough and Jonathan Lewis, two bowlers who would not feature in the tests, but were crucial elements of the limited overs set up. Gough, heart of an ox, a man who's fast bowling buttocks I have long admired, breathlessly put both openers back in their box in his second scintillating over.

The optimistic tones had re-emerged in the pub and were now in full cry. Then it was Lewis's turn join the party. He ripped out Symonds and Clarke. Then Gough, without another run being added had Hussey caught in the slips.

The Aussies were in the midst of an English-style batting collapse and how we revelled in it. The raucous terrace-like atmosphere in the Phoenix was cranked up to overdrive as Ponting swatted a loose one from Lewis to cover and collected a duck.

The east European barmaid collecting drained glasses from our table nearly jumped out of her skin when we leapt up as one and screamed a triumphant chorus. "C'mooooon". She grinned, collected frayed nerves and dropped pint mugs and sought solace behind the bar. But there was no refuge in this pit of nationalistic fervour. Everyone was savouring the capitulation of the baggy-greens. Wickets were tumbling regularly. Lewis with a four-fer, and Gough with three jaffas had reduced Australia to 31-7. Magical scenes.

England's win came sweetly enough, prolonged a little by some purposeful swishing from Australia's tail.

That Twenty20 victory was no informal preamble. It mattered. Even though Vaughan played down the victory in his post match interview, we knew what it would have meant to the dressing room. He spouted guff like, "well you know you can't get carried away… this is good fun stuff…. every edge seemed to go to a fielder and some days none of them do…. it's nice but it doesn't mean anything…" Lies, we said, all lies.

He was right though. To our utter disgust, it didn't mean anything. Come the test series, the painful reality of another dominant Aussie tour weighed heavily on us. Their too-comfortable win at Lord's in the series opener was only enlivened by Harmison genuinely striking the fear of God into the top order.

Otherwise it was grim viewing. Slumped over pints back in The Phoenix, the backdrop to our Summer, we feared the worst. Me, Nick, Bryn and Steve, amongst a cast of thousands, engineering late lunches and early departures to ride the Ashes train.

Thrillingly, and against our worst fears, England bounced back in style. At Edgbaston, the sight of Trescothick bludgeoning Lee and co to the four corners of Birmingham on the first day had the pub reeling and goggled eyed. That positivity led to the first 400-run+ day in the history of the Ashes, racked up at over 5 runs an over. That was a strong position for England. And yet Australia come back tenaciously when they bowled England out for 182 in the second dig. The stage was set for a fourth innings drama, with the Baggy Greens needing 282 runs to secure a 2-0 series lead. Reduced to 175-8 at the start of the final day, a defining England victory looked assured with only Warne and Lee at the crease.

It didn't go to script. In nerve-jangling scenes, the Australian tail defied and yet again defied England's victory charge, edging closer to a remarkable win of their own. Brett Lee stood firm, with first Warne and then Kasprowicz, repelling venomous missiles from Freddie, Hoggard and Harmison. Only a few deliveries remained when Harmison forced Kasprowicz into evasive action with yet another brutal throat-ball. It popped up to the keeper and England had won a ripsnorter by two slender runs. This was the second narrowest margin in the history of test cricket.

The scenes of victory included the now iconic (an over-used term, but possibly appropriate here) image of Flintoff consoling Lee with a word and a gesture. The scene captured forever those fleeting moments of poignancy in combat. It was the image that came to define that brutal series. When asked if England could now win the Ashes, the undoubted Man of the Match Flintoff replied: "We've got to!"

It is likely that the turning point in that game happened before even a ball had been bowled. In the warm up on the Edgbaston outfield, Ricky Ponting rolled a practise cherry to Glen McGrath who didn't see it and tripped over. In that moment, McGrath had ricked his ankle and was deemed unfit to play. McGrath, alongside Warne, was England's nemesis for a generation of Ashes series. The impact of that slip may have reverberated all the way to Sydney and back.

He was back for Old Trafford, although he made no inroads into England's first innings. We were treated to a majestic first day ton from Vaughan. England dominated; meanwhile Warne took his 600th test wicket and received a generous standing ovation. He also racked up a first innings 90.

McGrath was back up to speed in the second innings, ripping out yet another five-fer. By the last day, Monday, we piled down The Phoenix to watch as much of Australia's chase as possible. They needed a further 399 to pull off a World Record 423 winning run chase. England needed 10 precious wickets.

The pub was packed. This series had ignited everyone's imagination. 20,000 were locked out of the ground that morning. I think they must have all got on the train and emptied into our pub. The Polish barmaid, bless her, was once again overwhelmed and perplexed. Nothing in her career thus far had suggested a slow Monday lunchtime in a Westminster would unleash a blizzard of business. We tried to explain the significance of the quickly unfolding events. We failed. England failed, too. But only marginally. Australia were nine down as the overs ran out with Brett Lee – again - and Glen McGrath fending off Steve Harmison and Freddie at full throttle. As thrilling a draw as you could ever wish for.

Still one-all, then. On to Trent Bridge. England were again off to a flyer. This time Flintoff hit a blistering ton, and England forced Australia to follow-on for the first time in 17 years. Matty Hoggard and Simon Jones reverse swung England into the ascendency on a peach of a Sunday afternoon. That left England to get 129. Which, in the spirit of the series, became another nail-biter. Hoggard and Giles saw England nervously home. We counted down the runs single by single.

That was a great day all round. Nick and I had taken our families to Aldburgh in Suffolk for the Bank Holiday weekend. Great weather, great apartment, outstanding company. On the Sunday morning we informed the wives that we were off to play golf and that it would be great if there was Sunday lunch on the table when we returned. Incredibly, that is just what happened. After a tense nine holes at the majestic, salty-aired Aldburgh golf club, we returned to tuck into delicious roast beef and all the trimmings. There was a bit of giggling and knowing looks from the wives, yet we thought nothing of it. But as soon as the plates were licked clean, they shot out of the door with a barbed "OK boys, see you later...maybe!" and disappeared, leaving us with a mountain of washing up and the kids in need of entertainment. Turned out they had ensconced themselves in a beachside pub with a bottle of wine and spent the afternoon tittering about their perfectly executed revenge.

Well, the flip side suited Nick and I perfectly. Once the DVD was running on the other telly and a few cans of Boddies had been acquired, we blissfully rose and fell on the tide of England's fortunes in Nottingham. The perfect outcome for all concerned! The beers were for us, not the kids. I'd just like to be clear about that.

The decider at The Oval caused some family consternations of a slightly higher order. Those tickets Ben had speculatively pouched back in March for what we thought would be a dead rubber had suddenly taken on a glossier sheen. It was nice, for a change, to be spectacularly wrong.

However, the merest hint of anxiety pinched at my temples when I dug out the ticket. Sunday 11th September…rang a bell, somewhere. Ah, gottit. Hallow clang. Clapper out of tune. It was the day of Daughter No 1's 8th birthday party. She was having a dozen or so hyperactive friends over for a couple of hours of cake eating and screaming.

"Got anything on that day, Dad, or shall we move it to the weekend after?" had said Mrs A, sometime in mid-August.

"No, no that's fine. Can't see what else would be happening then", I blithely replied. I can even remember thinking that the cricket season would be well over by then. I had forgotten that in a bizarre twist of scheduling, the one-day series intervened before the final test.

Just to put this in context, tickets for this match, the decider in the finest series seen in a hundred years, were changing hands on e-bay for a minimum of £500. I did a shameful thing. I sold my ticket for a grand. No I didn't! Ha! No I didn't.

I went to my lovely daughter, put a comforting arm around her shoulders and said "Would you mind if I didn't come to your birthday party, darling? I'd only get in the way." See? Shameful! "No, that's OK, Daddy. I think Granny and Grandma are coming". Helen looked at me with narrowed eyes and a thin smile. "You'll pay!" she murmured. I still am. In many ways. My act of familial betrayal is aired every time we turn our attention to planning a party for either daughter.

Because of rain interruptions, the match was finely poised by the time Sunday 11th September came around. Me, Bryn, Ben and a couple of his mates took our seats in the Lock Stand and soaked up the atmosphere. Team England had risen to the occasion. Vaughany and his troops bounded on the pitch to the rousing thump of 'Jerusalem'. The day belonged to England. Early and timely wickets from that man Flintoff and Hoggard stopped the Australian charge in its tracks.

By mid-afternoon, England were batting. Shortly after Warne bowled Strauss, the umpires conferred in the middle under glowering clouds. The light was offered to the batsmen and they headed straight for the pavilion. The place erupted. Never had I known the crowd rapturously cheer a decision to suspend play. The irony was not lost on us and we couldn't shake the grins off our chops. Every minute was precious and this was a key moment. Play resumed for only a short session later in the day. Hysterically, the Aussies – Warne and McGrath most notably - came out wearing shades and sun block to hoots of approval from the crowd.

The next day we were predictably down The Phoenix as early as possible. My boss was there. His boss was there. Everyone was there. The place was stuffed. We coaxed Pieterson to his maiden ton, willed Warne to spill the one slip chance that came his way ("Warne's just dropped the Ashes"), and cheered England to a position of safety. The match was drawn and we won the Ashes 2-1. Cue the clichés: Epic, thrilling, heroic, intense, once-in-a-lifetime. And profitable: I'd backed the correct series outcome at 12-1. The reaction was, in truth, a little over the top. MBEs all round, open-top-bus-ticker-tape parade. But at the time I lapped it up.

And Freddie was Man of the Series. He had embodied the talent, tenacity and team spirit of the encounter. He had lived it large on the field and off. This was to be his finest moment. Those injuries mounted up and he never hit such heights again.

England tamely handed back those hard-won Ashes down under in 2007. Vaughan, out with a long-term knee injury was absent. For all Flintoff's force of personality and chin-jutting, lead-from-the front performances, was not an adequate replacement as captain. From the moment Harmison hit second slip with his opening ball, the series was over. Freddie's credentials as a leader were further exposed during the World Cup later that year when his infamous late-night drunken joyride in a pedalo cost him the vice captaincy.

With Strauss now at the helm, and back on home turf, we reclaimed the Ashes in 2009. Freddie played a less decisive role than in 2005, but a five-fer, a half-century or so and a thrilling run out of Ricky Ponting in the last innings cemented his place in Ashes history.

So, bigger than the Pope? Well, my Mother-in-Law didn't think so. At about the same time Freddie was going to bed to sleep on his retirement decision, she was getting up to board a 2.30am coach and battle through multi-tiered security checks so that she could sit in a field in Birmingham and squint at a giant screen of the Pope preaching to her and 80,000 others about a dead vicar. I don't think Freddie quite commanded that devotion. But for a time in 2005 he was pretty damn close.

Looking back on that series from the perspective of the 2015 home Ashes win, it is not hard to conclude that it really was a cliché-busting 'once-in-a-lifetime' clash. The series recently completed has been spectacular at times. It has sparkled with passion and electricity. However, it has not evidenced the class, quality and intensity of that epic encounter ten years ago. Although the score line of 3-2 would suggest a close series, in fact not one of these tests was particularly competitive. Both teams took it in turns to be commandingly brilliant and then utterly hapless across the five games. Only one match made it to the fifth day. Three were completed inside three.

That is not to say the series win was not important for England. Any Ashes victory is, but coming off the back of an utter drubbing in the winter 2013-14, the Three Lions really needed it.

That 13/14 debacle was the worst I have ever seen. The Ashes were prised out of England's grip in 15 painful, sorry days. The dreadful scenes robbed me of far less sleep than anticipated. Early morning telly loyalty was betrayed too many times by the tourists' careless batting and inconsistent bowling. 'Prised' might be a charitable term for the way Cook's lightweights capitulated.

Some signs were well noted in England the previous Summer: the resilience of Haddin, the resurgence of Harris and the resurrection of Rogers. It pointed to a closer Ashes series that Winter. Credit to Johnson. He really found his mojo on those fast, hard and bouncy pitches of Australia.

But that still shouldn't have added up to humiliation.

Clarke's quirky decisions in the Summer of 2013 looked like captaining genius in the Winter. Such is the power of perspective. Exposing Carberry round the wicket; two mid-ons for Pietersen's leg-side flip; becalming Root. Clarke had by then formed a strong bond with coach Lehmann and the swagger and confidence was palpable from day 1. So was the antagonism and aggression on the pitch. Not one single player gave the tourists an inch. In their face at every opportunity. Clarke later apologized for some of the comments he made and the stance he took.

His behaviour did appear excessive in the context of Trott's illness and departure. Nevertheless, it was probably a response to England's negativity in style and attitude during 2013. I didn't like Cook's captaincy that Summer. No one did. It was unimaginative, unbearably cautious and motivationally bereft. It exposed fragility in England's dressing room: Trott returning home; Swann unforgivably spitting out the dummy mid-tour; lack of faith in Panesar; Pietersen's increasingly detrimental self-interest.

Australia had very obviously advanced, but not as much as England had retreated. It was a calamitous tour. Worse, as a spectator, than Flintoff's tourists that handed back The Ashes 0-5 in 2006-07.

How complete then, the restoration of Cook's captaincy skills in the meanwhile? Come the moment of Ashes regain this Summer, Cook was lauded as a bold, confident leader who was ahead of the curve and making things happen.

Another curious twist is the numbers game that underpins this ten-year Ashes battleground. Australia are 15-13 ahead in tests won since England broke the hoodoo in 2005. Yet in that time, England have won five series and Australia two. So who exactly does hold the ascendancy?

4. COMEDY OF ERRORS

I just wish to be left alone with my thoughts and the sincere hopes
that my liver,
which I mailed home by separate refrigerated container, will arrive
soon.
Alastair Down, Racing Post, 2011

This particular tale of race-going tomfoolery is quite hard to recall. As will become clear, certain factors came in to play that have rendered the literal reproduction of some of the day's events a little hazy.

The beginning is fairly clear. It was Bryn that powered the expansion of our racecourse horizons. Left to Bacchy, we would have stuck to the Grade 1 tracks and the decent meetings. Nothing wrong with that, naturally. Feel the quality, etc. Such aspirations, however, were not necessarily the priorities of everyone in the gang. Bryn was keen that we try somewhere new, so long as it was in easy reach of Clapham Junction. Day-jaunts to Cheltenham and Exeter had begun to test the stamina of some of the mug punters that employed a lower quality threshold on the action and a higher benchmark for ale consumption.

There was a sustained effort (though some persevered more than others, Nick) to identify a Friday fixture - essential - in the south of England before the Cheltenham Festival at a track we hadn't visited before. We finally identified an appropriate venue in the shape of the outrageous drinking den and sometime horseracing circuit that is Fontwell Park.

In the days leading up to the gig, wind lashed and rain soaked most of the country. The fixture was in some doubt. Nevertheless, track officials were upbeat on Thursday, and so we elected to go. The final all clear only came through on Friday morning. By then, we had begun to coalesce around Clapham Junction. I arrived via the cheeky four-car, once-an-hour service that snaked through Kensington

Olympia and West Brompton, Bacchy slogged over from furthest Essex, whilst Nick and Bryn rolled out of bed an hour later than us and arrived at platform 15 rested, fresh and with flecks of home-toasted butter croissants still decorating their chops.

If easy reach of London was one of the criteria, I'm not absolutely sure we ticked the box. Fontwell doesn't have its own station. The place is no more than a large farming village and our train trundled – quite literally – down obscure branch lines crossing wide fields of winter grass (probably). We tipped out at Barnham, found the only taxi in the village and fled to the track.

Agriculture and horticulture are dominant in the area, taking advantage of the area's rich soil. As if to prove the point, one of the local landmarks is the award winning Denman's Gardens and Plant Centre. Strange, as there is no record of Paul Nicholl's monster chaser ever having graced the track...

At the turn of the 20th Century, the racehorse trainer Alfred Day had his training gallops at Fontwell. In 1924 the gallops were developed into Fontwell Park Racecourse. There were only four days racing in the first year and this slowly increased with a mixture of one and two day meetings, generally in spring and autumn.

There are more fixtures now, of course – 20-odd per year - and there has been significant investment in the facilities. A new 90 box stable yard had been constructed by the time of our visit and we also enjoyed the newly refurbished parade ring, winners' enclosure and saddling boxes, reopened only that year. I see from the website that a 40 bedroom hotel and pub/restaurant subsequently opened next to an equally new spick and flash main grandstand, which has changed the look (and probably the feel) of the place.

The venue was pretty low-key then though. Break out of the corporate-powered ring of Grade 1 tracks in south west London and racing is still a rural game where a largely local crowd, linked firmly to the farming and country sports community, supports fixtures.

Nevertheless, there are one or two moderately sized names associated with Fontwell Park (apart from Denman's spurious garden centre legacy). Monaveen ran and won here: the first and only racehorse owned jointly by the Queen and the Queen Mother. I must confess that I'd never heard of him. Apparently there is a topiary statue in the main enclosure that commemorates his achievements. We missed it.

The dual Champion Hurdler, National Spirit is also strongly associated with the track. Now here's a horse I have heard of. He won five races at Fontwell, most notably in the Rank Challenge Cup, which he won three years on the bounce in post-war austerity Britain. Since 1965 a prestigious hurdle race has been run in his name here. A suitably fitting honour. The race was later won by Fred Rimmell's Comedy of Errors who also went on to collect a brace of Champion Hurdles. He has a bar named after him in the main Grandstand. Far more appropriate. We may have missed the hedge homage to Monaveen, but we certainly didn't swerve the alcoholic tribute to Comedy of Errors.

Piling out of the taxi, we all quickly appreciated the human scale and homely feel of the track. We might even have concurred with the regional grouping of racecourses who consider it one of the most attractive racecourses in the country, had we known it had received the 'Best Small Racecourse in the South East' gong 19 years in succession.

We did know that it was the only figure of eight jumps track left in the country. It was – and still is - possible to spectate from the middle of the course where races wind round the double loops either side of punters who are effectively hemmed in by the circuit. Value-for-money viewing. That day, punters in the middle of the park would have had more unfettered access to the area's celebrated fertile soil than they bargained for. The weather had reduced the circuits to large tracts of rolled mud. The few patches of grass poking through the gloop looked vulnerable and exposed. No wonder the stewards had thought twice about staging the fixture.

However, we didn't venture to the centre. There are no bars out there. This was a drinking day and scant regard was paid to the singular track configuration, nor the ability of horses to handle the undulating gradients.

The homely feel of the place extended to a couple of local real ale outlets and a series of butcher-owned sausage and burger vans. None of your gassy or greasy mass produced muck here. It proved to be our undoing.

Beer flowed with spectacular ease, even by this group's thirsty standards. It is at this point where I begin to lose grasp of actualities and specifics of the day; and where clouded vision and fuzzy logic sneak in. Nevertheless, subsequent conversations with the lads and the exploration of secondary information sources have helped to fill some of the gaps.

We certainly witnessed Alan King's Blazing Bailey hose up in the opening juvenile hurdle. By some distance, this was the only piece of class we saw all day. The horse went on to be placed in that year's Triumph, and later to win a Cleeve Hurdle, a Liverpool Hurdle and to make the frame in a World Hurdle. Hard to believe he went off at 9-4 that mucky day. I'd love to say I spotted all that latent talent and waded in with a fat bet that smashed his price down from 3-1. I didn't. However, there is circumstantial evidence that Bryn was all over those tempting prices.

There were other winners scattered amongst us as well. I'm pretty sure I was on Amanpuri from Alison Thorpe's yard. The German-bred gelding was a bit of a Fontwell specialist, running 26 times but only winning three times, each one at the Sussex track.

And then as the afternoon wore into a beery blur, we took root in the Comedy of Errors bar, a fittingly monikered venue for the whole sorry day, and bizarrely, not the last Shakespearean intervention in proceedings. We stayed in there partly through inertia, partly to insulate against the cold, but mostly because Bacchy had convinced us of some sure fire things running at Wolverhampton. We failed to emerge from the convivial lounge for the last couple of heats outside, watching on the telly instead. Then we all punted up those rotten losing donkeys in the Black Country sand as well. The writing really was graffiti-sprayed in big red tags on the wall by then.

So maybe collective dyslexia is the factor that explains why half an hour later we had sloppily spilled out of another taxi and into The Murrell Arms in Barnham. We really should have gone home. Instead, we asked the cabbie to find us a decent boozer near the station. He obliged with a charming country pub of exposed-brick, low beams and horse-brasses. And hand pumped ale.

I have a distinct memory of gathering round the open fire in high backed carvers where we collected sharp looks, clicking tongues and whispered comments from the locals faster than losers in the placepot. Our high-spirited banter, turned up a notch with every swig, did not go down well with the good folk of Barnham out for a quiet night in the local.

We eventually took the heavy hints and hauled ourselves out of those cosy chairs, only pausing when Bryn's jelly legs collapsed and he went down like a shot soldier in the middle of the road. He appeared unable or unwilling to move and it took Bacchy and Nick to sling an arm each over their shoulders to complete the relatively short distance to the station.

Whilst the incidents on the train home were hardly more sensible, they were infinitely more random. Firstly, the ever resourceful Bacchy pulled a battered old copy of Henry V from the recesses of his grey herringbone winter coat. A competition of sorts soon ensued, revolving around the best delivery of the 'Once more unto the breach…' passage. Bacchy himself had a pretty good stab at the rabble-rousing verse, striking a spittle and flem-spattered emotional chord. I suspected he knew the piece by heart. I, on a very different hand, struggled to recite the words at all, so loose was my beer soaked tongue. Worse. I couldn't read the words either. They kept jumping all over the page. They would not stay still long enough for me to focus on them. Blind drunk.

"In peace there's nothing so becomes a man

As modest stillness and humility"

The irony of the carefully crafted Shakespearian dialogue we were trying to enunciate was totally lost on us.

The few other passengers in our carriage moved to the other end as we became louder and more obnoxious, draped over seats like giddy fools, shouting the odds about any passing whim. We started yet another of those conversations about the point of gambling. This one essentially revolved around Nick's assertion that winning was all luck.

Like Fontwell's figure-of-eight, this was the dodgiest of circuits; and one we had been round many times. Right from the early days. But that night there was edge. Nick's aggressive tones and furled eyebrows wound me up. Chipped away at me. By the time I was getting off at Clapham Junction, I was almost foaming at the mouth and swearing my head off at him. Telling him he was a "fucking arsehole". I leered from the exit doors, hanging on to the poles for all I was worth. One foot on the platform and one on the train. I pointed at Nick and shouted, "You should just shut the fuck up sometimes. Tosser". I let the doors close and flounced away with as much dramatic effect as a day's hard drinking would allow me. Steve and Bryn mustered a heavy-lidded look of partial surprise.

I woke with a thick head to a text sent by Nick after my departure. "You c**t. Why so rude at CJ?" I spent what remained of the morning like a cat on hot griddles (© Mick Fitzgerald) veering between trying to compose a crushing, obliterating reply and choosing to heroically ignore the text and claim the high ground.

In the end, we both caved in and sent pathetically apologetic texts, prompted by Nick's missus who was stood with him in the freezing rain watching their son play Under 11 football. "For God's Sake! Grow up you pair of idiots!!" was the summary of her sage advice.

A meeting that left its mark.

5. RASCOT

Horse sense is the thing a horse has which keeps it from betting on people.
WC Fields (attributed), cited in Readers Digest, 1942

Royal Ascot. Or these days, Roy Lasckut, a top-hatted and tailed fellow-me-lad with a clipped second syllable (now that Channel 4 have been instructed in the proper pronunciation) and he comes rapping his silver-handled cane at my door every year.

I have a love/hate relationship with this sprawling flagship of the social calendar. Ascot is where the fashion pantomime and society mash up all but swamps the finest five days of flat racing in the land. Insufferably posh debs, nobs and freeloaders in rented finery cram into the Royal Enclosure, jostling for vacuous attention with 27,000 other mates of Her Maj. The rest of the stands are spilling over with tacky bling and tattoo encrusted imitators, hell-bent on early oblivion courtesy of crap, expensive champagne.

And yet at its best the showcase can present a refined symbol of what Britain does best. A chance to shimmer and glow at an occasion given dignity by the daily attendance of The Queen. As a punter, and having been to Royal Ascot only once before, I know which camp I am in. There is no doubt that my one and only trip (as described at the end of Mug Punting) left me a little scarred and a lot bewildered.

Nevertheless, racing is absolutely dependent on such set pieces. These stunning races would be watched from half-empty stands were it not for the toff-inspired glamour and gaudiness that underpins the event. (But they might at least recognise what they were looking at…)

My good friend Julie and her book club decided to hit Ladies Day at the Royal meeting the year it relocated back to Berkshire. They chose to do so in some style. The full limo and Prosecco experience was whistled up from Red Letter Day excursions, or some such.

In 2005, the royal meeting had moved pretty much lock stock and barrel to York. Ascot was in the throes of a complete – and well overdue - redevelopment. In preparation, the racecourse at the Knavesmire had to be realigned and an extra section added past the home turn so that it became a complete circuit rather than an elongated horseshoe. This meant the track could be used for the fixture's longer races.

The switch of venues was a success, though not without some whining about lower attendances (the Knavesmire is significantly smaller than Ascot) and problems with the racing surface (the weather changed from wet and miserable to humid and sticky in 24 hours).

So it was with a soupcon of irony that I noted complaints after the first day of the newly rehoused royal meeting back at new Ascot about viewing problems on the main grandstand.

The racecourse refurbishment cost £185m and was delivered against a timetable tighter than Nell Gwyn's corset. The course reopened just in time for the meeting. However, it quickly emerged that the new stand, with a capacity of 30,000 and sharing some characteristics with Heathrow Terminal 5, had problems with visibility. Over 1,000 members complained about poor sight lines.

There were one or two notable profiles amongst these complainants. For instance HM Queen was unable to watch the racing from the Royal Box. The front parapet of the seven storey edifice meant that Her Majesty, at 5ft 4in, was unable to see over it.

The problems were rectified later that year with raised steppings and seating, but not before the Ascot communications department had caused chortles and smirks about the options to improve viewing that included the rather serious step of "the lowering of the concourse".

One of the interesting side stories to the vociferous outcry from this small but vocal community was the effrontery and dispossession they felt by the wider changes at Ascot.

For instance, journalist Peter Oborne reported that "one wife of a racehorse owner complained: 'I don't want to be snobbish but wherever you go you meet the hoi polloi' ". Another member of the county set moaned that his car park space no longer existed.

The new Ascot had pruned some of the worst extremes of privilege by incorporating progressive design features in the redevelopment. Oborne again: "The old Royal Enclosure formerly opened out towards the parade ring, giving the rich and titled special access while everyone else was forced to walk through a sweaty and crowded underground tunnel. The paddock was now readily available for all." And for the ordinary racegoers, there were far more bars, restaurants and open spaces.

The architectural glitch that meant Royal Enclosure goers (primarily there to see and be seen) were unable to (even) view the racing had merely exacerbated their sense of outrage and prompted the sniffy complaints.

Maybe the Ascot Set's worst fears about dumbing down are, in part, justified. A few years later, I chuckled at the reporting of a drunken brawl that broke out on Ladies Day. The fight had been captured on camera, with around six men throwing punches and one resorting to the use of a chair leg. The Daily mail observed that the incident "took place beside the Victorian bandstand near a champagne bar" suggesting it may have been OK if it had been behind the bogs in the cheap seats.

One female observer remarked that "one guy just kept going, 'Are you mugging me off? Are you mugging me off'. The tone of his voice was really aggressive and then they started pushing and shoving. We got out of the way and then suddenly our table with a newly-bought bottle of champagne went flying."

Not the newly uncorked champers!

"They were biting and kicking each other. It was quite scary."

The Daily Mail, articulating its perception of the nation's conscience, wrote that whilst Royal Ascot had been the "highlight of the summer calendar for the well-off and well-connected for 300 years", its reign may be coming to an end – with the event now attracting 'a much less distinguished breed of racegoer'.

"A quick glance across the terraces reveals a sea of flesh and unsightly tattoos", it continued, "of women in cheap, tawdry dresses and men who have shunned the expected top hat."

As usual 10 years out of date and 10 miles out of step, DM. Wake up and smell the cheap perfume.

Back to Julie's debut appearance at the spanking new track…

As befitted my self-appointed purveyor of bullshit tipping advice, she quite rightly asked me for some selections that she could comfortably discard in the pursuit of narrowing her punting options.

Given my relationship with the meeting, I was only too happy to oblige and with a pen dipped deep into the inkwell of sarcasm, I offered up the following well-meant but largely appalling preview.

Evening Julie!

Hope you've got your tiara buffed and stilettos sharpened. Or is it the other way round? At least once you've polished off the case of Bolly you can recycle the box as a viewing aid. Stand on it and you just might be able to see the winners scampering up the home straight over that posh new parapet. Don't be surprised if Her Maj elbows you out of the way for a better view.

Looks to me like Ladies Day came a day early. Both Ouija Board and Soviet Song, two of the finest mares in training, spread-eagled the fields in their respective Group 1 races today. Spine-tingling stuff. Fills up the soul. Not a dry eye in the bookies. Certainly not mine an hour later when my speculative 14-1 shot Stronghold got beaten by a flared nostril (attached to another outsider) on the line. I've never backed the winner of the Royal Hunt Cup and I suspect that will be as near as I ever get! Don't ask if I backed it each way! I know you would have!

So, with nerves shredded like cabbage in doner kebab, I'm pinning fragile hopes on tomorrow's 'official' Ladies Day card, back where it belongs at Royal Ascot. Despite my rock-solid northern-bastard credentials, this event is pure home counties pantomime and York should be saved for the real thing. We don't do toffs and chavs with anything like the panache of the southerners.

And what a mouth-watering card it is. Chock full of thoroughbred class. Three group races, two ultra-tough handicaps and a listed event for the youngsters.

Some race thoughts, then, for the Cheddington contingent to ponder, discuss and challenge in your stretch Hummer whilst stuck in a traffic jam alongside other gaudy limos somewhere near the M4. I hope any analysis here contributes to a meaningful, structured debate in which you arrive at your selections in a considered and balanced manner. None of this alliterative guesswork please.

It is worth stating here than Julie has stuck relentlessly to her Mother's tried and tested method of picking a Grand National horses based entirely on common first initials. Red Rum, Rhyme 'n' Reason, Party Politics and even Hedgehunter - the last a bit dubious in my opinion - bear testament to the partial success of the approach, though somehow she passed over Mon Mome at 100-1, which would have tipped the system well into the black.

2.35 Norfolk Stakes (Group 2)

This opening race is for babies. The two-year-olds at this point in the season are an unproven, unexposed bunch. As such, the race could be messy, with horses running 'green', flicking their heads about and skittering over the track as if their steering column has snapped. Jockeys are often to be seen wrestling with the reigns to keep their mounts on an even keel. Stand back from the rail is my advice. This will be over in a flash, too. Five furlongs is the minimum trip and will be run on lightning quick ground.

It's quite an open event in which Hoh Mike, Dutch Art and Sonny Red are likely to dominate the market. A tricky little event, really. I would be tempted to have an each-way bet on HOLDIN FOLDIN who absolutely hammered a poor field on his debut at Musselburgh earlier this month and undoubtedly has improvement in him.

It might be easier to put your bets on at the Tote. There will be loads of booths in the posh end, and it will be quicker if you don't fancy the scrum at the rails bookies to get your fistful of fivers on the nag of choice. Remember to give the nice Tote lady (who will have a Geordie accent. Try not to look quizzical. It's just one of those things) the horse number. They don't deal in names

(pet). An each-way bet is a win and a place bet, so a £5 e-w bet costs a tenner because it's two bets (Am I insulting you? Apologies.) (If not, I'll try harder).

Holdin Foldin went off at a very handy 12-1 and finished out of the frame, a game but outclassed 7th. Dutch Art, Hoh Mike and Sonny Red filled three out of the first four places, but merely mentioning them in passing afforded me no credit whatsoever.

3.10 Ribblesdale Stakes (Group 2)

An absolute belter of a race, dripping with quality. This is Royal Ascot's version of the Oaks. It's for three-year old fillies and is run over a mile and a half. A win bet on SCOTTISH STAGE would be my selection. Trainer Michael Stoute has an excellent record at this meeting and this is the pick of his two runners in this year's renewal. Scottish Stage ran a decent Oaks trial last month on ground she hated and that will have put her spot on for this. Lump.

Oh God, please don't tell me she lumped. Scottish Stage went off favourite at 5-2 and got absolutely smashed in running, not once, but twice. Fallon is master horseman, but could not find a clear run on this one and went down by an agonising neck. I was in up to my elbows and this one hurt. Maybe the ladies had enjoyed cheering on a live chance. Maybe.

3.50 Gold Cup (Group 1)

The showpiece of the day. A race for stayers over 2m4f. To these tired old eyes, I don't think the race is as strong as that run at York last year where Distinction was 2nd. So logic would invariably suggest that horse will dot up this year. But I'm not so sure. That performance surprised a few people and it's possible to pick holes in the form. He's a bit 'in and out' as they say and I'm not sure this is his ideal trip. I fancy REEFSCAPE on a win bet. This French raider has consistent form, group class pedigree and has been laid out for this race.

Another runner up. This time at 10-3, but no hard luck stories. Reefscape was thumped 11 lengths by O'Brien's brilliant staying legend, Yeats. This was the first of Yeats' four consecutive Gold Cups. A feat unlikely to be matched for a very long time, if ever.

4.25 Brittania Stakes Handicap (Class 2)

Nightmare. Absolutely impossible. 30 lightly raced and frisky three-year-olds will break from the stalls like an equine tidal wave, split into two or possibly three groups at equal intervals across the track and will helter skelter towards the stands in a series of impenetrable thrusts and counter-thrusts. Make sure you know your colours and focus on nothing else for the full 4 minutes otherwise you will have no clue what the hell is going on. Great this racing malarkey isn't it? I'd have minimum stakes each-way bets on MOTARAQEB (another Stoute horse) and GANDOR (will love the strongly run race), both at big prices. Tote and bookies will pay out on 4 places.

Unsighted. 23rd and 26th. Oh. My. God. Total carnage.

4.55 Hampton Court Stakes (Listed)

Unlike me to go for a favourite, but IVY CREEK looks like he has been kept specifically for this race after being unlucky at Chester last month. He looks a progressive sort and should go close. If your luck is in and you fancy an outsider in the race, Hopeful Purchase should go on well from his maiden win three weeks ago.

Ivy Creek did indeed go off a warm favourite. Warm in many ways. He sweated freely in the preliminaries, raced keenly and was forced too wide. Lost his chance before entering the stalls, after the break and in the business end too. Did well to hang in for 6th. I'm sure that's exactly how the good ladies of Cheddington saw it too.

5.30 Buckingham Palace Stakes (Class 2)

Another big field handicap, as if things weren't difficult enough. 7 furlongs is a tricky distance and it often pays to go for proven distance winners. A low draw may help here, as they are likely to head for the stands rail. Candidates who are not overburdened with weight at attractive prices include Goodenough Mover, Paper Talk, and UHOOMAGOO who is worth an each-way gamble. If there is no pace in the race he could be the one to pounce late. But not an overly confident pick!

Oh, why did I not sound a little more confident! A winner at 25-1! This time the official neck winning distance, though shrinking with every nano-second, went in our favour. Neil Callan rode a pretty poor race, getting trapped in behind runners, finding a lucky break in the wall of horses and then going home far too early. Somehow, even though edging right, this battle hardened handicapper held on. Oh boy, did I need that!

And then it's all over. Don't forget to drink Pimms by the bottle and stop off on the way back to spend your winnings on a tattoo or too. That way, they'll let you in for free next year.

Good luck!

She had a great day and God knows how, but she stuck with the tips until the last. I was vindicated. And relieved.

I pulled off a similar trick at Bath a few months later, though the results were less tangible. Again, with her book club pals (I do like the ambition of this particular social gathering), Julie asked if I had any hot tips for the meeting. Bath racecourse, the highest flat track in England, is more celebrated for its imperious aspect over the Mendips than its quality of racing.

I had a look at the card all the same and texted Julie a couple of likely sorts from Richard Hannon in the 2-y-o maidens and one or two outsiders who might like the drying ground. One of the Hannon runners won, admittedly at a skinny enough price and then in the very last of an eight race card, Powerful Wind screamed home by 3 lengths in a 5f sprint at 8-1. I was feeling very smug. My phone rattled and I clicked to read the surely congratulatory text.

"Thanks for the Powerful Wind tip." I scrolled down. "Unfortunately we left before the last."

This was not the first time I'd experienced such a thing at Bath. A good few years ago, I'd bunked off early from a conference in the area to catch the action at the track. I'd asked sprint specialist Bacchy if he had any advice. He came up trumps in the last, some dodgy class 6 5f event. However, I had had a wretched afternoon and, faced with a long journey back, cut my losses and headed home. Bacchy's tip Hello Roberto scrambled home by three parts of a length at 6-1. I felt sick.

6. PREVIEW

Out of everything I've lost, I miss my mind the most.
Ozzy Osbourne, Black Sabbath

The build up to the Cheltenham Festival is a precious period dedicated to form study and stable whispers; to ante-post staking; to fretful Oddschecker glancing; and to general loin-girding.

Sometimes I get distracted though. There are many reasons for this. I remember a 40th birthday bash shortly before one Festival that caused a significant diversion. "Fancy dress" it said on the invitation. "1970's". "Hoho" I had replied. "I'll just dig something out of the back of the wardrobe, then" I wittily replied. The same joke had been attempted by at least half the guests, it transpired. Humour is a shared experience I always say.

I thought about going as Red Rum. But even the town's well-stocked, overworked costume emporium couldn't meet my exacting requirements for the right shade of chestnut coat and sheepskin noseband. So 2nd choice was a barely passable tribute to Prince of Darkness, Ozzy Osbourne, complete with a plastic bat in my pocket for head-biting photo opportunities…. of which, sadly, there are none to report. Mrs A had a startlingly good punk makeover and would have given Souixsie Sue a run for her money in an identity parade.

Things nearly ended in disaster before we even arrived at the party. Walking down our side passage, my nylon wig became entangled with the metal gate and I had a good five minutes tug of war before I could extricate myself. Mrs A was no help, doubled over with mirth, hugging her convulsing, ripped-t-shirt-clad-ribs and tears ruining her carefully applied black eye-liner. There was still a fair chunk of the wig wrapped around the latch a week later, showing distinct signs of split-ends.

I gave the fire pit outside the venue a wide berth, given the incendiary potential of the plastic mop atop my head and recent clumsiness with the gate. But plenty of people were making good use of both that and the adjacent mouth-watering hog roast. Inside, we found all manner of 70's refugees. I was not alone: at least three Ozzies (with whom I respectfully and unspokenly knuckle-touched), supplemented by two Angus Youngs for lead guitar duties, Kiss's Gene Simmons on bass and Aladdin Sane-era Bowie on backing vocals. That's a super group I'd love to see. Add to that mix, ¾ of Abba, a few white Jacksons and a whole suburb of Village People and you start to get a flavour of the night.

With a sore head and a guilty conscience, I recognised the need to get my Festival prep back on track. I managed to blag some tickets for a festival preview evening in the Sports Café, Haymarket.

Festival previews were already in full swing back then and the last few years have seen the phenomenon grow to an industrial scale. Wider reporting in the YouTube and twitter-blogosphere has led to them becoming watered down and plumped up affairs. I'm also getting a bit fed up of twinkly eyed, winsome smiling trainers who are happy to fob off the betting public whilst tipping their owners the wink and feeding exchange insider dealings. Forums just seem to be another medium in which to do this.

On the other hand, previews are a cheeky route to garner the odd pointer from those on the inside track and they certainly help to feed the Festival anticipation. They can be very entertaining and the key is probably not to take them too seriously. More grist to the mill and all that.

So I pitched up at the Sports café along with about a hundred others and we were introduced to the panel comprising Geoff Lester, Journalist and name-dropper par extraordinaire; John Francome, then Channel 4 Racing presenter and the evening's resident babe magnet; Dan Skelton, then Assistant Trainer to Paul Nicholls and joker in the pack; Tanya Stevenson, Channel 4 Betting Ring correspondent; and Andrew Thornton, Gold Cup Winning Jockey.

The night was good entertainment in a venue with loads of atmosphere. Maybe too much atmosphere at times. The hubbub of a noisy sports bar in full swing on a Friday night drowned out the chat on the odd occasion. Whether I missed any panel pearls of wisdom was highly debateable, the value of the views on offer being mixed at best. Separating the gossip and rumour from gold-plated information required the wisdom of Solomon and a fine grained bullshit sieve.

There was much mirth at Tanya's selection of 250-1 shot Kawagino in the Champion Hurdle. He infact finished a very game 5th at 100-1.

Amongst a few misses, the panel landed a big hit or two: the Arkle (My Way de Solzen), RSA Chase (Denman) and the Gold Cup (Kauto Star). On Denman, Dan Skelton earned a cheer when he said the horse was his bet of the week, even at evens. "My Only worry is AP following Ruby on Dom D'Orgeval. AP will probably follow Ruby around all week, even out of the toilets!"

There was no real chance for questions until after the formal close of proceedings, when I took the opportunity to reminisce with legend of the saddle Andrew Thornton about the game Sir Rembrandt, one of my favourite staying chasers. "Don't forget him in the William Hill he said". In the end, I couldn't bring myself to back the old timer against those young handicappers.

Ruby Walsh has made preview nights his own. I heard some of his choice observations about the 2009 Festival. Never short of a refreshing view, even if it's not always on the money:

> Supreme – *"I imagine Cousin Vinny runs here and if so he will take all the beating. Go Native won't get up the hill."*

Go Native won and Cousin Vinny was unplaced.

> Arkle: *"There is no future Champion Chaser amongst these. Kalahari King has been winning donkey derbys, Forpadydeplasterer won't win but can be placed."*

Of course Pady won by a short head from Kalahari King. There was indeed no Champion Chaser in the line up, though Pady went close when he was runner up to Big Zeb the year after.

> Ryanair: *"Vor Por Ustedes is a cert. Imperial Commander is a handicapper, Monet's Garden gets lost outside of Aintree, Tidal Bay ran like a hairy goat last time and Our Vic ran terribly on his only run this season."*

Imperial Commander won from VPU, but Monet's did absolutely get lost in the race. The Commander went on to win the next year's Gold Cup amongst three Grade 1s.

This is unfair though. Ruby had a superb festival in 2009 and in the preview he also tipped up the winner of the Gold Cup (Kauto Star), the Champion Chase (Master Minded), the World Hurdle (Big Buck's – his 1st victory at 6-1), the RSA (Cooldine) and the Champion Bumper ("Patrick Mullins has ridden in a lot of bumpers this season and I know he fears Dunguib" – 6-1). Maximum respect.

I didn't always build Ozzy Osbourne in to my Festival prep. Although when nerves got the better of me and I started to jibber like a confused fool about crumbling logic resting on a series of crazy accumulator perms, I took strength from Ozzy's wisdom. For he once said "It could be worse.... I could be Sting." Less comforting, the big man from Birmingham also said "Out of everything I've lost, I miss my mind the most...."!

7. TEXAS SCRAMBLE

Columbus went around the world in 1492.
That isn't a lot of strokes when you consider the course.
Lee Trevino, major-winning golfer

"To play golf is to spoil an otherwise enjoyable walk." A caustic quote that featured in H.S. Scrivener's 1903 book 'Lawn Tennis at Home and Abroad', later more famously attributed, in truncated form, to Mark Twain.

Did you notice how casually I dropped in the reference to our golfing morning in Aldburgh a few pages back? (Keep up at the back there…) A few years ago, that would never have happened. I might have agreed with Mr Twain. I might have enjoyed hacking round a par three two-club pitch and putt for a fiver at Great Yarmouth once a year, but that was about as far as my golf went. Even armchair participation was limited in scope: the US Masters (a bit), The Open (a bit more) and of course, the Ryder Cup (quite a lot).

The Ryder Cup is always a thrill. It consistently contrives previously unknown twists that a tournament with a rich 125 year history has no right to keep inventing. The come back at Medina, for instance. Records tumbling and emotions soaring.

The one before that at Celtic Manor was Monty's finest hour; and where he won a few new admirers. The final Sunday was so wet that the event spilled into a fourth day for the first time in its history. That morning I was listening on the radio. I wasn't alone. I gather another 28 million others tuned in to events at Celtic Manor. Johnny Inverdale was the ring-master, whipping up the atmosphere and encouraging his audience to skive off work a bit longer. That's what you get for a Monday finish. He was also responsible for classic piece of radio journalism early in the day. John was queuing up for a bacon butty and indulging in a bit of open mic vox pops. "Hello Sir, can I ask you how you managed to get here today? Have you come far? Do you have an understanding boss? inquired our intrepid reporter. "I'm a marshal here actually", came the straight faced reply. We can only hope for John that he wasn't wearing his Day-Glo high-viz jacket with 'MARSHALL' stamped across the shoulders in six inch letters.

By then, I'd been playing badly, but with enthusiasm - for a little while. I think the first catalyst was my Bruv taking up the game. Initially I took little notice beyond scoffing that he'd asked for golf shoes for Christmas. Ponce. At one family get together, he and my Uncle Roland were chatting with an array of animated gestures. They'd always got on well enough, but such enthusiastic conversation was quite uncommon. I tiptoed nearer, mince pie in hand, where a couple of overheard comments helped to explain things. "Yes, I can't think of any finer feeling anywhere than a proper, full-blooded connection with the driver off the tee". Bruv nodded. "I know. Just one makes up for all those scuffs and shanks."

It wasn't long before a niggling curiosity about the ancient game crept up on me like a middle-aged desire for Ferraris, parachute jumps and tattoos. The well of intrigue sprang a leak one night when flirting with Bid Up TV.

Shopping channels are one of the strangest manifestations of satellite telly. I'll admit to a brief phase of fascination with the medium that revolved around laughing at the histrionic efforts of the bling-heavy, spray-tanned pantomime motormouths charged with selling piles of tat. It was a throwback to the TV of shifting props and visible microphone booms. If Mrs Overall had wandered in from stage left, no-one would have been surprised. Indeed, I think David Dickinson was involved at some stage. Almost the same thing.

And then one night when, after perhaps one beer too many, a shiny-suited daytime TV wannabe spoke to me directly from the shopping portal in the corner of the room about a set of oversize Dunlop golf clubs, a bag to put them in and a trolley on which to wheel them. Mrs A saw the glint in my eye. "Shall I?" I said, as if I needed an answer. Part of the hook is the auction process itself. I've read of e-bay junkies who get off only on securing a winning bid and have precious little interest in the goods they have bought. It's about the rush of winning. As a small-time gambler I can absolutely identify with this.

Bidding was a little hard to grasp at first. Once you'd been ensnared by the super-enamelled smile and pseudo-comedy pitch (the best sellers knew they were flogging absolute crap), there was a sort of proxy bid over the phone. Instead of bidding an actual price, the system would automatically bid-up to a maximum value and the clock would count down until all the units had been sold. At the end of the auction, everyone paid exactly the same price. I got to see my name scroll through the bottom of the screen when my bid was accepted. Showbiz!

I 'won' (this illusion was a significant part of the trick) my golf clubs for under £100. I felt that it was a crazy price and I was delighted with them. And unlike those e-bay mugs, I did use them. As I did the three-piece hard-shell luggage set acquired shortly after, and, indeed, the 64-piece stainless steel cutlery set a little after that. Then I quit. I had no need of therapy sessions for chronic withdrawal symptoms beyond the initial six months…

Bid Up TV has gone. It was a fairly short-lived medium in the scale of these things. I read later that this and its many sister channels had received 33 rulings against them by the Advertising Standards Authority. The two main types of problem were misleading pricing claims and misleading product descriptions. Pretty fundamental issues for a shopping channel!

I told the lads about my purchase the day we went to see England v S Africa at the Oval. They chuckled heartily. But a seed was sown. It wasn't long before the boys joined me. Nick and Bryn both bought sets (through more conventional retail routes) within weeks of each other.

Nick took to golf with gusto. Not only getting out to the range and on the course as much as he could, but spending his free time down at his nearest US Golf megastore buying up cheap, innovative and sometimes gimmicky clubs. A new putter was fair enough but the hybrid pitching/lofting club was dubious enough – a Titleist Pro V1 nearly split my face in two propelled from its face on the 17th at Ivinghoe one day - and the metal weighted swing training contraption was just mysterious. Nick also eschewed formal lessons and put his faith in sheer muscle. He engaged everything when unleashing his swing and gave the ball the sort of raw propulsion I could only dream of. It reminded me of a story that my mate GC told me after he'd been for his first lesson. The coach had been stood behind GC as he cranked up for his opening shot, gripping the club like a broadsword and unwinding an almighty white-knuckle, gritted-teeth drive. The coach looked at him and asked, "Do you play all your shots like that?" GC nodded. The pro went on, "Jesus, you must be wringing with sweat after the first hole!"

Bryn, on the other hand, took the methodological approach. He presented the golf pro at his local course a challenge when he pitched up and said, "I'm partially sighted. What can you do for me?" To his credit, the coach was brilliant. He devised a set of routines that were all about set up, repetition and alignment. Pretty sound skills for any budding golfer. Bryn couldn't see the ball at his feet very well, but he knew when he'd hit a good one off the tee.

We were all pretty crap, to be fair. But we'd certainly got the bug. Being crap all together helped. We were all learning and so were at a fairly similar level. Ben and Adam joined us too and eventually there was quite a gang of us tearing up fairways, quite literally sometimes around London and, well Aldburgh, at least once.

In fact, we'd got the bug so much that Bryn decided that his stag weekend should be a golfing weekend. And so the Arundel Masters tournament was born at Avisford Park in a quiet corner of Sussex.

The golf might have been short of quality, but the competition was never lacking in needle. It started early. Long before we got anywhere near those manicured green carpets. Deciding the format and teams for the main tournament of that first stag weekend consumed us with the dedication that we should instead have been applying to booking a strippagram or handcuffing the groom-to-be to a lamppost, naked and shorn... Is that too much information?

We settled on Texas Scramble. The only other offer on the table was an incomprehensible variation of Stapleford using a handicapping system that Harvey Smith would have plenty to say about. The collection of reprobates that had pitched up to mark Bryn's forthcoming betrothal fell into natural groups of those who could play pretty well, those with some ability and those with bugger all. Texas Scramble suited the construction of teams with members from each of those loose collections, captained by lads who, it was rumoured, could play a bit.

The format's key attribute was a variation on a foursome where the captain chose the best shot and everyone took the next dubious swing from that lie. Crucially, everyone had to get in four shots off the tee. This meant that there was no over-reliance on the captain's qualities. It also meant that it was a genuine effort, with everyone required to play a part.

If that was the rules agreed, aided by alcoholic inspiration, the team composition was next. Bacchy, Ben and Paul self-selected as captains. That was the easy bit. Sorting out their supporting cast involved matching perceived ability with actual vision. Talent, or lack of it, was corralled into a rough hierarchy (sparing no-one's feelings) and then cross-filtered so that each team had fully-sighted players balanced the partially sighted lads – Bryn, Pete, Ad and Andy, collectively known as the blindies. (Forgive this apparent affront to political correctness. It is a term of affection – mostly - used by the guys themselves.) The elaborate matrix was aided by physically drawing names from some brass-ware receptacles liberated from the oak mantelpiece of the Black Horse's lounge bar fireplace.

We swayed back from the pub to the hotel up the road. I imply 'up the road' as if it was a relaxed stroll. It was, infact, a busy road. In the dark. No speed limit and no footway. Half of us were blind. All were blind drunk. It took a while…

…Nevertheless, come the appointed time on Saturday, out we strode into a gorgeous September morning, fuelled by a monstrous fried breakfast, Nick's single malt-filled hipflask and Andy's 1.5 litre bottle of rum and coke.

Stood on that lonely tee, at that moment, we non-captains prayed for just one break: to get a good clean shot away off the first. In truth, anything over the ditch a mere 80 yards away would do. It was not much to ask. But there was a lot at stake. Ian Poulter's fist pumping and heart thumping Ryder Cup shenanigans would not have been out of place here.

Bacchy, arguably the best amongst us (having once held that mystical stamp of greatness - the handicap mark) set the highest standard on that hallowed first tee. He was the first to step onto the plate, when the tension was tightest, the nerves most taught. Bacchy addressed the ball confidently, twitching his vintage wooden wood with a worn metal plate held in place by tiny cross-thread screws. He squatted over the ball, poised like a coiled spring; drew back his cocked arms and described a perfect arc with his smooth and fast swing. The outcome was a beautiful, clinical and absolute air shot. No contact at all with the little white ball sat smugly on its spike. The club face whooshed into the beautiful follow-through accompanied by hysterical hoots and the sound of apprehension bursting.

As if in sympathy, all our team's first shots were a pile of cack too. One spannered left field, another limped apologetically past the ladies tee and the last slammed into the ditch on a trajectory never more than six inches above the turf.

The round wasn't all as bad as that. It offered up sporadic encouragement in the form of acceptable drives, chips, lofts and putts. These were mostly overwhelmed, however, by a litany of duffs, tops, slices and shanks. Little balls were pursued from rough to scrub to bunker and finally to green and hole with relentless enthusiasm and expletives. GC, he of the gritted-teeth swing, called me from Berko as I was trudging up the excruciatingly long par 5 4th. "Got any tips for the St Leger today Dave?" I didn't have any information for him, but we had a chat anyway. I mentioned the hangover, the wayward golf, and the fast-emptying hipflask. "All going to plan then!" he chortled.

Hole 13 was the biggest challenge. It was only a par three, but between the tee and the green lay The Ravine. The Chasm. The Gaping Canyon. Across that weekend of three rounds, we variously christened this hole – with only the barest hint of melodramatic overplay – the hole of doom, the valley of gloom, and that f***in' 13th. We lived up to its billing. Some went right, I hit many trees, others scooped into the bottomless pit. We took painful drops under the sheer cliff face of that impossible green. (From the top, given the state of our game, surely one of us peered over the edge uttered that immortal line, 'Have you ever thought of tossing yourself off?') Our disintegrating game was only cheered up by the grim looks on the faces of our other teams behind and in front. Knitted brows, stony stares, monosyllabic banter. And more nips from the hip flask.

Somehow we ended up being the winning team. Beers were bought in the clubhouse and a topless golf DVD was produced as the prize. I'm pretty sure Paul snaffled that and it has not been seen since.

The bar in the hotel was OK, but still a sterile hotel bar when all said and done. Bitter like dishwater, prices like holy water. After dinner, we revisited the Black Horse. Puerile stag behaviour half-heartedly reared its head when Bryn was lined up for a night with the two gay landlords.

He escaped his rendezvous and instead we spent an inordinate amount of time playing some farcical word game entirely based around making up new names from footballers merged with drinks. Lowlights included Lomana KahLualua (genius Brynaldo) Highland Park Ji-Sung, and Boddingtony Adams. I think we even strayed onto planets at curious stage (JuPeter Schmeichel, Marc OverMars). Dread to think what we came up with for Uranus... Future European Ryder Cup captains could do a lot worse than call us in for motivational talks before the singles finale.

Whisky finishes back in the bar almost battered our stag party into submission. And yet we roused ourselves for an epic Bits n Pieces pop quiz in mine and Nick's room. Rock and Roll is not dead. Avisford Park Hilton had thoughtfully provided each room with a complimentary 1/3 third bottle of cheap red wine. The lads all brought their contributions along. I think three of us had done the name-that-tune tapes and Nick had brought his ghetto blaster along. So, fuelled by thin Cab Sauv we identified our way through snippets of Motorhead, REM, Kylie and God only knows what else until the night porter brought events to a swift close. He'd had enough of complaints about crap 1980's europap emanating from room 213.

I suspect it was very late, but I don't know for sure. I do know that a few short hours later we were more or less woken up by urgent thumping on the door and shouts of "Morning lads. Sleep well!" Our neighbours leaving early, I guessed.

No-one made the golf course that Sunday morning. Bacchy and I could only muster a weary glance at the Goodwood card. The track was just down the road, but any beer talk in the bar last night about pitching up for an afternoon's racing had quickly evaporated in the sharp, headache-inducing September sunlight.

A few weeks later, the Richmond Hill hotel played host to a screaming night for Bryn and Debs' post nuptial party. Mrs A and I stayed over. Just as well. Nick's wife Den was in fine form. So much so that she needed to borrow our room for a chuck up and lie down after the red wine got the better of her. Nick was none too pleased about having to whistle up a cab and leave the party early. His eyebrows were doing the dance of doom across his forehead. We all thought it was hysterical to see him sucking up a bit of his own medicine for a change.

Den was pleased that Bryn's wedding was a one off. Thankfully, the Arundel golf weekend remained a fixture for a number of years.

8. ROYAL WINDSOR RACES

The price of a decent seat at a West End theatre is £35;
for the cost of six seats, you can have a goodish time on a
racecourse
and not have to talk to, or buy ice creams for, five people in the
interval.
Clement Freud, Freud On Course, 2009

Sometimes you plan a trip to the races and everything conspires against you. The trains are truculent (Huntingdon). The weather is miserable Towcester). The beer is gassy (Catterick). The horses lose (Everywhere). When the plan comes together though it is worth doffing one's cap to the moment. A rather splendid, perfectly executed, borderline classy trip to Royal Windsor Racecourse one fine August day was just such a moment.

It was a sparkly day of azure skies, dazzling whites and lush greens and smart-casual. The Summer of 2007 had been pretty damp all round. So, as GC remarked to us, sipping a pre-race Pimms and fruit salad creation (and doing remarkably well to avoid poking himself in the eye with a sharp straw), "The wettest, coldest August in a generation and we organise perfect high summer weather for one day only? How does that happen then?" He was right. I composed a smug grin, the effect of which was slightly tarnished by stringy pineapple bits and strawberry pips wedged in my teeth, left over from my own Pimms & fruit punch encounter.

I may be over-emphasising the literal detail of the summer cocktails here. But you catch the mood, I suspect.

Indeed that mood had been perfectly cast the moment we left for the track. No-one wanted to drive with those alcoholic fruit salads in prospect, and training our way to Windsor and Eton Riverside BR was always going to be too convoluted for comfort. So the taxi alternative was an easy decision. But Mrs A and I were certainly not expecting the shiny Mercedes-Benz S class parked outside Bex and GC's place, nor the grey suited, peak capped, leather gloved driver holding open the doors for us. This was no mere taxi. This was a chauffeured limousine! Turns out GC and Bex knew Rob the driver and had asked him for the full works.

And that is precisely what we got. Apart from a couple of moments of anxiety, trapped in the never ending, budget spiralling M25 road-widening works, we breezed over to Berkshire. The highlight of the journey, I recall vividly, was being waved through the barrier by Day-Glo-jacket man as he peered through the windows of our Merc to see which celebs were being chauffeured in. We pulled up hard against the main entrance whilst the poor mugs in the hail-a-ride jalopies behind were tipped out at the barrier. I swear Mrs A crafted a regal twist of a gloved hand for the crowds as we cruised through.

The champagne cocktails and Pimm's frivolities didn't last long. Guinness (always my real-ale stand by), red and white wine were soon flowing faster than the adjacent Thames. Normal service resumed.

Windsor has surprisingly few weekend fixtures. Most of its meetings are shoehorned into the increasingly popular end-of-work to end-of-daylight slots during Summer evenings. So it felt like the locals had made the effort to capitalise on this gorgeous day by turning out both in force and éclat. There was enough exotic headgear to put the pimms fruit salads in the shade. Nice to see Mrs A and Bex easily surpassing the standard, though. Blimey, they scrub up well (given a clear brief and sufficient lead in time, that is…)

It wasn't a day for serious punting. The four of us ponced around the paddock (or was that just me?), schmoozed through the bars, lingered by the running rail and joked with the oompah band…. generally soaking up the vibes and bantering the day away.

The racing was a good enough middle-ranking mix of handicaps and maidens, with one conditions sprint chucked in for a nod to quality. My nap for that race, Galeota came a fairish 2nd (and went on to win three times in the remainder of the season unburdened of my cash on each occasion). It was his first outing for 2 years having failed at stud after shooting jaffas! I didn't get any closer with the straight bets, but I didn't half give the placepot a scare. Smirfy's Gold needed to make the frame to land me what I suspected would be a decent dividend. He was fast out of the blocks and gave me a real thrill before fading out of the places in the final furlong. A frameless 4th. The divi was £146 to a £1 stake. I had a wringing wet two-quid ticket welded to my sweaty little palm. A very, very, near miss.

GC had much better luck. We crossed to the far side of the track for the feature handicap. Nice perspective from there back to the packed stands. We watched the field flash past us at close quarters, to collective groans as we racked up more losers. But no, not collective. GC was grinning like a Cheshire cat! He'd only bagged the 12-1 winner, Muhannak! Where had that come from? Fantastic!

After racing, we joined most of the other punters on the very pleasant boat trip back up the Thames to the town centre, passing giant riverside spreads with cruisers privately moored at the bottom of manicured grounds. The refined residents must have loved the bawdy and full throttle racket emanating from these ferries lurching their way upstream.

Windsor really is a lovely spot and we unearthed a pleasant little restaurant for dinner tucked away and down a side street.

After troughing heartily we inexplicably concluded that another drink was needed. Of course! We'd only been on the sauce for about six hours! I remember winding up Castle Hill and stopping to tell Bex, GC and Mrs A about a Waggamama restaurant that used to be a kebab house. I lamented the fine, hand-crafted produce that this place used to purvey. Last time the lads and me were here, Bryn had a unique thing called a kebab roll. I'd never seen anything like it before…. a flat bread and kebab meat creation with no salad. Fascinating. I turned round from staring in disgust at the new restaurant to find myself alone. Bereft! Those bloody fast-food philistines had high-tailed it off to the Horse and Groom. I soon caught up.

Time fizzed by and my recollection gets hazy. But I do remember GC flicking open his phone, saying something like "Beam us up Rob" and miraculously the Merc appeared right there, right then to teleport us home. Fan-bloody-tastic. And then, we staggered out of the car straight into The Lamb, round the corner from our house. I don't know why. I sort of recall the four of us lording it over the place, telling anyone who would listen that we'd had a top day at the races but that we'd only had one miserable winner to share between us. I also remember trying to square the debts of the day with GC at the bar.

"Two tickets for the races equals half a cab fare plus a quarter of the dinner. I'll see you and raise you."

We were in no fit state for such high finance. GC, mate, I still don't know if I ever properly settled this one...

There are photos in circulation that present circumstantial evidence that we ended up at ours, sinking into oblivion in the wee small hours. A fitting end to a very smart day out.

9. THREE DAY WEEK

The Gods have spoken! It is the return to the three-day festival!
John Randall, Racing Post journalist, 2008

These pages have described in heart-on-sleeve tones just how special is the Cheltenham Festival. You know, the "highest quality racing in one of nature's great amphitheatres played out in front of a raucous crowd packing the stands to the rafters and gambling their every last penny…" stuff. It's all true.

The festival is also a test of endurance. In the days of the three-day Festival I would collapse in a heap on the train home. Bacchy in the seat next to me, neither of us able to raise much more than an incoherent gabble about shifting fortunes as depicted in the annual Schedule of Shame™ bet spreadsheet.

I would usually return emotionally drained, physically shattered, mentally overwhelmed and sometimes financially bankrupt.

When the full-fat high calorific four-day Festival became a reality in 2005, it was one-day further than I was prepared to go. I knew my limits. So the Festival in 2008 provided an interesting return to the three-day format in the most unusual of circumstances.

Everything had been proceeding to plan. After a full day's intense action at Prestbury Park cheering home a new Arkle hero in Tidal Bay and a new Champion Hurdler in Katchit, we pitched up at Auntie Mona's to be greeted by a table resembling the deli counter at Waitrose. Every year since the turn of the century, Mona had been welcoming Bacchy and I into the bosom of her home and treating us like kings.

We fell in to the routine easily. After a bite to eat and the well rehearsed banter between Mona and Bacchy about tea drinking ("Ah now, you're the funny lad who doesn't like tea. Paul, will you fetch that percolator down from that there top cupboard and make the boy some coffee...) we headed off to pubs in Gloucester for some more well rehearsed banter with the ever present Irish lads who would tell us what a rubbish bunch of novices they had this season, and then we would watch them all yag home over the next couple of days...

Next morning seemed to be following the format as I emerged into the kitchen to play out Mona's morning joke:

"How did you sleep Dave?"
"Like a log, Mona."
"Woke up in the fireplace, eh?"

Events, however, were not conforming to the template at all.

"Seen this Davoski?"

Bacchy was pointing at The Morning Line which showed rows of corporate tents with roofs stripped bare by high overnight winds. Temporary stands were looking precarious and bits of girders and struts were poking out of the tented village at curious angles. The winds had whipped up a good deal of frenzied action at the course early on that Wednesday morning. Edward Gillespie, Cheltenham's Chief Executive was on the Morning Line by 8.30am reporting danger everywhere: flying debris, collapsing sub-structures and tented village mayhem. The site had been declared unsafe and Champion Chase day had been cancelled.

Or not cancelled, but, as it emerged later that morning, postponed, dismembered and stitched back together with Friday's card in some crazy Frankenstein's monster of a meeting. Tickets would be refunded in full and all Wednesday's races would be rescheduled for Thursday and Friday, grafted on to the rest of the festival programme. That meant ten races on Thursday and nine on Friday.

John Randall, the Racing Post's historian, archivist and resident anorak, texted the delicious Tanya on the Morning Line to credit a higher authority with the interventions. "The Gods have spoken! It is the return to the three day festival!"

We didn't yet have tickets for the Thursday. We had planned to pick them up at the track early on Wednesday. Now we were thinking that every man and his dog would want to be there to see history being made'.

We headed over there early and in truth we had nothing to fear. We were at the course in plenty of time to bag a ticket for the following day. But it was a tingly moment. I clasped the ticket in my sweaty hands and let out a little yelp of joy at the prospect of this monstrous card of Grade 1s, 2s and stunningly competitive handicaps from dawn till dusk the next day.

There was time to poke about the racecourse for the morning. We wandered through the National Hunt Hall of Fame for an hour, soaking up some nostalgia (Dawn Run nicking the Gold Cup from Wayward Lad) and reliving past glories (Michael Dickinson's 1-2-3-4-5 in the '80s). There were plenty of folk about doing the same as us, too.

The Course was all dressed up with nowhere to go: the bars were open, the bookies were taking bets on Huntingdon and Southwell; there were enough fluorescent-bibbed security guards to demand the wearing of sunglasses; the Centaur conference suite was playing the Best Mate Story on a giant screen to a three-parts empty room of disinterested punters shuffling around aimlessly. The enclosures were off limits (back to the dangerous winds), but we snuck a peak through the gates near the Best Mate enclosure at a deserted concourse just before 2pm, the scheduled off-time for the Ballymore Hurdle. Surreal.

Cheltenham town centre was similarly ill at ease with itself: 40-odd thousand punters had to go somewhere. Every pub was rammed. The bookies were overflowing. I even struggled to get a cup of coffee in the back-street Starbuck's. At the station a fleet of double-decker buses were parked neatly in line by the entrance waiting to shuttle hordes of eager racegoers that did not turn up.

Bacchy and I regrouped at Mona's. There was time to have a relaxed few beers and plot our way through the new cards. And eschewing the usual kebab option, we even found a decent curry house for some grub.

Next morning, Edward Gillespie informed us on the Morning Line that everything was OK for racing. Early start though. First race was 12.30pm. Despite our clamour to get tickets for Thursday, the restructure seemed to have an impact on the attendance. The crowd was distinctly thinner than the Tuesday, though the roar that accompanied the tapes going up for the first race was no less enthusiastic. Was it tinged with a little jeer, or was that just my imagination?

The day didn't disappoint. Right from Old Benny's grinding win in the opening 4-miler, through to a thrilling finish when Cousin Vinny gave Willie Mullins yet another bumper success in a race completed in near darkness and through streaming drizzle.

Master Minded delivered an absolutely remarkable performance in the Queen Mother. This, year after year, is my favourite race: seasoned chasers streaming over fences with pinpoint accuracy at high cruising speeds. Master Minded left the rest of the field for dead today. When jockey Ruby Walsh eased down his mount coming home, the horse was still pulling away from the game but outclassed Voy Por Ustedes in 2nd.

Ruby's pixelated face, magnified ten-times on the big screen, betrayed astonishment. This was a breathtaking display. But for emotional intensity, what about Inglis Drever landing his third World Hurdle crown? A feat never achieved before. And how he had to work for it. On ground softer than ideal, hitting a longer flat spot than usual and boxed in between Kazal and My Way de Solzen, Inglis somehow raised his game, jinked out from the hole and outstayed Kasbah Bliss back up the hill. Not a dry eye in the house, I swear. Marvellous scenes.

And what else? A first, overdue, festival success for Sue Smith with the evergreen Mister McGoldrick who absolutely bolted in at 50-1; Our Vic who finally landed a Grade 1after donning blinkers for the first time at the ripe old age of 10; and Evan Williams breaking his Festival duck with High Chimes.

Me? Nine losing races out of ten... Kazal's 3rd in the World Hurdle saved me a complete blow out. But I was in serious debt after 16 races. So going home after only two of the three days still felt as draining as the full Monty.

The prospect of settling down to watch the Friday extravaganza in a big-screen—comfortable-pub environment was very welcoming. However, in a mad moment of scheduling amnesia, I had to go in to work for a morning meeting. On normal Festival Friday this would have been achievable, but with a near-dawn start on that extended day, I had little chance of making the opening races. Added to this, my hollowed-out Festival demeanour was detected immediately I walked in the door. "Are you sure you should be here?" inquired my boss.

I scuttled out of the meeting as soon as polite and flattened a cycle dispatch rider on my screech to Old Street tube. (Revenge, barely noticed at the time, for the many such encounters that had gone the other way.) The clock was ticking too quickly. The mares' hurdle was kicking off at 12.30pm. I leapt out of the tube at Euston and took the steps two at a time to the first floor William Hill's in the quad outside the station. Whiteoak's short-head victory at 20-1 was almost as breathless as my cross-London charge. She was gifted the race by an idling Refinement and as I flew back in to the station I briefly chastised myself for deserting McCain's mare whom I had backed a couple of times that season.

I had 35 minutes to make it to the boozer for the Ballymore Hurdle. One of my red-letter races in which Trafford Lad was my flag bearer. The Victoria Line was so slow and packed to the straps. Waiting outside Victoria with twitching nerves it became obvious that I wouldn't make it to Laddies in time. A working knowledge of every bookie in central London came to my rescue and I made it to the Billy Hill's near Buckingham Palace Road to see the final circuit.

Trafford Lad ran well enough and I began on the come-back trail with a little return on his 3rd place. He was behind an epic struggle between Venalmar and Fiveforthree, which I glimpsed through bobbing and weaving heads in the bookies, They were hammer and tongs over the last few furlongs, with the latter just prevailing under a driving Ruby Walsh ride. One of the best finishes of the week.

There was some immediate, although fleeting compensation for the Trafford Lad defeat. I swaggered in to the pub having landed the second leg of a fantasy festival double with Fiveforthree, which put me in pole position for the prize. Or so I thought. I blew out in the Gold Cup later. Nevertheless, I took the opportunity to remind the lads that I was firmly on the premises. I was so full of myself that I failed to register one of the toughest reversals of Bacchy's pro-punting escapade.

He had witnessed Venalmar's defeat in the Ladbrokes next to the Jugged Hare. He had a lot of money riding on the Mouse Morris beast, ante-post. Bacchy celebrates winners and mourns losers with pretty much the same intensity irrespective of the stake. When Venalmar was chinned, Nev was standing next to him. In one of those deeply perceptive observations with which a casual observer might not credit him, Nev sized up Bacchy's emotions. He looked with slow deliberation, and after a pause said: "That one meant a lot, didn't it?" Bacchy said "Yeah". They exchanged glances, but they were already on their way back to the pub and nothing more was said. I knew later how much that one had hurt him.

It took me every one of the nine races on that Friday to get myself back in profit. Remarkably, I ended the peculiar meeting back in the black.

The sight of Nenuphar Collonges plugging on up the hill to claim victory in the 3 mile novice hurdle when every other beast was treading water will stay with me for a very long time. That was the big winner I was searching for. The Coral Cup was close. Ferdy Murphy's Naiad Du Misselot somehow got up to beat Kicks For Free on the line by the new distance of 'a nose'. Junior was third to land me some place wedge.

So by the time the Gold Cup came round I was quite relaxed. I could enjoy the spectacle. And I did. Watching Denman gallop reigning champion Kauto Star into submission was awesome. The horse was simply relentless. A juggernaut. Maybe it wasn't quite the race some envisaged. There was no dramatic moment as Kauto Star cruised up to Denman's shoulder. No opportunity for the nation to hold its breath for six seconds and wonder what would come next. But it was no less impressive to these old eyes.

The Fantasy Festival had gone in the Gold Cup when a couple of the guys outpunted me with big stakes on Denman. I played too conservative.

Bagging a 33-1 winner in the Foxhunters was just sheer spawn. I remembered Amicelli as a decent novice chaser for Philip Hobbs. So a few quid on him for that reason was enough. I don't think I even looked at the rest of the card. And up he trotted. Easy as you like.

Another marathon day of punting ended in a blur of London Pride and dodgy kebabs. That was about the only predictable part of this particular Cheltenham Festival when, with apologies to the Spice Girls, four became three.

10. CELEBRATING THE KEBAB

Hear 'Fancy a takeaway?' and for a split second feel
like your outsider has just won the races.
Just Eat, London Underground advert, 2015

I harp on about the humble doner kebab in these pages so much that I feel it is only right to devote a little formal appreciation to this extraordinary culinary delicacy. The catalyst for this tribute is the generous coverage that accompanied the passing of Kadir Nurman in 2013 in Berlin, aged 80.

Kadir, a Turkish immigrant to Germany, was a pioneer in popularising the doner kebab. The idea of grilling huge lumps of meat on a rotating skewer was not new but, so the BBC reports, "Nurman had the idea of selling the sliced meat and salad sandwiched between flatbread so that it could be eaten on the move." Genius, of course.

Nurman apparently set up a stall in the German capital back in 1972 so that late night Berliner revellers might partake of "something to offset the effects of large quantities of beer." The number of kebabhauses in Berlin now tops a 1,000. Those Germans eh?

The explosion of taste derived from juicy, loosely lamb-related product, carved generously from a thick rotating skewer of the stuff, combined with pitta, salad and piquant chilli sauce is now an indispensible modern day classic. Nurman's achievements were rightly recognised by the Association of Turkish Doner Manufacturers in 2011. However, he apparently distanced himself a little from the current manifestation of the beast he created, claiming they had begun to use too many ingredients.

I'm probably on the side of Kadir.

The UK's first bona fide kebab shop opened in Stoke Newington in 1966. Once Nurman's doner-on-the-go invention had reached these shores, the industry soon powered up. It currently employs about 70,000 people, supplying and running 17,000 outlets and is worth more than £2bn a year to the economy. Tory MP Nadhim Zahawi recently co-organised a competition to celebrate the achievements of the industry, along the lines of the British Curry Awards. Those Tories eh?

And yet the doner still does not garner the respect it deserves. It came as no surprise that the furious horse meat scandal of that same year would sooner or later engulf the humble kebab shop. Long the butt of jokes about the quality and identity of their meat, it turns out that some may have received 100% horse meat - labelled as beef or lamb - from a UK slaughterhouse and meat factory. Horse meat, in my view, is far from the worst ingredient to be found in take away food.

I remain a staunch supporter of this fine product.

> *The Bella Doner*
>
> *My favourite kebab house, 'The Bella Doner' is only two minutes stagger from the tube, but it is on a side-street, and food snobs and vegetarians never seem to find their way there, even on Saturday nights.*
>
> *Its customers, though fairly eclectic, are mostly 'regulars' who indulge in the same savoury treat every visit and go there for the quality as much as the convenience.*
>
> *If you are asked why you favour a particular kebab house, it is often the shish that is mentioned first, but the thing that most appeals to me about 'The Bella Doner' is that giant spit of dripping roasted meat itself, or what people often call the 'elephants foot', amongst other less charitable names.*

The whole architecture and fittings of this kebab house are uncompromisingly practical. It has no grained woodwork, ornamental mirrors, subdued lighting or sham Michelin-ia.

On the contrary, it has glass fronted counters, Formica tables, plastic panels and other modern simplicities. The stained floors, the chipped chiller-cabinets, the neon fly-electrocutor, the peeling ceiling stained dark yellow by griddle-smoke, the stuffed pickle jar on the fridge. Everything has the transient functionality of the late twentieth century.

In winter there is generally a fierce heat coming from at least two of the grills, and the corner shop lay-out of the place means you don't have to queue outside should there be other customers. On the illuminated price list there are doner kebabs, shish kebabs, shami kebab, burgers, deep-fried chicken, 'extras' and humus for those too bashful to risk eating kebab meat in public.

There may be a video game machine tucked away in the corner, but it is on low volume so doesn't disturb the general ambience of the place.

In 'The Bella Doner ' it is usually quiet enough for conversation, but no more than pleasant small talk. Instead, you watch the telly in the corner showing an obscure game-show. Even on late nights and such occasions the chatting that happens is of a decorous kind.

The shop proprietors don't know any of their customers by name, and try not to take a personal interest in anyone. They are all middle-aged men. Two of them have three days facial hair growth and builders clefts big

enough to park a bike in. They call everyone 'mate',
irrespective of age and avoid eye contact. ('Mate,' not
'Matey': kebab shops where the server calls you 'Matey'
always have a dodgy raffish atmosphere.)

Unlike most kebab houses, 'The Bella Doner' sells
kutluma, pakora and samosa as well as chips, and it also
sells condoms, 'morning after pills', and is obliging
about using the loo in an emergency.

You cannot get beer at 'The Bella Doner', but there is
always the glass-fronted fridge where you can get coke,
lucozade and even kefir (a speciality of the house), as
well as tea, hot chocolate and that bitter, weak coffee
that only seems to exist in take-aways.

The special pleasure of their doner kebab is that you can
have home made chilli sauce with it. I doubt whether as
many as ten per cent of London kebab houses make their
own sauce these days, but 'The Bella Doner' is one of
them. It is a sharp, piquant, fiery sort of sauce and goes
perfectly with the meat.

They are particular about how the kebabs are served at
'The Bella Doner' and never, for example, make the
mistake of serving them in a polystyrene tray. The
modern trend is for a deconstructed kebab with pitta,
meat, salad and sauce piled on top of each other in a
closed polystyrene tray and then suffocated in a plastic
bag. But in my opinion a kebab tastes better out of a
paper wrapping. Apart from the usual pitta bread, The
Bella Doner' also serves some of those pleasant doner
wraps rolled in flatbreads.

The great surprise of 'The Bella Doner' is its restaurant.
You go through a narrow passage leading out of the

take-away, and find yourself in a fairly large room of plastic tables and chairs with framed pictures of Turkish landmarks hanging on the walls.

Here, you can get table service, for example, mixed kebab, or chicken kebab with shredded salad and chips served on real crockery and eaten with a knife and fork for about a six quid.

On late evenings there are no drunken rowdies. You can sit in the restaurant or at the little metal tables out the front of the shop and tuck into your kebab feast without being disturbed by loutish behaviour and foul language.

Many as are the virtues of 'The Bella Doner' I think that the restaurant is its best feature, because it encourages a cross section of society to go there, instead of being the preserve of late night junk food drunks.

And though this is regulated and processed food, some horse meat inevitably sneaks into the doner mix. This, I believe, is against the law, but it is a law that deserves to be broken, for it is the puritanical nonsense of excluding this perfectly reasonable and nutritious flesh that has to some extent, reduced the quality of the doner and therefore its reputation.

'The Bella Doner' is my ideal of what a kebab shop should be at any rate, in the London area. (The qualities one expects of a regional emporium are slightly different.)

But now is the time to reveal something that the discerning and disillusioned reader will probably have guessed already. There is no such place as 'The Bella Doner'. That is to say, there may well be a kebab house of that name, but I don't know of it, nor do I know any house with just that combination of qualities.

85

I know kebab houses where the shish is good but you can't sit down, others where the chicken kebab is to die for but which are dripping with noisy and unruly crowds, and others which are quiet but the doner is generally greasy. As for restaurants, offhand I can only think of a dozen London kebab shops that possess them.

But, to be fair, I do know of a few places that almost come up to 'The Bella Doner'. I have mentioned above qualities that the perfect kebab house should have, and I know of one that has eight of them. Even there, however, the chilli sauce is bland and the restaurant is not open in the evenings.

And if anyone knows of a kebab house that has a wide range of juicy kebabs, home made chilli sauce, take-aways served in paper wrappers, a restaurant and eclectic clientele, I should be glad to hear of it, even though its name were something as prosaic as 'Kebab Machine', or 'McDonners'.

Should anyone recognise the structure and nuance of 'The Bella Doner' as described above, all I can say is that I am paying homage (and huge apologies) to the memory of the great George Orwell, born 110 years ago this June. His outstanding essay about the perfect pub 'The Moon Under Water' was published in the Evening Standard in 1946.

11. UP HILL ALL THE WAY ROUND

*I'm afraid the dramatic uninterrupted view of the horses going out
into the country
and returning up the punishing hill has been ruined
by dumping a dog track in front of the stands.*
Trip Advisor review of Towcester racecourse, 2015

Towcester racecourse received a very positive airing in the first
collection of these rambling tales. The phrase 'up hill all the way
round' was a tongue in cheek quote from a trainer bemoaning the
extremity of the circuit. I was tickled to discover that betting chat
rooms are regularly baited with the wind up "which jumps track is
uphill all the way round?" When posted to a football forum, the
question received 3,000 replies.

Towcester is my local track and I still have a soft spot for it. Though
circumstances are changing and how much longer I will love its
rolling acres and friendly charm is open to question.

Over the years, the track has hosted any number of our outings. For a
small town gaff track, it can often punch above its weight. I've
mentioned my mate GC in an earlier chapter. Towcester played a
part in our 50th birthday present to him.

When the time for gift-giving arrived, we left the precise details a
little hazy. His instructions were clear: to arrive at our house
(accompanied by Bex) prepared for the elements, no passport
needed, and packing swimming trunks, just in case.

The budgie smugglers were, of course, a complete red-herring (oh
how we laughed) but would GC know that? Subtle, eh? They made a
verbal appearance amongst many other futile wind ups as we took
the train northwards. Passing a flooded gravel pit:

"GC, your present is actually a wreck dive over there in Leighton Buzzard. Did you bring your wet suit? No worries. You can borrow mine. Only I'll be wearing it at the same time."

"Not a problem, Mr A. Back to back or front to front suit you?"

We disembarked at Wolverton where there should have been one taxi with Granny inside, waiting to whisk the girls away and another waiting to whisk us on to the venue. There were none. Only a blustery rain-lashed car park. I looked at Mrs A who offered a supportive smile. We waited in an open fronted corrugated iron shack serving as a ticket office, avoiding drips from the leaky roof. Wolverton used to be home to the mighty BR workshops turning out rolling stock for the finest railway in the World. Most of it has gone now. Including, one dark night, the removal of the station roof and fittings. Pulled down, despite being listed, to save repair costs. It was a bleak station then.

I glanced at GC. Hands thrust deep into pockets. Trench coat collar turned up. Double woolly balaclava hugging his gnarled face. OK, I made the last bit up. He was gritting his teeth though. And I swear I could hear him humming 'Happy Birthday to me....'. He surveyed the windswept scene and asked with a grin "Is this the bit where I say thanks for my birthday present?" How we hooted. Nervously in my case.

Just then, the SpeedLine taxi cavalry came over the hill and we were on our way again. I'd bagged the nice roomy front seat because I was in charge of directions. Very important. I looked behind as I uttered something witty (possibly) and noticed that, GC, a bit bigger than me, was slightly cosier. Elbows tucked in and hunching over, neatly wedged between Mrs A and Bex. A thorn between two roses? A fart between two cheeks? Hard to say really.

By the time we'd navigated the Old Stratford A5 roundabout, GC had worked it out. "I think it's Towcester races" he beamed.

I was getting worried about the rain. Squally showers kept bumping into each other, blowing in from the west on a sharp breeze. The ground at Towcester was already heavy. Many more minutes of steely stair-rods and we would have been flirting with abandonment. My jitters didn't calm much as we scampered through rain bouncing off the tarmac to get to the Empress Stand.

But once inside I was happy. This was all new. Towcester was a track I knew very well and loved. I had always been with the proles next door, though. I'd never passed through the 'hospitality guests' entrance before. I positively flounced up to the reception, puffed out my chest and said, "We've got four reservations for the Empress Restaurant please".

We were shown upstairs, through double swing doors and into an open plan, well appointed dining room. There was a bar at one end and a huge glass wall leading to private balconies at the front. Betting stations with TV screens were strategically placed around the edges. The dining tables were beautifully set and already had waist-coated waiters fussing around seated guests. We introduced ourselves and were shown to table 16, handy for the bar, the telly and the betting booth.

I think GC was impressed. He didn't stop grinning until his first race loss. He must have secretly feared an afternoon of pot noodles and fizzy lager on the steps of the wind-buffeted grandstand. I was impressed too - and a bit relieved. It's not always clear exactly what you get in these circumstances. But I have to say, Towcester put on a top show.

There was already wine on the table, but I went to the bar for some aperitifs. And received a verbal cuff on the ear for my trouble. "Take a seat, sir. We'll serve you at your table", said waist-coated lady, mildly surprised at my procedural gaffe.

A young, fastidious chap called Mike arrived to take our drinks order. He looked after us wonderfully. And when the main course was a bit late, he brought us a complimentary bottle of wine and was full of apologies "I'm so sorry for the delay, the kitchen's full." We wondered what that meant, precisely. Cooks jammed in right up to the rafters, all vying for hob space? An explosion of expanding insulation foam, pinning an army of sous-chefs against the wall?

The wine was a welcome, but in truth, unnecessary gesture. We were there all afternoon and would rather have good food cooked well than rushed. And indeed it was. Smoked salmon with a crab and coriander salad; chicken breast in mushroom, garlic and Madeira sauce with fondant potatoes, butternut squash and roast beetroot; followed by espresso panecotta with chocolate sauce and Viennese biscuits. I guess they were all out of arctic roll…

Our betting rep was called BJ (no smirking at the back there, please). He was also very attentive. "That's a nice watch", I said, dazzled by a glittery pink metal bracelet holding a face the size of an Olympic discus. "Fank you Sir, I left my gaudy one at home as it's a Sunday". BJ was a good laugh. He helped out Bex and Mrs A when they did that time honoured, doe-eyed 'I-don't-know-what-I'm-doing–this-betting-is-so complicated' trick, merely because they didn't want to queue at the booth. Shameless. Mrs A thought she recognised something in his camp manner, his rolling gait, and his sizeable girth. "He would remind you of Peter Kay in a not-remindy kind of way, don't you think?" We all merely blinked back, trying to picture what that meant, exactly.

Not that Bex and Mrs A needed any help on the betting. Bloody hell! Bex bagged the winner of the first, a lovely looking prospect called Whoops A Daisy, trained by Nicky Henderson. The horse glided through the mud as if on rails. And later she picked up again when Round The Horn cantered up by the length of the straight. A few near misses for GC and for me, but they don't seem pay out much for those.

We'd been watching the races from the private balconies running across the front of the restaurant, removing us from the hurly-burly of the steppings below us. Our vantage point provided a superb view to catch the races, but also opened up the vista over the track and down to Towcester town nestling in the valley. It may not be Goodwood on the Downs or Cheltenham in the Cotswolds, but this is still one of the finest aspects in racing.

Back at the table, just in case we were getting peckish – obviously a real risk - afternoon tea had arrived. Hardly seemed a moment since lunch. Life is just such a struggle sometimes. I tucked into scones, jam and clotted cream with the gusto of a half-starved waif, ready for the next race.

Mrs A was sticking to her tried and tested strategy of backing long shots. So how did she miss Tuvalu who won the 2nd at 40-1? Because she was on already on Fantastic Morning at a slightly more conservative 25-1 is why. But there was no jeering when Tarabela won in some style at 28-1! Mrs A went to collect her winnings from that nice BJ man in the Ladbrokes booth and she positively swaggered back to the table before slamming down the fattest wedge of crinkly greenbacks I've ever seen. Well, as fat as £60 can be, anyway. We declared that she was an absolute genius of the track and I was a bit worried she'd gatecrash my trip to Cheltenham. But only a bit.

On a sourer note, the green screens had gone up around Panzer who fell after the last. This is always disturbing, and particularly so in front of packed grandstands. It usually only means one thing. But thankfully the horse was no more than winded and was soon led away, none the worse.

And then it was time to go. Blink of an eye and all that. We got our bets down for the last before heading for the taxi. SpeedLine were late and we had connections to make, so that was a frustrating. On the up-side it meant we just about caught the race on the big screen. Bex ran over to give us a running commentary, but we couldn't hear her properly back up at the gates. Wisps of 'red hat'….'stripey top'….'over there' drifted on the breeze, accompanied by random gesticulating and interesting facial expressions. We got the message, though. Mine and GC's pick, our nap of the day Syndication from the Venetia William stable - Towcester specialists - hosed up. The lucky last! The get-out stakes! Thank you very much!

So we all went home happy.

We finished off the day with a few drinks back at GC and Bex's and staggered home stuffed, watered, merry and rich (well, in experience if not exactly in money!)

I've been happy to fly solo at the track too. On one occasion, between jobs, I conspired a handy opportunity on a day that broke blue, clear and gorgeous: a clean Spring day with hot Summer temperatures in a climate changing world. I did a spot of gardening before making for the track. Potting on the poppies sowing the sunflower seeds before reaping a harvest at the races. Well, that was the plan.

Public transport isn't always the easiest to railway-free Towcester. The bus connection at Northampton let me down. I ended up flagging a taxi. Cabbies are always worth a laugh. This one was no exception. "Gambling, eh?", he says. "Gambling. I went in that casino last month." He nodded over the road. " 'Do you wants some chips?' says this girl in a short skirt. 'No thanks', I say. I've already eaten! Harrharrharrggghhh!" Everyone's a winner. It turned out that he was studying for a psychology degree and he wanted to work with autistic children. Never judge a book, as they say.

Towcester Racecourse's free entry policy had been paying off handsomely by increasing the attendances at meetings right across the season. That day was no exception. There was a good crowd in time for the first race. The gaggle of girls by the running rail in skimpy outfits and high spirits could have been mistaken for a hen party if it wasn't a Monday afternoon in the middle of Northamptonshire.

As befits a Monday, the racing was cringingly poor. In the first race a rank outsider called Chain won in what the race announcer described as 'dramatic fashion'. That' was dramatic as in Laurel and Hardy to my eyes. First the leader blundered the 4th last, leaving his pursuer clear in the lead until, with two fences left to jump, he ejected his jockey via the side door. The new leader was the favourite Carthy's Cross who was miles clear coming up the hill for home. But he began to lose interest all by his lonesome and, despite the frantic urgings of his jockey, he virtually stopped. The hitherto tailed-off Chain suddenly scented an unlikely victory. He closed down Carthy's Cross and snatched the race with 200 yards to run, accompanied by cries of anguish from the legion of punters who were all over Carthy's Cross.

This set the tone for the day. Not only did I fail to find a winner in any of the six races, but I also managed to ladle vinegar all over my burger. An easy mistake. Who would expect a brown squeezy bottle to contain anything but brown sauce? Even a pint of John Smith's Smoothflow, purchased from the well-appointed, newly constructed grandstand bar couldn't swill the taste of acetic acid from my mouth.

Towcester does surprisingly well in the PR stakes too. AP McCoy rode his 4,000th winner at the track. I'm old enough to remember when he was known simply as Tony McCoy. So we go back a way.

Alongside all the deserved plaudits about drive, determination, will to win, tenacity, mental strength, indestructible body, etc etc, we should not overlook the impact he has had on tactics and race riding.

An elastic continuum of murky practices sadly continues to straddle racing. It has dodgy runs to protect handicap marks at one end and stretches mercilessly through to blatant doping and surgical maltreatment of horses at the other. Punters, I'll wager, have never had any doubt, from day one of McCoy's career, at any gaff track or aboard any outside rag, that he was ever doing anything other than riding to win.

Time after time he has conjured victory from certain defeat by dragging reluctant beasts up finishing straights by sheer force of will and brawny muscle. When I started watching jumps racing, so often you'd see a horse make the early pace and fade to nothing. McCoy changed all that with bold front-running performance that took complacent, muddling-paced races by the scruff of the neck. He gave race riding a competitive kick up the arse and changed it forever.

Peter O'Sullevan was erudite and precise in marking the occasion of the 4,000th winner on the Today programme the morning after. What a master of language he is compared to the generation of gaffmeisters and cliché peddlers that inherited his microphone. He said that McCoy rang him on his journey back from Towcester and, amongst other chat, offered his record breaking riding boots to O'Sullevan for the latter's racing charity. There is the measure of the man.

Achieving his remarkable feat at my local track gave me a peculiar little thrill. Given that McCoy hallmarked his career by turning up and riding just as hard at the byways and cul-de-sacs as at the major centres, it seems fitting that Towcester played host and not Cheltenham. They all came the same to McCoy.

The track's marketing department was aware of the opportunity presented by the countdown to the Champ's landmark. They had been trailing the potential climax to #AP4000 at their meeting for some while. The chips fell the right way and it provided a massive boost for the course. Seven thousand ecstatic punters cheered McCoy and Mountain Tunes back to the paddock. JP McManus allegedly offered to buy them all a pint.

Fates conspired to prevent me attending. A regret. And now he has retired in a rarely seen flurry of genuine, unalloyed respect. He leaves a massive hole in the punter's armoury. His are boots that Dickie Johnson, Tom Scudamore and the like will never fill. Sandown's old Whitbread Gold Cup meeting was the last day of the domestic jumps season and they conspired with Channel 4 to play up the retirement of McCoy to full effect: guards of honour, Champion Jockey presentation, family photos, interviews… Only a fairytale last day winner was missing. I couldn't begrudge him any of that. I hope The Champ doesn't waver on his beautifully conceived notion to go out at the very top. Something sportsmen rarely carry off with dignity.

So the times are a-changing and a new order is settling in weighing rooms up and down the country. And a new order at Towcester too. They have just built a new £1.8m greyhound circuit inside the existing racecourse. Entry to the dogs – like to most of the racing fixtures – is free. On the face of it, this is a good move and increases my leisure options considerably. It comes as part of a £15m refurbishment at the track. What's not to like? Well, the down side is that seven of the venue's 17 current fixtures have been flogged off Arena Racing to help pay for the work. This includes its two prized dates of Boxing Day and Easter Sunday. As an extended family we have enjoyed many days at the track on these high day and holiday meetings, so their disappearance is a sorry loss.

On the other hand, Lord Hesketh sagely pointed out that "If this place is going to survive and prosper, it's going to have to operate for more than 17 days a year." That is fair enough. Maybe Towcester's enterprise should be commended. Though possibly not the raw enterprise shown by it's Chief Executive, Kevin Ackerman who was recently found guilty of corruption, along with three others, when they used insider information to place bent bets at Kempton and Wolverhampton. Bad publicity about the high number of injuries experienced by dogs at the new track can't have helped either.

Ultimately, I'm not at all convinced by this move away from a focus on racing. Give me the horses over the dogs any day. I've nicked a quote from a Trip Advisor reviewer at the top of this chapter who shares my instincts. This is a bit injudicious as, to be fair, most of the comments were very positive about the new Towcester. So despite my deep scepticism, maybe I'll hold any further fire until I've seen the set up in the flesh.

12. A PIVOTAL YEAR

Given the choice between the experience of pain and nothing, I would choose pain.
William Faulkner, The Wild Palms, 1939

2008 was something of a game changer. At around the same time that I was negotiating a mature exit from gainful employment to become a freelancer, my Mum was diagnosed with terminal lung cancer.

Anyone who loses a parent knows how shattering the experience is. To see the life sucked out of my effervescent Mother by that vile disease was crushing. I was a fervent and assertive anti-smoker before her diagnosis. The bitter irony of the smoking-induced carcinogens that ate away her lungs was just a further twist of the knife.

Needing to establish my own business during this traumatic time probably gave me something to focus on outside my Mum's treatment. Apart from a bizarre phone call from a mildly stroppy client that I took at the top of Sutton Bank on the same day as the funeral, everyone was very understanding.

I was not subject to the day-to-day agony of her treatment and decline. Being based down south, that painful process fell to my Dad and Bruv. They were remarkable and kept up a stoic positivity long after I had given up hope. Something to do with the geographical proximity and daily contact, I suspect.

I spent many hours' on solitary train travel that year, up to Yorkshire and back. It provided many opportunities for people watching. And listening. I overheard this on a journey to York one Saturday evening about 9pm:

> *Oh, hi. Hi Mike. Yeah, I wanted to catch you, man.*
> *Thanks for calling. Yeah, yeah I'm good thanks. Yeah, no*

worries. Well, sort of. Look, I can't give you the key...
I've locked myself out, yeah, and well, with the key on
the inside. No, the key's on the inside. [pause]

Well, it doesn't matter how it happened, does it? It just
did. Well, I don't know how I did it. No, I'm on a train
now, heading back to my folks. I had to leave earlier
than planned.

OK, Mike, look it doesn't need to spoil your evening,
man. Just keep a level head yeah? It doesn't need to be a
big deal, yeah? There's no need to get worked up man,
just take it easy. No, no man, doin' your nut on me ain't
gonna help... [click].

The young man shrugs, puts his phone down and returns to his Terry
Pratchett novel, leaving his mate to an expensive evening with the
locksmith.

On another occasion I had come up from the West Country and was
changing at Birmingham.

I was busting for a pee. My train had lurched and rolled into the
airless, soulless subterranean stench that was Birmingham New
Street Station 15 minutes late. I knew I wouldn't have time for both a
leak and a lovely spicy sausage butty from the Sbarro booth before
my connection to York. The decision was easy. My hunger could
hold out longer than my bladder. So I skittered between hapless,
luggage-laden families and 1st Class lounge-seeking Thursday
afternoon business travellers on my way down the concourse.

I was too desperate to worry about cultivating my resentment
towards the barriers guarding the gents. Indignation at paying for a
wee had to wait until after I'd scrambled a 20p coin from the hidden
layers of my suit. But I couldn't gain access until the joker in front of
me wriggled a coin from his pocket. One of the turnstiles was out of
order and I was queuing up behind the dithering git at the only
available entry point. It really was the limit. If I had to fork out
wedge just to have a jimmy-riddle - let's face it, a basic human right

97

- then at the absolute minimum I expected some reasonable standard of service. Not that shoddy farce.

The blonde-haired youth - no more than 18 I'd say, once I cared to look a bit closer - was getting a bit edgy himself. His agitated fingers were working through all the nooks of his denim jacket and crannies of his Levis. He couldn't locate the magic coins. At a time like that compassion kicks in. I fished the appropriate denomination from my loose change and tapped him on the shoulder. He took the ten-pence pieces with respectful thanks and flushed relief. Merely a small token on my part, I thought. If he was suffering anything like me, 20p was a small price to pay. Shared experience and all that.

The toilets had been flooded with some vile nuclear-strength Domestos derivative and the sharp, stinging odour assaulted my nasal passages like a pencil up the nostril. I thought my eyes would pop out. But even that could not dilute the satisfaction of completing my mission. Once the hiss of high pressure bladder evacuation had given way to a tap dance of drips on the metallic urinal, relaxation spread through my mind and body like a sedative. Tense muscles eased, furrowed brow given a metaphorical cold flannel. I probably said 'aaaahhhhhhhh...'

I zipped up and headed for the exit. I passed the bloke in the denim jacket on my way out. He was stood in front of the 'Condomi' rubber johnny machine, filching his pockets for more small coinage. Only this time he needed 50ps to satisfy a different sort of demand in the underpants area. I shook my head as his imploring eyes meant mine. And I chuckled. Now he really was taking the piss. There's only so far you can stretch compassion…

… My last north-to-south rail journey, as Summer had slipped into Autumn, was a few days after Mum's funeral. Leaving Dad and Paul behind at the station was unexpectedly tough. When my Mum exhaled her final breath with the three of us around the bed, we said 'It's just us now'. Departing the café on platform 1 to return to my own family, I achingly felt like it was 'just them now'.

We had made a strange pact that afternoon, born of the need to establish some normality and a mechanism to connect. We began an annual 40 horses to follow competition, running over the course of the main jumps season, October to April. Forty horses cherry picked by each of us to form a stable whose combined net profit or loss to a level £1 stake would determine the winner. I had been doing something similar for myself over the previous couple of years and was very confident. Needless to say in the seven renewals of this competition I have not won once.

Mum, knowing her final decline would be swift, had asked just one thing: for someone in the family to say a few words at her funeral service. Standing up there, and the room was packed, to talk about her in front of the coffin was the most challenging speaking engagement I've ever undertaken.

Auntie Wendy, Mum's youngest and favourite sister, got up first and did a great job of remembering the tender, funny, compassionate core at the centre of my Mother's being.

We had all agreed. Mum was so full of positivity and good spirit, what was the point of being mawkish in her final scenes.

In closing, Wendy had said how proud Mum was to have children and how she had play-bitten the lovely soft flesh on the bum of her first born – me.

I got up and stood on the rostrum just vacated by Wendy. 'I've still got those marks on my bum!' I said. Thankfully, everyone chuckled and it broke the grip of tension squeezing my stomach. I was able to deliver my informal eulogy without too many gulps, convulsions and teary sobs.

We all wanted to try to get across the warmth, humanity and humour of my Mum. Everyone in the room already knew all that, but it still needed to be shared. I said:

...She wasn't a bad cook, either, me Mam. Best Yorkshire puddings ever. And not afraid to experiment. I remember when we first had this foreign concoction. Lasagne it was called. Heck, it was good. A big deep tray-full, the size of a small satellite dish between four of us. But Mam didn't forget the tradition. It was all served up with mash potato and three veg as well! We never went hungry...

And when I found out that I'd got my first job in London, Mum's homely ways came right to the fore. I was enjoying an extended Summer break after completing my degree at North Staffs Poly. Sat in the sun at the top of the garden, Mum called me in to take a phone call in the kitchen.

That was also the room from which Mum ran her hair-dressing business. One craggy old Yorkshire battle-axe was sat under the hairdryer, whilst another was facing her with my Mum pruning and shaping her grey locks. I picked up the clunky red receiver fixed to the wall at the back of this galley kitchen and had a conversation with the Civil Service Commission. I was told I had been 'allocated a post' (such was the language of the Civil Service in those days) in the Local Government Boundary Commission in London, part of the giant, long-gone Department of the Environment then under control of that gnarled old Tory stalwart, Nicholas Ridley MP.

I told Mum the good news and went into the living room, closing the door behind me. I could hear the conversation unfolding through the door.

"What's he say, Heather? Enquired one battle axe.

"He's got a job in London!" said my proud Mum.

"That's champion. What's he doing?" asked the other.

"Department of Environment!"

"Oh, great! What's that then?"

"I'm not sure, Ethel. Drains and the like, I think."

"Oh…That's nice."

I had to hold my sides. Fantastic.

And here I was exactly 20 years later, setting up my own one-man band and putting myself back together after a generation in that Civil Service mincer. Mum had been pleased for me, but worried that I was taking a risk with my young family. A typical Mother's viewpoint.

The business tottered onwards that year and I was grateful for vital support to a host of former colleagues in various organisations. Flying solo gave me what I hadn't realised until then that I was craving: flexibility, independence and some personal responsibility.

Above all, freedom from clockwatching and marking unproductive time at someone else's desk. Being able to manage my own time was crucial. And not in a management-speak volley of 'working smarter not harder' bullshit. There was more to this than altruism. Bacchy had by now become a full time pro-punter and an injection of flexibility would enable me to find more time to join him at the races!

So, although 2008 was by turns, painful, grief-laden and seismic, there was an upside. I just had to look at it in the right way.

13. PRO-PUNTING

It's one thing to ask your bank manager for an overdraft
to buy 500 begonias for the borders in Haslemere,
but quite another to seek financial succour to avail oneself
of the 5-2 they're offering on Lie De Bourbon for the St Leger.
Jeffrey Bernard, 1978

When I snapped shut the laptop on the first volume of Mug Punting over a decade ago, I was already thinking that the next collection would be all about Bacchy's rise to fortune as a level-headed, steadily accumulating pro-punter. If there was a loose, frayed thread running through the previous book, it was the relentless progress of Bacchy and the spirited dust cloud the rest of us kicked up in his betting tracks. He was the antithesis of mug punting.

These tales do indeed pick up that theme, though the outcome was not entirely what I was predicting.

Bacchy's carefully tended dream of professional punting had been nourished on honest Cheltenham value, ruthless flat-track nous and murderous exploitation of the international markets. The value of his points-based staking plan had steadily increased with each successful campaign. The betting bank was swelling.

Nevertheless, progress was slow. Bacchy remained tantalisingly short of the capital needed to launch his new career with a wet sail. Then came redundancy. In one of the many 'bonfire of bureaucracy' culls of the Civil Service that the last Labour Government undertook – no more than sleight of hand in terms of real savings – many departments shed posts across the board. I had taken advantage of this a year before. Now Bacchy was able to step away from the rat race and use his modest, but hard earned lump sum to bankroll a place in the stalls for a very different sort of race.

I tried to imagine the sort of negotiations that took place in Bacchy's mortgaged home where he was father of three and hitherto bringing home a steady and valuable income. Where mentally constructed statements like "I've been made redundant and my plan is to use the wedge to subside a gambling career. That'll be all right won't it Debs?" might have needed more careful handing at the point of verbalisation.

Somehow, those discussions were concluded satisfactorily and the new career steamed ahead with his wife's blessing. Support even. Albeit with some boring old commitments about regular contributions to domestic expenditure. Mortgage, blah blah. Yawn.

I followed these developments with real fascination, unequivocal support and green-ish envy. Green-ish because whilst I loved the boldness, the freedom of this venture, I knew I'd never have the confidence in my own punting to embark on such a thing. I was far from covetous of the pressure that bringing home the bacon via the bookies would entail. But to witness the journey at second hand was pure theatre.

Bacchy's approach was to build on what had served him well up to that point: a rock solid staking plan. For this he took his cue from Kelly. Bacchy had read deeply of the mathematician John L Kelly. In 1956 he had developed the Kelly Criteria, the crucial ingredient in the Kelly Staking Plan. The criteria are designed to maximize the growth of a punting bank over the long term, by determining the optimum stake on a bet. The fundamental assumption underpinning Kelly revolves around whether the punters' estimate about a horse's chances are better or worse than the bookies' estimate.

At the point where the serious form student can determine that value is on their side rather than with the bookie, then the Kelly Criteria will tell you the optimal amount of your bank to bet.

This is the formula in its raw state:

$f^* = bp - q / b$

... where f* is the fraction of the current bankroll to wager; b is the current bet odds (fractional); p is the probability of winning; and q is the probability of losing, which is $1 - p$.

Let's say that your bank is £10,000 and the current odds of the beast you are interested in is 5. You've had a look at the form, weighed up the ground, checked out the colour of the jockey's cap and thus determined that your edge is 25% or 0.25. In other words, you think that the selection has a 25% better chance of winning than the bookies do: you think the horse should be 15-4 (i.e. 3.75-1) rather than 5-1.

Then: f* = (((5-1)*0.25) - (1-0.25)) / (5-1) f* = 0.0625

With me? Good. Multiply this fraction by the start bank to find your stake:

Stake = 0.0625 * £10,000 = £625

I can grasp the maths. And the logic behind it: you think you have found some value and this formula determines the optimum wager based on your judgement. There are many web-inches dedicated to this model, including other ways of expressing the formula. There are also variations that aim to reduce some of the perceived risks with Kelly where it requires a large number of percentage estimations - so the stake can still be too high. The variation, called 'Proportional Kelly' (of course!) divides the percentage by a given factor (say 2) to minimise the risk. The key to the Kelly Criteria is that it optimises your stakes providing you are able to predict with a high degree of accuracy.

There's the rub of it. Nowhere in any of the screeds of advice on this model is there any solid formula to identify those crucial overrated 'value' bets, or how to calculate your 'edge'. Bloody systems eh? More questions than answers.

Nevertheless, Kelly remains a vital tool in the armoury of those who know what they are doing. It became an important plank of Bacchy's pro-punting career.

For two or three years, his serious punting unrolled, with me hanging on to the coat tails. At some point he optimistically declared "I don't see why I shouldn't be able to manage a fun trip to the races every fortnight or so…" Bacchy's 'fun trips' involved a stash of the folding stuff crammed into a crumpled brown envelope that he would pluck from the inside pocket of his jacket. Harry Redknapp had nothing on Bacchy's style. Slapping down gaff track each-way doubles, across-the-card combinations and fruity perm exactas. Fun indeed.

Of course the fixture-a-month schedule could never be maintained. Work intervened on my part; and Bacchy had a few too many family health distractions. Nevertheless, we did pretty well criss-crossing southern England in Bacchy's low slung jalopy.

Some were new tracks to me like leafy Lingfield and its three-track flat, all weather and National Hunt combination. We pitched up there on a quiet jumps day when there was better racing on the telly in the bar from Fontwell and Newcastle. We could have gone to Fontwell, where Synchronised finished 3rd in a novice chase. He went on to win the Gold Cup in the following season. In the last race of that decent Fontwell card, we also watched Cue Card win the bumper at 6-1 on his racecourse debut. We didn't take either of these hints at the subsequent Festivals. We did enjoy the charms of Lingfield, though A stalwart venue, providing the backbone of grassroots racing. Less charming was the way Venetia Williams' Flanagan cost both of us a handsome return by booting away his healthy lead at 14-1 through every hurdle in the home straight. That was the best chance of the day.

Other tracks like Huntingdon I had not been to for years and where I had never witnessed a decent race. So the chance to see the Peterborough Chase - the track's only quality card - was not to be passed up. If only to show support for decent mid-week racing over packing out the weekend fixtures. This is a dilemma for small courses trying to maximise their income. Thankfully, despite a flirtation with a Saturday fixture, the Peterborough Chase is settled back into its Wednesday slot and attracting both decent fields and respectable prize money. The renewal we saw found Deep Purple in a rich seam of form, trouncing a classy line up that included Albertas Run, Tidal Bay and Racing Demon.

I was also delighted on a personal level to navigate Bacchy to my local track at Towcester where we really did indulge in the more humble fields of lower league national hunt. I felt very paternalistic towards the track at the time and we had a good day.

It wasn't all gaff tracks, though. There were a few trips to Newmarket's July Course. I had never been to either this or the Rowley Mile before. Having been to both since, the warmer, more personal and less exposed July Course gets my vote every time. Renovated Victorian grandstands set a relaxed tone, bedecked with begonia-stuffed hanging baskets and hosting punters in straw boaters and cream trousers.

The July Cup meetings saw a number of memorable moments. The race is now run on a cluttered Saturday that is more likely to make racing fans stay at home so they can watch all the fixtures on telly rather than go to the track. Shame. Huntingdon and the Peterborough Chase, take a bow.

The closest finish we saw was when favourite Marchand D'Or squeezed out US Ranger by a head on good ground in 2008. Ten minutes later the sky fell and we experienced a monumental thunderstorm. Sheet lightning filled the air and rain exploded off the tarmac like mortar fire. Whilst everyone was running for cover holding drenched racecards over their heads, Bacchy and I were scouring the form for soft ground horses. Between us, we found Profit's Reality in the closing handicap who ploughed home by half a length at 14-1. A rare racecourse coup.

But the day strangest incident came in Bacchy's placepot strategy. He needed Frankie to guide Zelloof into the frame in the penultimate race. Through the deluge out on the track and the torrents of gushing off the roof in front of us, we could just make out Zelloof passing the post at no more than a canter. Missed the break, we assumed, tailed off and brought home tenderly by Frankie. Bacchy shrugged his shoulders and tossed his ticket away.

It was only later that we learned the horse had actually been withdrawn. The lancing rain caused problems for Zelloof behind the stalls and he didn't race. The weather also obscured our view of events and we didn't pick this up. Bacchy's placepot token had transferred to the favourite who had hit the frame. Bacchy had a winning ticket! Except he didn't. He had chucked it and we were already homeward bound.

Those lovely red-coated ladies at the Tote did him proud though. After Bacchy explained the situation in a long and involved phone call, the Tote were able to identify his bet from the till records and duly stumped up his winnings, paid out at £90.20 to a £1 stake! Hope Fred Done is planning to maintain the same levels of customer care...

My most recent trip to the lovely July Course was with the girls for a music night. The weather had a hand in that meeting too. We counted ourselves mildly fortunate to see any action at all. During the week, weather forecasts had stubbornly predicted heavy rain for southern and eastern England on the Saturday in question. I heard the slap of precipitation against our bedroom window early that morning. For the next few hours I monitored the grey skies leaking moisture that alternated between downpour, stair-rod and bucket. I kept checking the Racing Post website, but there were no hints of an inspection at Newmarket (though Redcar had already been abandoned).

We set off, grimly determined. Me, Mrs A, Daughters No 1 & 2 and their friends Callum and Zoe, repeating the racing and music trick that we had pulled for the girls in two previous Summers: Kempton and Olly Murs; Sandown and Jessie J. This year McFly would provide the musical port and cigars after a feast of racing.

The M25 was nose to tail. There was so much rain and spray that it resembled driving through a car wash. The M11 was worse. A bad crash on the southbound carriageways had caused a major tailback on our northbound route of rubber necked ambulance chasers slowing down to get a good look at the carnage. We missed the first race, a 2yo maiden. But as we climbed from the trusty Zafira in the car park, the rain had subsided to a drizzle. The atmospheric and metaphorical gloom were both lifting.

Being a generous sort, I funded the younglings at £2 per race and they could keep their winnings. And that's what they did. The three girls cleared over £50 between them, backing 7 winners in total. Callum, in many respects my punting protégé, had brought his own stash to top up my contribution. Good lad! He loves a day at the races. We discussed jockey bookings, the impact of the rain on the going and some of the finer details of form. He told me that he often didn't pick a horse just on the name anymore. His plan was to keep some of his stakes back for a big bet on the lucky last. Marvellous stuff. "Mug punting indeed!" I beamed. "Isn't that the name of your website?" he asked. He went home potless. As did I.

Zoe, on the other hand, was a revelation. There were six runners in the 2.45 nursery handicap, so we did the sensible thing – backing one runner each. Zoe picked Safety Check who held on soundly from Callum's Ticking Kate. It was as near as he got all afternoon. Zoe was overcome with joy and leapt around the enclosure, bucking and squealing like a yearling. She had never been to a meeting before and expressed surprise that there were so many races. "But when the Grand National is on there's only one race", she said. Interesting perception from a teenager about the prominence of the race in a really good three-day meeting.

Though everyone missed out in the next, a valuable class 2 handicap (the kids all wanted to back Mankini – not on form logic, I suspect – and were disappointed to see him declared a non-runner), winners came thick and fast for the girls for the rest of the afternoon.

The best race of the day, a listed sprint, was savaged by defections as the ground changed. We walked over to the parade ring, decorated with hanging baskets and shadowed by the thatched roof weighing room. Zoe was applying some thought to the afternoon and wanted to make an informed selection based on gait, gleam and girth width. I wanted to look an old friend of mine in the eye and see whether she still had what it takes. Mince was sensationally progressive as a three year old the season before, but seemingly had not trained on. I was sorry to see she also was a late withdrawal. I didn't get my heart to heart.

Tropics went off favourite and landed the race by a comfortable length. Tropics went on to become a very smart horse indeed in subsequent seasons. It was Daughter No 2 that benefitted there and then. I'd been backing outsiders all day and Master Of War was just about the best run I got out of any of them. A decent third I thought and I added him to my list for the rest of the season. Which probably explains why he only won once more in 11 runnings.

Zoe was back on track with Lancelot Du Lac in the next and after studying the card she observed "That's the second time that jockey has won on one of my horses today." She was right. Mikael Barzalaona was in fire. "Also Zoe", I added, "he won the first race before we got here". The three girls' eyes lit up and they scoured the card for his next ride. "Here it is! Greek War!'" she declared. "I'm following Zoe", said Daughter No 1. "Me three!" joined in Daughter No 2. And so it was that three teenagers roared Charlie Appleby's charge down the centre of the track, furlong purple in face and hoarse in voice to land their healthy 6-1 spoils. They were delirious.

Mr Barzalona had no mount in the final race, but the girls' attention was already drifting. No sooner had Peace Seeker crossed the line then they were off to find a pitch front and centre for the McFly boys.

Callum, Mrs A and I wandered over to catch a few numbers from a more modest distance. The band plied a perfectly respectable brand of energetic pop punk with some catchy vocal hooks and an assured swagger. There were plenty of Mums and Dads happily foot tapping and shimmying their approval too, though the predominant register when it came to end-of-song screams was definitely high end. Dogs ran screaming. Thankfully the drinks glasses were plastic (if you see what I mean). They were a massive hit with the girls, evidently.

The rain returned only towards the end of the set and it seemed like we had cheated the weather. The Guardian carried photos the next day of extreme flooding in Essex. We had had a lucky escape…

Back to Bacchy... His proper bets, as oppose to the Lingfield and Towcester frivolities, were the ones that mattered. I remember a few of us met up for beers in Victoria to watch Royal Ascot in 2008. Bacchy had punted the (then) Spanish trained Equiano for the Kings Stand based on his form in France. He took a huge price a few weeks before the race. The horse under Olivier Peslier made all under the stands rail and never had a moments' bother. The SP was 22-1. Bacchy had a good bit on at 66-1.

The winnings paid for the mortgage for that month and plenty bit else besides. Bacchy was exuberant and maybe a touch relieved as well. Even then, in the early days of his pro-punting career, Bacchy admitted that he was struggling to get the big stakes down. Sometimes because the bookies wouldn't lay bets at their standout prices for the sums he was trying to get on; and sometimes because he went for Kelly Lite rather than Kelly Max: too cautious.

There was plenty of real punting at Cheltenham. Goes without saying. That is where it all started.

The lovely Auntie Mona had passed away in late 2008. Only a long struggle with that vile disease cancer finally breached her tenacity and spirit, well into her 80s. Her death brought to an end many things. Not least some celebrated Festival stays for Bacchy and me with her in Gloucester. Mona's family all said that we should continue the tradition and lodge with any of them in and around the Gloucester area. We would have been welcome and we knew it. When the time came, however, we felt that the visit just wouldn't have been the same without Mona's hospitality. Irreplaceable.

For the next couple of festivals we stayed in cottages either side of Stroud. The first year on the outskirts of the glorious village of Painswick and the following year in the small town of Nailsworth. Both lovely places with excellent pubs for real ale, steak pies and racing chat with other Festivalites residing beyond the Cheltenham hurly-burly.

The bus route from these villages to Cheltenham was absolutely crucial. There was one an hour into town and by riding the 10.25 we could wolf some home-rustled brekkie and still find time for an hour's internet research and wagering in Cheltenham's central library. The days of widespread free wifi were then still a distant dream.

Other technology was slightly more widespread, but no less reliable. On one occasion we met up with Bacchy's brother-in-law, Dave and Jane who had somehow blagged the loan of a very smart Bentley coupe for the day. She insisted on giving us a lift back to Painswick and wanted to show off the in-car sat nav. Only she insisted on overruling the directions every time the mellow, seductive recorded voice gave a breathy "at the next roundabout take a left turn" or some such. We ended up on both the M4 and M40 on a circuitous journey back. Although Bacchy and I were enjoying the ride, we both hooted merrily as the luxury coupe came smoothly to rest outside The Falcon right behind the Arriva South West service bus we would have got from town anyway.

We bumped into Bacchy's pal Intersky Andy (one-time syndicate-sharer of the Champion Hurdler Intersky Falcon) a couple of times. Good bloke and great to share a pint with. He came over from Tatts and marvelled at the relaxed demeanour that accompanied Bacchy's Pro Punting career. Did he seem a touch sceptical or was I imagining it?

Both years were amongst my best punting Festivals. 2009 was especially hot – though it didn't start off so well. The Supreme (which I have sill never won), was the subject of a side bet between Bacchy and I. Whoever bagged the best result in the opener also claimed the double bed in the cottage. Medermit, under a mesmerizing drive from Robert Thornton screamed up the hill. But couldn't real in Go Native, punted by Bacchy. The put-u-up beckoned. It barely mattered to be fair. Later that afternoon we both celebrated Punjabi's narrow margin win in the Champion Hurdle. I also had Cooldine in the RSA and Big Buck's impressive first win in the World Hurdle, amongst others. Nicholls was in his pomp that year and he trained Kauto Star to become the first horse to regain the Gold Cup in a scintillating victory, chased home by the redoubtable Denman.

2010 saw a good bet on Peddlers Cross come in. One of those rare moments when we were both hock deep into the same horse and could celebrate unreservedly. That was an emotional win as I'd developed a strong affection for the gutsy horse all season, as well as collecting on the betting front. That day he looked destined for stellar greatness. Until he ran into the Fly.

A last-second, spontaneous punt on Albertas Run in the Ryanair also worked out well. How that horse loved Cheltenham. I also had a crazy acca that landed me a dubious-but decent three-figure pot. It set me on the road to ruinous festival-acca bets that I still tramp. This was the year of Binocular's outrageous Champion Hurdle win after being declared a non-runner by Nicky Henderson in January (without scratching him from the race) and Imperial Commander's party-pooping Gold Cup victory over Kauto and Denman.

I didn't know it then, but that would be the last Festival I shared with Bacchy for a good few years.

14. CLASSIC HEROES

It really was a twelve-way dead-heat.
You see, everything is perfect in Paradise, and that includes the handicapping.

Tony Morris, journalist and writer, in 'A Horserace Made in

Heaven', 1994

The Ebor meeting is one of the highlights of my flat racing season. As an unreconstructed professional Yorkshireman, I have a predictable affinity with this sublime, stylish and mature track that some refer to as the Ascot of the north (if comparisons must be made then surely it is that Ascot is the York of the south?) (And Guildford is the Wakefield of Surrey....).

The 2010 Yorkshire Oaks was a classic encounter of the nation's top middle distance fillies. A favourite of mine, the previous year's dual Oaks winner, Sariska was lining up against old foe and globe-trotting multi-grade 1 winner Midday, as well as the star of that season's classic filly crop Snow Fairy.

Sariska was the star filly in 2009. Beautiful, graceful...profitable. She probably counts as one of my few genuine and unmitigated successes on the flat. She came to my attention during a listed event at Newbury where she broke poorly, slowly and late, but made up acres of ground to finish like a classic mug punters' con-trick: the fast finishing fourth. Well, I took the bait. She went in to the mental notebook in Caslon Openface, 16pt, bold. Next up, her trainer Michael Bell, not unfamiliar with classic glory, put her in the Musidora at York, a famous Oaks trial. So I went in on the juicy betfair prices on a multi-lateral basis. A fiver on her Musidora odds and a fiver at her massive Oaks odds.

She won the York trial in - even at the time I thought this – convincing style. I was very optimistic about her chances in the Oaks in early June.

My partner in crime, Bacchy had spotted the same thing and had waded in with a pro punt. We had made a number of memorable and mostly profitable appearances at Oaks day on the Epsom Downs across the years. But we'd been a little lax in attendance since the heady days of Casual Look in '06. So 2009 saw a welcome return to form.

Not before some full force griping about the new bloody stand though. Epsom's redevelopment had produced the Duchess Stand, a £40m carbuncle designed to cosset even more disinterested corporate freeloaders in exaggerated comfort and service at the measurable physical and financial cost to proletariat punter: worse views, increased no-go zones, hiked entrance fees, deeper disgruntlement. Scum bags.

Revenge, however, was swift, fortuitous and whiskey-soaked. I was pretty confident about Sariska's chances. This is a regular trick my mischievous mind chooses to play on me. Nevertheless, I was convinced that she had the best form on offer. I wasn't disappointed, though not without a few solid scares along the way.

Jockey Jamie Spencer had the filly well positioned gunning down the straight. She came to take long time leader Midday at the furlong marker and I honestly thought that it would be all over right there. But Midday wouldn't go away. Blimey, did she keep coming at Sariska. Exhilarating fireworks down the straight and a heart-stopping tight finish. The Michael Bell filly held on, but by a diminishing head.

Still, it was enough to provoke Bacchy and I into a fit of demented leaping and lurching, safe in the knowledge of a perfectly executed coup. And then the dreaded 'bing bong' over the PA announcing a stewards' inquiry. We watched the replay. A bit of scrimmaging over the final furlong, but nothing to worry about and we breathed a sigh of relief.

But the inquiry went on. Word spread round the track that the incident of concern was way back on the bend. And it wasn't

Midday that was the victim, but the pre-race favourite Rainbow View. On-course TV finally dredged up the pictures for the big screen that showed Rainbow View squeezed for room on the bend and stopped in her tracks as she tried to angle out for a run. Sariska, piloted by Jamie Spencer, who couldn't have been more obvious if he was clutching bench-vice, was squeezing her back against the rail. After a good deal of depressing, confidence sapping tension, she kept the race. Cue more back slapping and glib 'never in doubt' comments. But it was close.

We headed for the drink sponsors' tent. The tasting bar had been drunk dry - no more free samples available. So, befitting the spirit of the occasion, a fine bottle of their Woodford Reserve bourbon was purchased instead. In apologising for the lack of freebies, the salesman proffered us two plastic cups and a cheesy grin. The remainder of the meeting passed in a blur of sour mash and straight exactas. Happy days.

Sariska and Midday had locked horns on two further occasions with Sariska prevailing each time. Legend.

Bacchy and I returned to the Oaks meeting a couple of years later, together with our mate Bryn and his Father-in-law Sid. Only this time we opted for the cheap seats in the Lonsdale enclosure.

Sariska ran well in the Coronation Cup against the boys. But couldn't overhaul the impressive Fame and Glory for the all-powerful Aiden O'Brien yard. There were no bourbon-soaked celebrations of big wedge payouts. But we had a good day. Sid in particular enjoyed his first visit to the Oaks meeting in 40 years!

And so to York's Knavesmire and the fourth meeting between the two. Sadly the fireworks were lop-sided this time. Midday was sensational. She confirmed herself at the peak of her form with her second Group 1 victory in three weeks. Sariska? She refused to leave the stalls. No run for my money that day. Still, I was well in credit with this lovely mare.

Later that season, the chapter closed. The end of my love affair with the gorgeous, classy and now it appeared, moody, Sariska. Her refusal to start in the Yorkshire Oaks on the previous occasion was a significant blot on her imperious reputation. Nevertheless, trainer Michael Bell was clearly persuaded to give her another chance. "We have nothing to lose", he said of the dual classic winning filly. So she lined up in the Grade 1 Prix Vermeille at Longchamp, once again facing old foe Midday.

Joining these two warriors was the unbeaten French filly Sarafina and soft ground-loving High Heeled. But it was a rerun of the Yorkshire Oaks with Midday winning authoritatively and Sariska again planting her sourpuss feet and refusing to start. There was a great photo in the Racing Post of Jamie Spencer looking like a right turkey in the stalls, blinking tamely back at the camera as the rest of the field tore down the track.

Michael Bell was, under the circumstances, genuinely hilarious when he called time on her career by saying "It is rather annoying as we know we can potentially beat that lot. It's rather like having a Ferrari with no keys." Fantastic. Like a fool, I still loved her though. What memories. This undeserving and faintly comical final curtain simply added a smidgeon of mystique to her reputation. In some ways, the only loser is Midday again. Whilst Sariska refused to race there will always be the smallest trace of tarnish about these victories. I know you can only beat the ones that turn up, but what if Sariska's Ferrari engine had started….

So whilst we are on the subject of Classic Heroes, I feel a tribute is in order to one who hit nose-bleeding heights the year that Sariska bagged her Oaks, but in truth put her firmly in the shade. Sea The Stars' achievements in 2009 felt like a once in a generation event. Bacchy sent me a bit of heart-felt prose from a pretty hard-nosed gambling acquaintance of his. It's lovely stuff:

Awful game this...

We get pissed off with how it's run. We get pissed off with those who run it. We get pissed off with clerks who can't run a tap (or run it too much!). We chunter about bent races and question bad rides. It costs us an arm & a leg to go see it happen and when we get there it's crawling with drunks, way too packed and the traffic was sickening enough for you to swear you're never going again...

You wonder why you bother?

In my case, I 'bother' because it's all the family have 'bothered' about since I was born.

When I was little & the old fellah used to take me along to the races with him & I didn't really have a clue what was going on.

Gradually, I got to like it & took more interest in what was winning races & took notice of what the old fellah was backing. I wanted to find out more about it & started asking the old man.

The most interesting stuff was when he told me about the great horses. There were only two he kept going on about: Sea Bird & Vaguely Noble. Told me Sea Bird thrashed a horse at Epsom (Meadow Court) that would have been a decent Derby winner most years. Proper thrashed him. He'd seen great horses: Dante (got a photo of him with that one at home), Crepello, St Paddy, Nijinsky. But he never put any of those up with his 'big two'.

*Over the years, I've seen a few good uns:
Alleged, Troy, Shergar, Dancing Brave, Dahlia, El Gran Senor, Oh So Sharp, Nashwan, Generous, Pebbles, Nureyev, Blushing Groom.*

Probably more that I've forgotten about, but they made the study & wet days at Nottingham worthwhile. They (when racing's pretty much all you 'do') light up your life for a while. None of the above really passed the old man's 'litmus test' though & made me think "Jesus, that's special".

I thought that was it.

Then this one came along.

I'd known about him long enough. Final Furlong & Irish Whisper were all over him like a rash before his debut & told me he was something else. It took the Guineas win to convince me he could shift & I've been sold on him ever since.

I've only backed him once. In the Derby, & never had a moment's worry.

He impressed me more at York after the race when he looked as though he'd done nothing more strenuous than had a bloody good shit. His opponent that day, Irish Guineas winner Mastercraftsman looked like he'd been in a collision with a truck.

He then wiped the floor with the Ballydoyle 'tag team' in the Irish Champion & set the seal on his true greatness today in the Arc when overcoming traffic problems that would have found out a whole host of 'best horses in the race' with the minimum of fuss.

My old man followed this sport for 55years.

The year he died (1987), he was still talking about the best two he'd seen.
That tells you how often these buggers come along.

I don't think half of us would be doing this, but for the chance of horses like this popping up & let's be fair, when they do, the betting means nothing.

Make sure you take all this in. Might be thirty years till you see another one!

I never got to see Sea The Stars in the flesh. A shame. Nevertheless I have personal memories and thrills woven through this wonder horse's spectacular six month reign-supreme. I backed him for the 2,000 guineas at, with hindsight, a generous 10-1. His turn of foot in the last two furlongs marked him out as something special. He was already being talked up for the Derby, where I backed him again in a race where Ballydoyle famously got the tactics wrong.

With STS pulling Mick Kinane's arms out of his sockets, Aiden O'Brien's horses simply wouldn't make the race a test of stamina. STS had never run beyond a mile. He was not a guaranteed stayer. Ballydoyle's number one contender Fame and Glory certainly was. But he was tucked up behind STS. They had Irish Guineas winner Mastercraftsman in the race too. Three out, Kinane's mount was travelling so smoothly. Like a dream. He picked off the Ballydoyle pacemaker and won without sweat; the Ballydoyle big two having not landed a blow between them. As the beast crossed the line, the camera cuts to his trainer Dr John Oxx. In a maelstrom of whoops, cheers, flung hats and punched air, John calmly looked into the middle distance and nodded briefly. A nod that said, "Yes, job done. That's what we expected".

My admiration of the dignified Dr Oxx grew as the season progressed.

By this time, I was also riding high in the Tote Ten to Follow competition, courtesy of STS, Sariska (of course) and a couple of other handy winners. Sadly, my appearance in the Racing Post leading entries column was not repeated. Lofty prominence declined soon after. Unlike STS who went from strength to strength. The horse's 5th straight group 1 at Leopardstown in the Champion Stakes possibly his most devastating. Absolutely crushing a decent field, including older horses (as he had done in the Eclipse at Sandown and the Juddmonte at York. I didn't back him for those, nor had I any intention of doing so for the Arc, likely to be his final race.

But I was leaving a job in Camden and the crowd there bought me an ante-post slip for the horse in that race as my leaving present. I tell you straight, I was filling up. What an inspired gift! Even more touching when I learned that Kiran and Miia had decided to place the bet in the local William Hill having never set foot inside a bookies in their lives! The good lady assistants in there talked them though the transaction with, I hope, understanding and tact. For inevitably I knew them well!

So when Sea The Stars completed his perfect six having his most arduous passage and one again displaying that crushing acceleration, I had a sentimental moment all to myself.

He finished on the best possible note. Each time he ran I became more and more nervous. I'm so pleased his owner and trainer resisted the clamour to go to California for the Breeders Cup. I also say yah-boo sucks to the pundits attempting to pour cold water on his level of greatness because he won each time only by a comfortable distance and not the 20 lengths they need for their ratings analyses. Bollocks. He did what he needed to do with complete authority and confidence over different distances, underfoot conditions, tracks, countries and against all age groups. He's the best thing I've seen on four legs since Lassie Come Home.

And, just to prove that once in a generation can be twice in a generation, along came Frankel. That's a whole other story...

15. RACING UNDER PRESSURE

You know, somebody actually complimented me on my driving today.
They left a little note on the windscreen. It said 'Parking Fine'.
Tommy Cooper, 1978

My driving instructor was going on about gees-gees the other day. I'd let it slip that I was a fan of the horses and liked a punt.

"It's so cruel though. The horses bleed from their noses and suffer burst blood vessels every time they race."

"Well that's not exactly true", I said, struggling to maintain the correct line on Hemel's Magic Roundabout at the same time as fiddling with the blinker thingy.

"And when it comes to the jumps, there are just too many deaths. I disapprove".

"Yeah, but things are improving, these horses have the best possible care - whoops!" Grinding noises suggested I'd engaged an inappropriate gear. Again.

It was no use, Russ had me at a disadvantage. There was no way I could refute his arguments whilst trying to turn off the radio turned on by mistake and peering through wipers set to intermittent on this beautiful day.

Driving for me is a bit of a saga. Truth is I've left it a bit late to learn. My overstuffed brain is a stuck in its ways and doesn't want to pick up any new tricks. Like clutch control, for instance. It seems unable to communicate simple messages like STOP to my right foot. Or is it left? I'm outside my comfort zone inside that Ford Focus and I don't much like it.

I tried learning to drive for the first time over ten years ago. Mrs A was expecting daughter No 2 and I thought I'd just hop into a motor, grab a few lessons and pass my test in time to be a useful 2nd driver in the family. Just in time for the baby to pop out. Well that little fantasy crashed and burned - not quite literally – one Saturday just before Christmas on the unsuspecting streets of Tring.

"Never mind the f***ing handbrake! What about the f***ing steering wheel?" screamed my soon-to-be ex-driving instructor.

I was gently manoeuvring the car towards a small crowd of Christmas shoppers staring back at me with rising panic. Seems that my grappling with the sticky handbrake after a tricky uphill junction had knocked me slightly off course. Anyway, disaster was easily averted with a hasty spin of the wheel and we wobbled off down the High Street.

"Could you pull over here, please?"

Guy's voice was now a little less panic-stricken. I executed a perfect kerbside stop. Guy cleared his throat in a rather embarrassed way.

"Mr Atkinson" (he always called me Dave) "I'd like to apologise. I've never sworn at a client before. …Have you thought about learning in an automatic?"

That was pretty much it for that set of lessons.

So back to Russ. Does he have a case? It's a fact that on average one horse a day dies in training or on the course. That's pretty harrowing. On the other hand, there are about 17,000 racehorses in training in the UK. They are bred to race. Without racing there would be significantly fewer horses. They are beautiful, magnificent animals that grace their surroundings and it is a privilege to see them in full flight. The vast majority are incredibly well cared for with excellent facilities and devoted stable staff. The authorities are incredibly hot on trainers who abuse or mistreat their horses. Look at the treatment rightly meted out to that old rogue Howard Johnson. Casualty rates are declining, too, despite what Animal Aid will have you believe before every Cheltenham and Aintree Festival.

I tried to make these points to Russ. "It's a much safer sport than it used to be. Look how they've tamed the Grand National course". He gave me a side-long glance. Yeah, but one death is one too many isn't it? That was great clutch control." I beamed inwardly. "You stopped to let that car through and moved off again perfectly. Only you were in second gear. You should have been in first!" I stopped beaming. I was never going to convince him that these sad deaths were the acceptable price we paid for the thrills and adrenaline rush of a spectacular sport.

But it's true that those running the game have been too complacent, too out of touch with issues of concern around rehabilitation, welfare and safety at the tracks. Mistakes are still being made.

Take the whip abuse issue of 2011-12. What a shambles. There was a hastily convened whip review and swiftly implemented 'reforms' to deal with a public outcry over use of the whip. It did nothing to lift the game out of the hole it had dug itself. Initially welcomed by all as valuable clarification, jockeys were soon protesting, handing in their licenses and threatening strikes. The word 'draconian' had not been bandied about as much since Slade guitarist Dave Hill's fringe was last spotted.

New rules originally introduced in October 2011 were about as popular with jockeys as George Osborne was at the Paralympics. A new set introduced in March, which followed a lengthy series of tinkerings and adjustments finally began to make a difference. By October, the number of whip offences in Britain had fallen by 34% compared with the same period in 2011, whilst the occurrence of weal marks on horses had virtually disappeared. This is overdue, but nonetheless very welcome news.

It is interesting that the Green Party's manifesto for the 2015 General Election promised a complete ban on use of the whip in racing and a full review of the sport from top to bottom. The issue remains live and worth noting that the Greens picked up more votes in 2015 than in 2010 (OK, only 3% more…!)

Amongst the vitriol and opprobrium at the peak of the whip crisis, I remember spotting an amusing tweet which suggested that Paul Carberry would be unlikely to ever pick up a whip ban on the basis that the tweeter had "…never seen him smack a horse seven times in a whole meeting, let alone one race". Backers of Harchibald in the 2005 Champion Hurdle will chuckle, no doubt.

The trouble is that for as many positive, touching stories that breach into mainstream media about horse racing, there are as many negative ones. The issue of alleged cruelty within the sport has rumbled on for some considerable time. It usually peaks with the Grand National. A couple of years ago, coverage of the tragic deaths of Dooneys Gate and Ornais was played out in the full glare of the public spotlight. Ballabriggs, the brave winner of the race that year had to be dismounted after the finish line and his jockey received a lengthy ban for whip abuse. This was part of the catalyst for the whip orders that emerged during the flat season that Autumn.

High profile casualties and bad press generated by the Grand National will not go away easily. After the incidents in the Ballabrigs race we had to bear the deaths of the Gold Cup winner Synchronised (after which McCoy said "I cried, I was in a mess, I didn't ride for days") and top handicapper (and a big favourite of mine) According To Pete in 2012. Those pictures created a massive welfare and PR problem. The debate about racing's track record of duty of care has not been well handled under the intense glare of media questioning and public opinion. This is where racing's separateness from the wider world can cause mistrust and suspicion. On one hand the 'ignorant and uninformed general public' were berated for jumping to conclusions about how racehorses are treated. On the other hand, 'aloof and unsympathetic toffs' were vilified for closing ranks.

The race remains a thrilling spectacle, underlined by a photo finish in which Neptune Collonges prevailed by a snotty nostril in the same race as those deaths. More fence modifications have followed, and changing the start to a jig-jog start (which remarkably worked, despite many a sceptical remark) may have turned the corner for this great old race. There is plenty of evidence that reducing the field size would improve matters further, but this has been left alone for the moment. The 2015 running was seen as a success. Authorities will have breathed a sigh of relief.

Another sour subject that broke into the mainstream was the perennial Achilles heel of race fixing. In the year that three Pakistani international cricketers received prison sentences for spot-fixing bribes, British racing undertook the largest investigation of its type into suspicious betting patterns. Four jockeys, including girlfriend of Keiron Fallon, Kirsty Milczarek, received bans ranging from 6 months to 12 years for fixing a series of races in the Summer of 2009. Trainers Maurice 'Fred' Sines and James Crickmore, the central characters in the scam, received 14-year bans. Five others – Nick Gold, Peter Gold, Shaun Harris, David Kendrick and Liam Vasey – were also found guilty of 'corrupt or fraudulent practice'. What's interesting is the nature of the reporting by the tabloids, which focused on Milczarek's relationship with Fallon and her 'racy' publicity photos, rather than the complexity of the case or the scale of the investigation.

More recently, the revelations about doping and horse abuse prompted by Al Zarooni's steroid scandal in 2013 were painful. In Ireland, successful national hunt trainer Philip Fenton was banned two years after illegal medications were found at his stable during 2012. Hardly a swift resolution. Elsewhere, Fergal Lynch returned to race riding 10 years after being banned for deliberately stopping a horse, in collaboration with a crooked owner. Journalist Greg Wood prefaced the moment when he wrote, "a small stain will appear on the integrity of British racing as Fergal Lynch walks into the paddock at Ayr racecourse." The BHA's view that "Lynch has satisfied us…that he has successfully reformed his character" cut no ice with Wood who argued that "For the cardinal sin of deliberately stopping a horse there should never be hope or expectation of a second chance." Lynch continues to divide opinion. Particularly since he has enjoyed such a successful year in the saddle during

2015. There's no better way to change the minds of punters than by riding them some winners.

There's some way to go for the sport I love. Same goes for me and the driving.

Inevitably Russ got the last word.

"It's just a too exploitative for me. Bit too many revs there, Dave."

A young Mum pushing a pram gave me a nervous wide-eyed stare as I raced the rpm counter through the 6,000 mark trying to make a gentle uphill left. I only want to drive so I can get to a few more race meetings!

16. CAREERING

A punter can only be successful if they can withstand their longest losing run.
Unfortunately, luck comes in on a bicycle and leaves on a motorbike.
Anonymous pro-punter, thoroughbredvillage.com, 2011

By the time the 2011 Cheltenham Festival began to form a shimmering shape on the horizon, there had already been doubts about the nature of my participation. I had had a glorious Festival Decade with my (by then) pro-punting mate Bacchy: riding the highs and lows together; confiding intimate details of rash exactas, embarrassing Lucky 15s and salvage trade-outs; demolished monumental kebabs; tackled Auntie Mona's mountainous high teas; ridden the Queens Hotel party wave.

In that time Bacchy had graduated from a £10-a-bet punter, through escalating commitments of disposable income and strategy to emerge as a fully fledged, full-time gambler. Some journey.

Strangely, Bacchy's emergence as horse powered income generator hadn't changed the relationship of our punting. The common enemy was the bookie. He and I had very different profit margins and staking plans riding on our bets. But you would never have guessed so. An unremitting joy has been the camaraderie, competition and gentle rivalry in both the fervent Cheltenham build up and the four-day Festival hothouse itself. The period had been characterised by exultant moments of triumph – sometimes shared – and when not, genuine pleasure and/or knowing empathy in each other's individual successes and failures. All this despite the massively different levels of risk and exposure.

It became increasingly apparent in the countdown to that year's Festival that those days were over. After a couple of years or so at the top table, Bacchy had found it necessary to supplement the gambling income with regular paid employment. I completely understood that. His punting numbers had been big. But not quite big or regular enough. Cash flow, identified early as the number one issue in that line of work, particularly in a jumps game that suffers regular bleak-midwinter closedowns, was the persistent niggle. Like Melodic Rendezvous in a Champion Hurdle, Bacchy was always slightly behind the pace, out of his comfort zone and struggling up the home straight. Sometimes the big ones got away too. Like Venalmar back in 2008. And others besides.

One of his observations about moving from small time to big time gambler I had not appreciated at all. That was the struggle he faced to actually get a bet down. He had a particular beef with SportingOdds who were often a point or two better about some horses than their market rivals. Attractive. Until you tried to get them to lay anything more than £100 or so. The fancy prices were merely a marketing tool (of course) to attract small time staking. "A sad excuse for a bookmaker" was Bacchy's indictment.

I had not considered this angle before. If you are a value punter building a strategy around waging a calculated percentage of your bank at given odds, the least you expect is to be able to get your money down at the advertised price. Bookies' ultra conservative risk policy definitely ate in to Bacchy's profit margins on some occasions. Such practices violate the spirit of a transaction but do not actually break any laws.

This is not the only way bookies ensure the playing field is about as level as a Himalayan rock face. Since the advent of Internet wagering, the bookmakers' habit of shutting down profitable accounts has grown significantly. In the not too distant past, this would sometime happens to high rolling punters who wore their telephone account closure notices like a badge of honour. Many would have personal relationships with bookmakers and big business would still be done face to face in shops and on course.

Fully accessible internet accounts with transparent punting histories mean big winning bets are no longer anonymous or untraceably cash-based. It is a simple task for bookies to identify profit makers and through their carefully calculated risk analysis modelling, shut them down, no matter how loyal the punters have been. Significant can be as little as a few hundred quid.

Bacchy took stock of his overall gambling performance, together with these industry barriers and took a mature decision to find gainful employment back in the world of 9-5 sedentary paper-pushing. In those straightened economic times it was always the right decision.

That's where my sympathetic line ends. Because the job Bacchy secured was a business manager in a local school. It was a good job, I had no doubt. But the Cheltenham Festival is run in term-time. School staff don't get time off during the term. Apparently Easter Sunday fell as early as 23rd March in 2008. However the next one isn't until 2160. And even then, the schools would need to break up the week before to chime with the Festival. (I bet we'll still be working though...still waiting to qualify for a pension)

Worse, Bacchy had ended up working for his missus. Of all the predicaments to find yourself in, this must be one of the most challenging. Debs was the Head teacher at the primary school where Bacchy had secured his employ. We played out the prospects of Bacchy taking some tactical leave during this crucial Spring term on many occasions and over many subsequent years. I tackled Debs about it directly at Nick's 50th birthday barbecue, thinking that a few glasses of rose and a nip of Nick's famous Mojito mix might have loosened her resolve. No chance. I was sent packing with a "How can I have tea with the vicar when my husband is gambling the mortgage away?"

There was a brief respite in 2014 when Bacchy conspired to work for a different direct line manager, but by 2015 the previous scenario was back in place. The working relationship with his wife remained an insurmountable hindrance to participation.

During a pre-Festival drink down the Willow Walk, Bacchy himself offered up the phrase 'pussy-whipped' to describe his predicament. A crude, distasteful, slightly alarming term. Though none of us could think of a more accurate description. We shook our heads and drank more ale. And then whiskies. And then Nev bought me the largest, most tabasco-infused Bloody Mary that has ever been mixed. It came in a vessel related to a goldfish bowl and contained enough ice to warrant cramp-ons and an axe. Nasty.

Interestingly, on my trip to Aintree earlier this year with Bacchy and his missus, his defence about Cheltenham non-appearance almost began to unravel. Over a few well-earned nightcaps in the company of our hosts, Debs pointed an accusing finger and asserted that Bacchy hadn't even asked for the time off for the Festival until far too late; and that next year he should follow due process and put in formal leave request. There was much humorous scoffing on both sides, but then Debs showed her real hand. "How does it look if I let my husband go to the races and gamble irresponsibly when he is the business manager at the school where I am the head teacher…?" There's the bottom line. He needs a new job.

When Bacchy e-mailed me to confirm the grizzly truth back in the Autumn of 2010, I was in bits. I felt choked, breathless and dizzy. Hyperventilation and cold sweats. I would have wept if I wasn't a hard northern bastard. Bacchy must have been worse. It wasn't entirely a bolt from the blue. I had seen all this coming, I knew his new job was with Debs in her school, But that didn't soften the blow.

So that was it. No more festival antics for the deadly duo.

In my inconsolable grief, Mrs A was going witless. "Surely someone will go with you to the bloody festival." She didn't understand. "You don't understand. It won't be the same. It won't be the same", I wailed, rather pathetically. "You are going to be insufferable if you don't go. I don't think I can take it". There was no trace of mirth around her lips. She was deadly serious.

Slowly, from this wreckage, a tentative solution shimmered into view. Like the Champion Chase field cresting the Prestbury Park Hill.

Dad and Bruv were lapping up their enjoyment of racing like never before. Since Mum passed away, racing had become something for them to do and to bind them together. However, they had never experienced that magical Cheltenham atmosphere, that sharp thrill as the tapes go up on Tuesday afternoon; the need for nervy, incessant, barely comprehensible banter of utter, utter drivel before each race. Could this be the year?

I floated the idea just before Christmas. Dad and Bruv were warm to the prospect. Almost as if they'd read my thoughts. We toyed with a modest appearance on the Tuesday and then home for the coverage on telly. I could settle for that. Better than nothing and Champion Hurdle Day was always my favourite. Dad and Paul came down for Christmas. By Boxing Day we'd planned an assault on the first two days with an option on the third and a cosy rented cottage in Stroud. It felt like the cavalry coming over the ridge to save the day.

So the fires were stoked and soon I was watching the trials meetings and clench-teething "Come ons!" at various moments inexplicable to anyone else in the house. Just like every year. It wouldn't be the same. How could it be? But it would be excellent. Different. A new chapter. New experiences.

I told Bacchy there was room in the cottage for him in case he got a sudden reprieve. The chances were slimmer than a Monsignor come back (still burning up the gallops, we hear) but we kept a slug of Laphroaig in the bottle, just in case. He was delighted I was maintaining the Festival traditions.

17. FESTIVAL TOURISTS

How bad did it get? Well let me put it this way.
By the end of the first day all the money which had been hard won
over the winter through a careful campaign of abstemiousness
and selective investment that culminated in a winning Cheltenham
only a few weeks before had gone.
Not some of it. All of it.

Paul Haigh, racing writer, 'A Cautionary Tale', 1994

We settled comfortably into our base deep in the Cotswolds, readying ourselves for the first day onslaught. Bruv had been hard at work, poring over the Racing Post to construct elaborate each-way Lucky 15s and accumulators.

Our Festival bunker was in the hamlet of Maugersbury, tacked on to a south-westerly spur of Stow on the Wold, overlooking gentle hills and wooded valleys. We had Wi-Fi, which was by then a pre-requisite. Bruv was checking the decs earlier and said, "Ooh, Sedgefield tomorrow. I'll just have a look."

"Sedgefield!" I decried. "On the eve of the very greatest jumps meeting in the World, you are checking out sellers at Sedgefield?"

"There's some good racing at Sedgefield, I'll have you know", Dad piped up. "On a par with Catterick."

Hmm. Damning with faint praise as far as I was concerned.

Stow was a splendid choice. Handsome soft Cotswold stone buildings, pretty shops, fine pubs and restaurants. The town was experiencing its annual invasion of racegoers. We picked up our first festival tip within 15 minutes of arriving. In the Tourist Information, the Manager says, "Hi, are you here for the races?"

We grinned back. "Do you follow the horses much?"

We kept grinning. More nervously. Would she want a tip?

"I had a trainer in here the other day, looking for accommodation nearby."

Now we were interested. "Yes, a Mr Harty, I think. Can't remember his horse."

"Captain Cee Bee" said Bruv, quick as a flash. "I think it might have been Eddie Harty."

"Yes, I think that was him. He said his horse would win the Champion Chase on Wednesday!"

Settling down to the final decs, it was refreshing to focus on some action after months of anticipation and ante-post anxiety. Shaky at the best of times, my portfolio had taken hits with withdrawals over the last couple of days. My most confident bets were Peddlers Cross in the Champion Hurdle and Realt Dubh in the Arkle.

The first day at the Festival is simply the pinnacle. If I had to pick only one day to attend, it would always be this curtain-raiser. Four days of fine racing lay ahead and the expectancy and optimism had not yet been punctured. It was a perfect scenario. Alastair Down in that morning's Racing Post captured the mood perfectly:

> *Over the next four days the tumult will build to a series of spectacular crescendos…for sheer sustained ferocity of competition coupled with unbridled emotion, there isn't a sport that can get within hailing distance of this cherished week.*

Fills you up doesn't it?

We were up and about early. There were some last minute additions to opening day portfolios. Bruv was jabbering away about bets that could only hint at the chaos going on inside his brain: "If Cue Card wins the first, well that's the key and sets everything up. And

Menorah. Just can't see him out of the first three. I can see Banjaxed Girl bolting early and leading them all a merry dance. Need to get 'em in a combination."

These are classic signs of Festival Virgin Rambling. Slack-jawed babbling. I know because I've been there. As a veteran of 12 years, I was content to watch Bruv grapple with the scale and the enormity of the thing. Desperately trying to resist backing every horse in every damn race of this puntathon, chasing the big money.

We headed up to the King's Arms on the Square for a quality 'race-goers breakfast', including black pudding, lambs kidneys and a free Racing Post (served separately).

RUK was on the telly and presenter Stuart Machin was banging his head against a brick wall trying to get an opinion out of his studio pundit Jonathan Neesom. This non-committal sage simply would not put his neck on the line in any race for anything. Wasn't that his job? At one point Stuart looked straight down the camera and almost rolled his eyes in an 'I-can-only-keep-asking-the-questions' sort of way.

We hit the track early and found a good berth in the seats by the uphill fence. The track looked beautiful. Do I repeat these exact phrases every year?

The two festival virgins on my right were still trying to wind me up. "So that's the famous Cheltenham hill is it? Towcester's worse. One of these runners has good Catterick form. Are you going to mention that in your blog, Dave?"

Gaff track tourists. And there were more behind. A Welsh youth smartly turned out in tightly-cut shiny grey suite approached his mates with a fist-full of a placepot slips and cried, "OK boyos, who's the jo-ka who picked out numb-ba 11 in a ten rrrrunn-er race, right? You Dai! You twattt!"

Hoots of derision. Earlier they had asked us what the minimum stake was on a placepot.

"Can you do a quid, like?" High rollers from the low valleys. Can't knock value punting.

And then a bone shaking roar to greet the start of the opener. I'd spent long enough telling my folks about that spine-tingling moment, so I was glad the assembled Cheltenham choir didn't let me down. We were graced with a finish to suit the occasion. Four in line at the last. Sprinter Sacre looked like he might power away from re-hot favourite Cue Card – jockey Joe Tizzard's squeezed pips could be heard popping from at least the furlong marker – surely he had gone too soon? Next, Spirit Son stayed on passed him. Finally, seemingly from nowhere, Ruby Walsh galvanised Al Ferof to scream home for the Paul Nicholls yard. Nicky Henderson's horses 2nd and 3rd. Cue Card out of the frame. Hear that? It's the sound of a million combinations and accumulators being ripped up. Riotous laughter of celebrating bookies in the background.

I backed Sprinter Sacre. It was the last race in which he tasted defeat for two and a half years, running up a sequence of 10 straight wins. It says everything about my performance in this annual heat, losing over £50 in this one race alone! It says more about the quality of the race we just had witnessed. A whole host of these horses went on to feast at the top table for a good few years – and they are not all finished yet. Apart from Sprinter's spectacular achievements, Cue Card won a Haldon Gold Cup, an Ascot Gold Cup, A Ryanair Chase and a Betfair Chase. He was also runner up in a King George. Al Ferof was no mug either. Apart from this, he won some decent novice chases, the Paddy Power Gold Cup and a brace of Amlin Chases at Ascot. Even Zaidpour, labouring home in 7th has now snaffled close to half a million in prize money, mostly in Ireland.

The one subsequent disappointment was Spirit Son. He came out again that April and smashed up a good field at Aintree (including Cue Card), but picked up an injury in the close season and never raced again. What heights might he have attained?

The Arkle didn't disappoint either. Finian's Rainbow was prominent for a long way and briefly looked like he had got away from the pack, then Ghizao momentarily challenged. Eventual winner,

Captain Chris began to stay on after some right howlers early in the race. My boy Realt Dubh also stayed on, but didn't have the pace up the hill to catch the leaders. I didn't think the jumping of Captain Chris would hold together under that severe examination, but he won that well. Finian's Ranbow 2nd, Realt Dubh 3rd.

I backed Carole's Legacy in the three-mile handicap, but she couldn't quite get to Bensalem in a stirring battle up the straight. Bensalem's fencing was always deeply suspect, but he managed to jump through all the holes that Reve de Sivola had punched into the obstacles. Much to Bruv's disappointment.

I was so far into Peddlers Cross for the Champion Hurdle I could see what he had for breakfast. I was desolate that he couldn't nail this race. We saw an epic though. First hand, under blue skies, we witnessed a legend being made. The race panned out beautifully for my boy and there were no excuses. Hurricane Fly found more on the run-in than I was ever expecting. As the two met the last together, well clear of their desperate pursuers, Peddlers looked slightly the more fluent.

I was convinced Peddlers' proven stamina would come into play and burn off the Irish raider. He could have done with more of a test to bring that grinding attribute into full effect - the race was run in a time two seconds slower than the Supreme over the same trip an hour and a half earlier. He came back at the Fly up the hill, but the latter dug deep and was actually going away at the line. Great race.

I was a real fan of Peddlers Cross. I'd backed him off the boards both that season and the previous one. His win in the Neptune was a glorious moment. However, he never fulfilled his potential over fences, despite that sphere looking the obvious move. In a breathtaking fencing debut, Sprinter Sacre smashed Peddlers to bits in the Wayward Lad novices chase at Kempton. But many pointed to this Champion Hurdle as the turning point in his career. "Hurricane Fly broke Peddlers' heart" people say. There may be some truth in that. Though it's also worth remembering that Donald McCain sent him out again at Aintree, only three weeks after that punishing race.

He finished 7th there, after an effort 3 out. There is no telling how close to being bottomed the horse was at the end of the season.

The cross-country event was a sober antidote to a great race. The most notable incident in this renewal was the comedic value that Mike Cattermole tried to squeeze out the mildly amusing names given to fences on each of the tortuous ever-decreasing circuits, such as the Double Spread Hedge and the Stuffed Hurdle. The contrived, premeditated food-related observation The Catt that "One Cool Cookie runs out at the cheese wedges" was the low point.

The rest of the day was a mixture of small wins and near misses for the three of us. Quevaga was again imperious in the Mares Race. Dad got the placepot up, but only to small fractions, so he didn't go home rich. We didn't go home quickly either. Messy car park exiting.

But a few beers and a welcome fish & chips supper enabled me to lick my wounds, reflect on a very good day's racing, and reload. I was ready for Day 2 with a recovery strategy. Once more into the breach....

Dank, grey, impenetrable. Never mind the weather. This was my mood after the Champion Chase. A pall of low cloud hung over Prestbury Park obscuring Cleeve Hill, cloaking everything in cold mist and providing a perfect opportunity for this clunky simile.

We were only two today. Dad's leg was playing up and he decided against putting it through the rigours of another circuit of the racecouse. He sportingly drove Bruv and me to the track through fog and rain, and then returned to watch the action back at our Stow nerve centre.

Approaching the track from the town centre is a very different experience to the walk through car parks from the north yesterday. Then we wove through endless Range Rover tail-gate picnics of champers and smoked salmon, hosted by country couples wearing enough acreage of tweed and corduroy to carpet the home straight. Today, we dodged groups of lairy pint-pot screamers, fancy-dress debs and busking children (I kid you not). Bruv was unable to resist accepting a lovely yellow Betfair scarf handed out from a box in someone's front garden. Novice.

The crowds seemed thinner. The Best mate stands were as busy as I could remember on Tuesday, confirmed by the Racing Post that put the overall total attendance at over 53,000. Much more elbow room on Wednesday though. We watched the first from the rail by the winning post. I took a photo for a couple of punters at their first festival. She looked at the image on the back of the camera and exclaimed "Oh, that's not a very good one!" Her partner retorts, "Well why didn't you smile then you daft tart!" I handed the camera back and beat a hasty retreat. I would have hated to be the cause of a domestic.

The early races were nothing short of carnage on the punting front and at least two were unsatisfactory on the racing front, too. The four-miler saw a convincing win for Chicago Grey, produced expertly by his amateur rider. Bruv collected a little, but was also getting excited about a horse we've both backed, Pearlysteps. Only he was cheering on the wrong horse! Wrong colours, wrong jockey!

The Neptune Hurdle remains a profitable race for me and Rock On Ruby did pretty much everything he could to maintain the record before getting mugged right on the line by First Lieutenant. ROR would have scrapping for 3rd had not Oscars Well and So Young both slammed into the last, stopping their momentum as sure as ramming a gear stick into reverse.

My nap of the meeting, Wymott was up next in the RSA Chase. Oh what a shambles. He was never travelling. Not interested. Spat out the dummy. He wasn't alone. Red hot favourite Time For Rupert was lethargic and sluggish at his fences. And two horses fell when tanking along. This left Jessies Dream and Boston's Angel to fight out the finish, with the latter prevailing under a gutsy, gritty and determined drive. Despite a shocking show from my team, I was pleased for trainer Jessie Harrington who is a talented, self-effacing and engaging individual and who saw her charge, Oscars Well fluff his lines earlier with the race at his mercy. Another turn up result in the RSA. How many times?

Champion Chase, the best spectacle of the meeting for me, saw an emphatic performance from Sizing Europe. My punt, French Opera was not up to this class. How could I have ever thought he was? An ill-advised exacta perm was also a grubby little failed cash-grab.

A day and half into the puntathon and I was beginning to lose reason, judgement and balance. And that's not just a result of the emptied hip flask. I've been in that predicament many times before, and although Day 2 is so often the card where I get my Festival back on track, maintaining positivity and focus is often hard.

Bruv was having an equally bad time. Reflecting back on the first, he said, "Comes to something when the highlight of your day is cheering home an each way shout. And it's the wrong horse!" Even through my dark mood, I raised a grin. He goes on. "You know you're having a bad day when your get-out stakes is the Coral Cup!" I thought I'd cornered the pathos market.

Ah, the Coral Cup. 2 ½ miles and 27 unfeasibly handicapped runners. BUT NOT THAT DAY! Through very different reasoning and obscure circumstance we both managed to back Gordon Elliot's Carlitto Brigante in this minefield of a race. And he bolted home! We were celebrating long before the last-hurdle fall of his nearest rival that made the run-in academic. 20-1. That sounded lovely. Much high-fiving and back-slapping was set loose. We warmly applauded the horse home. (Just once, I'd like a winning jockey to doff his cap in the direction of the Best Mate enclosure. A small gripe, admittedly...).

My Bruv collected his wedge there and then, whilst I had that particular little thrill later in the Ladbrokes in town where I'd struck the bet. I love race horses. These animals are beautiful athletes, trained to perfection, running and jumping with fluidity, grace and verve. But sometimes that poetry takes second place to an outpouring of baseless, charmless, shameless and ugly greed. Filthy lucre.

"I loved this horse last year and backed him in the Triumph." I declared, swell-chested. "He's been handled tenderly this year."

"Is that so," says Bruv, "He first came to my attention because the Brigantians are the Celtic tribe that originally settled in our part of Yorkshire."

What kind of intellectual approach to punting-by-names is this?

"So what's the significance of Carlito then?" I venture.

"No idea, mate. Bounded up that so-called hill though didn't he?!"

That changed the day, of course. We prowled around the bookie avenues, having little 'fun' bets on the remaining two races and generally feeling pretty pleased with ourselves. Infact, nothing else went our way, but that didn't matter.

We met Dad down the town and he ferried us home, after enquiring whether we needed to hitch up the trailer for all our folding stuff. Back at the ranch, we wound down over a few beers and a medium rump steak with all the trimmings.

A couple of days later, I was climbing off the Festival crazy train. It didn't mean that I had quite come back to earth. Just like blinking back into daylight after a twist on Disneyland's Aerosmith Rock n Rollercoaster, reaclimatisation was needed. The head had to stop spinning and the brain needed to reacquaint with its surroundings.

The sun was out on that beautiful post-Gold Cup Saturday morning. It was time to pause for breath.

For me, the relative success of a Festival is judged by the interplay of a number of factors across the full four days: the ebb and flow of financial fortunes, the heart-stopping spectacle of the racing in the championship events, the mouth-watering illumination of potential in the novice events… and of course, the craic, the banter, and the company. Balancing all those criteria, I've never had a bad one. And that year was up there with the best.

On the wider stage the true barometer of success comes down to one race: The Cheltenham Gold Cup. Sat in the garden, welcome sunshine was making the newsprint of my Racing Post dazzle and glare. This was as much about the quality of the writing as the weather conditions. For a change. The RP exploits its dominance of the market place to dish up some pretty average, hackneyed, shallow and at times, I'd argue, partial reporting. But if there was a need to understand the significance of the Gold Cup to the industry and to the majority of the public, then it was writ large in that Saturday morning edition. I noted the sage remarks of Robert Whaley-Cohen, the owner of new champion Long Run,

> *This is the greatest four days of jump racing, this is the most important day of the four, that's the most important race of the day. What can be better than to win the best race on the best day at the best meeting?*

And if you had the stomach for unashamedly dramatic and touchingly sentimental race reviews, Alastair Down's tour de force was an absolute joy. He's not everyone's cup of tea. But as a journo, he knows when to switch on the humility and needs no second invitation to go for the emotional jugular. In this piece he blasted both barrels in order to stake a claim for the race's place in history.

> *...At Cheltenham yesterday an absolute epic of a Gold Cup lifted our sport to heights you might dream of reaching perhaps once or twice in a lucky generation.*

My own festival experience always has more twists and turns than this one great race. Dad, Bruv and I drew stumps on Wednesday night I was back home on Thursday morning in time for the first race of the third day. I can't remember the last occasion I was at home for a day of the festival. At least 12 years ago. But I enjoyed the change.

I enjoyed the pattern of the afternoon: baying at the telly in the Jewson, urging the gorgeous and talented Noble Prince up that lush hill and away from the stout Wishfull Thinking to land me a win single and the last leg of an each way Lucky 15. Then having to open the door to the dining room and apologise to Mrs A and Steve for disturbing their important music businessing.

The latter part of that pattern rather became the norm: the baying and the apologising. Less so the winning: my hollering was insufficient to see Kalahari King collar Albertas Run in the Ryanair, nor to urge Fiveforthree to threaten the remarkable Big Buck's in the World Hurdle.

"Sorry guys! Bit exciting in here".

This wasn't the only repeating pattern either. Both Albertas Run and Big Buck's had won their respective races on the same afternoon last year. Buena Vista leading the field a merry dance in the Pertemps final – as he had also done last season – gave the day an eerie feeling of déjà vu. How I failed to back Buena Vista in that is a mystery to me. I was all over him last year and nearly chewed the long suffering Bacchy's ear off about how thrilled and stunned I was to have finally cracked the Pertemps conundrum.

Bacchy's Fantasy Festival Competition was hitting top gear by day 3. A good few of the lads had entered. It was a simple, inspired and original competition based on fantasy wedge to punt over the four days. Rather than pro-punting, Bacchy should have parcelled this up and sold it off to one of the big bookies or newspapers as the perfect fantasy game.

The e-mail banter had been electric already and plenty of good scores had been notched. Winner would take all come the heady, charged denouement in a Westminster boozer on the Friday afternoon.

Nev, perennial bridesmaid, was desperate to win. He had backed Albertas Run and Big Buck's to open up a £200 quid lead on the rest of us, but Colin, also courtesy of Big Buck's was handy in 2nd. I was off the pace, but had notched the first leg of double through that lovely Noble Prince. Landing the 2nd leg would put me back in the mix. Nick was lurking. He's good at that. Colin was well aware of all this and was on the text to me:

"Who's the second leg on, mate?"

"Sorry, not declaring that till tomoz afternoon. Adds spice don't it?"

"I don't want f**king spice in my afternoon!"

The banter on Facebook was quality. On Bacchy's timeline:

Bryn: "Nev will blow it, he won't be able to resist a hefty punt along the way and then the pressure and booze will get to him."

Colin: "I will psyche him out, get inside his head space, take him to uncomfortable places."

Uncomfortable places! What Guantanamo talk was this? Cracking stuff! With this chilling encounter in prospect, I arrived at the Barley Mow. Nick and Colin were already there and had baggsied the comfy leather sofas in front of the giant drop down screen. Nev was next and then the rest of the lads arrived and the action at Prestbury Park began to unfold.

Despite my own extensive personal punting strategy for the afternoon, Fantasy Festival always dominates this day. It's not the money; it's the pride, the thrill and the matey competition. The lead often swaps faster than a Coalition Government policy position. Indeed the psychological warfare that Colin and Bryn have alluded to is something that party strategists could learn a lot from.

Zarkandar bolted up in the Triumph. Lovely looking prospect. He was lung-burstingly roared home by me, Nev and Nick. Exposed to this full force wind tunnel, the gaggle of young ladies and gentlemen who had been sat under the screen quietly moved elsewhere.

In the County Hurdle, Final Approach somehow managed to get his lovely nose in front right on the line with a very late lunge. I'd backed him, but wasn't celebrating. I couldn't see that he'd got there in time. Even the cameraman was focusing on Get Me Out Of Here. I was already bemoaning my luck to Nick, "Every punter groans about the ones that get away and there's another one to go with Rock On Ruby. Tssk." I was still whinging, when the result of the photo was declared in favour of my boy. Colin said he heard me shriek from the bogs. Two out of two. In the Albert Bartlett, red hot favourite Bobs Worth showed real class and smoothly ran out a handy winner. I didn't have any real money on him, but this big bruiser of a horse landed the second leg of my Fantasy Festival double. That put me right in the frame.

Heady stuff. And although I didn't get another winner for the rest of the afternoon, I was delirious. Gold Cup manoeuvres in the dark den of the Barley Mow were by then in full swing. Nick had overtaken Colin and was seriously in the hunt. Nick has previous in this event. Harder to crack than Nev, too - Colin's prophecy about him came true. Nev's uncomfortable place was an ill-judged, wide-eyed grab for glory at £150 notes each way on the Commander. The reigning champ burdened with the leader's hopes and fears at 4-1. Madness we all thought. Infact I think we tried to talk him out of it. "Shit or bust. You know me Dave". And we did.

The race, of course, quickly became seen as a classic. The brave old guard replaced by the new. The best horse in training landing an epic from two glorious ex-champions. Perfectly scripted. When Kauto Star led them out on the second circuit. Colin and I exchanged glances.

"What's he doing? This isn't Kauto's game!"

But we were grinning. The 11 year old was serving it up to the field, pouring on the pressure. Imperial Commander was on his shoulder, Denman and Long Run tucked behind. Commander's blunder at the fourth last provided the impetus for Denman to stake his claim. There was an audible gasp in the pub as this tank, absolutely flat to the boards, ranged up and past Kauto.

"Gooo on Denman, Gooooo on son."

Independent shouts of encouragement rang around the pub for this gutsy warrior that were inspired by sentiment, not profit. For a moment, we thought he might do it. And then Long Run swept through. He rose beautifully at every fence when asked big questions by his articulate, well-groomed and thoroughly likeable amateur jockey, Sam Whaley-Cohen. He sizzled up the hill and won in a track record time. We all knew we'd seen some race.

Only the briefest of respectful pauses was granted before we knuckled down again for the decider in the Fantasy Festival. Nev knew his chances had now gone after the Commander had been pulled up. This left me a tiny few quid in front with only the Grand Annual to go, the festival closer, at 5.15. Bacchy, architect of this Fantasy Festival feast arrived in the pub a little before the off.

It was great to see him, his participation in the four days having been limited by a punishing work schedule.

So, we were 'all in, all in' for the decider. It is traditionally done by secret selection to avoid any advantage being gained by the leader. Bad news for Nick. He and I managed to select the same horse and to the same stake. In a field of 23, this is some feat. It was a crusher for Nick, who now couldn't win. In the end, none of our selections got close. Nev's Anquetta briefly threatened, but the frame was filled with outsiders. This meant that I'd managed to cling on to the FF trophy by a few spawny pennies.

Late afternoon became early evening and then dark night in a blur of Doom Bar, Brakspears and celebratory double-Glenmorangies. The time came to lurch home from this marathon session that had been, by turns, exhilarating, satisfying and shattering. At the end, we made big promises of a mob-handed return to the track next year, just like the old days. Bacchy had achingly missed the thrill and had taken the absence stoutly on the chin. So we'll both be there next year. Bryn put his hand up for a couple of days too. Col fancied it and did I hear Nev say the same? I reckon my Bruv will be back as well. So that sounds to be very much like a formidable army to go to war with next March.

Sitting in that Saturday morning reflective sunshine, I noticed an unread text message on my phone. I checked it out:

"I love u 2 Davoski".

Oh no. Warning bells. A quick flick to the sent box confirmed it. Yep, sure enough, a raft of emotional, sentimental, guff-filled texts has been dispatched late the previous evening, presumably on the train back home: "I really love you guys…. what a brilliant day…great comp…. love your enthusiasm…. wouldn't be the same…." And so it went on.

As a post-script, the schedule of shame financial analysis, updated for the final time that Saturday morning, revealed a rather pathetic bottom line: I had paid the price for some sizeable and rash plunges on the Supreme and the Champion Hurdle and some ridiculous combinations. £515 staked in 53 separate bets covering ante-posts, wins, doubles, each-ways, accumulators, Lucky 15s, exactas and placepots to give an overall PROFIT of £14. FOURTEEN QUID.

Blood, tears, toil and sweat. Good research, bad information, ugly judgement. Near things, sure things, things can only get better.

And some exultation, redemption and reward too. Is it worth it? You bloody well bet it is!

18. CELEBRATING THE CHASERS

Have you got any more like him at home?
Paul Nicholls on meeting the breeder of Kauto Star, 2008

Long Run's Gold Cup felt like the dawn of a new chasing era. Both Kauto Star and Denman gave best to this young star with just six summers on his back and the world at his feet. Yet barely 8 months later, Kauto Star had completed one of the most remarkable resurgences seen in top level jumps racing.

After mustering third in that memorable Gold Cup and then pulling up in the equivalent in Ireland, many expected to be penning his racing obituary. I was amongst them. I respectfully wrote him off at Cheltenham, and hailed the new breed. I shook my head and called for well-deserved retirement after Punchestown.

Team Ditcheat knew different. Owner Clive Smith and trainer Paul Nicholls decided to keep him in training and throughout the Autumn the horse was the subject of incredibly upbeat reports from the yard. He reappeared in the Betfair Chase at Haydock in November. Once again I argued (alongside many others) that it was a race too far. I didn't want to see an ignominious end to a great career.

That was the start of the renaissance. After his thrilling victory – and I mean thrilling: jumping as an art form, front-running as breathtaking spectacle – connections revealed that they had indeed considered retirement and that this race had been his Gold Cup. Nicholls was emotional, pumped and vindicated. Days like those are why he sticks with a game that delivers more than its fair share of knocks.

Connections had no option, swept on a tide of emotion, but to take the King George route on Boxing Day. Like a killjoy naysayer, high on pooping parties, I again felt he couldn't win. He needed longer between his races… Long Run and other pretenders would be fitter… blah blah. I was wrong. The betting public was right. My mate Colin, a true believer, was right. Again Kauto put a fine field to the sword. Long Run got much closer this time. But the result was the same. The outpouring of emotion was the same.

His upwardly mobile profile during the second half of 2011 was more akin to the breakthrough of a six-year-old novice, not a battle-hardened chaser who would turn 12 a few days after that King George victory. Despite the age burden, this wonderful son of little-known sire Village Star ended the year with an enhanced reputation amongst a swirl of glittering accolades that an average Oscars' night would die for.

This proved to be the zenith of the remarkable revival. The Gold Cup was of course the only place to go after those victories. But the fairy story was over. Firstly there was a fall in the Spring whilst working that put in doubt his Gold Cup participation. Then the race itself in which he was sensibly pulled up. Everyone breathed a sigh of relief. This time his retirement was confirmed.

That was not nearly the end of the Kauto drama. Clearly the relationship between master trainer and single-minded owner had been deteriorating for some while. This spilled out into press as a full scale row over how Kauto Star should spend his dotage.

Nicholls gave a quivery, emotional interview to Alastair Down on the Saturday after the events had gone public. The toothy Mr Smith had chosen a dressage career for the now retired legendary chaser, and this had upset the trainer and his team. It is the owner's right to do as he wishes with the horse, of course. That's not something old pumpkin head was disputing. Though it seems the way the decisions were made and subsequently announced had wound up the champion trainer and his team beyond measure. He packed off Kauto to his new home with Laura Collett, a dressage rider of some repute and promptly stuck his bottom lip out.

The subsequent volleys of accusation and counter charge were highly entertaining. Who discussed what with whom…Where was the best home for the horse… Who loved him the most…it all added a touch of drama to an obviously emotional set of circumstances.

John Francome had his own inimitable take on the jousting between trainer and owner. During his brief training career he said that owners should be treated like mushrooms: fed lots of manure and kept in the dark!

Even the premature death of Kauto Star could not simply be mourned as a tragic accident. The horse broke his pelvis and neck in a fall at Laura Collett's yard. No-one saw the incident and five days passed in which Kauto's condition worsened, before he was euthanised. This revelation was seized upon by twitter trolls and conspiracy theorists to invent stories of collisions with brick walls and criticize the treatment of the horse in the aftermath.

Desperate stuff. A bitter final scene in the story of Kauto Star, the greatest steeplechaser of the modern era. He was the best over a range of trips, tracks and underfoot conditions. He won more Grade 1 chases than any other horse. Time after time, he proved people wrong. The horse was a sensation.

He wasn't my favourite though. Denman, who retired shortly before his stable mate, held that accolade. The two sparred many times and served up some scintillating performances. I find it hard to express why I loved Denman the Tank so much. Something to do with belligerence, running style, guts and attitude. I won more money backing Denman than I ever did on Kauto and that may be a factor too. I felt enormous loyalty to the beast.

Denman's Gold Cup was an awesome display of unrelenting power. And those Hennessy wins! Arkle's remarkable back-to-back victories in the 60's were achieved under a specially devised handicapping system that had him weltered with 12st 6lb. Denman achieved what was almost a comparable modern day double under a mere 11st 12lb in 2007 and 2009. The latter was an exhilarating, freewheeling performance of bold jumping and relentless galloping in which he gave away 13lb more to his rivals than he had in 2007.

Denman loved the broad, expansive furlongs of Newbury. The next year, the Tank almost repeated his Hennessy tricks when hiked up the ratings a further 8lb. He tired to an emotional 3rd.

His retirement also looked like it would be painfully short when he contracted a potentially fatal bone and blood infection. However, he recovered well after five months in an equine hospital and was last spotted lapping up the limelight with another stable star, Big Buck's having a day with the Blackmore and Sparkford Vale Hunt.

19. A FORCE FOR GOOD

He wore a wing collar with a green smock
and listened to Vivaldi while singing The Jam. He was brilliance up
close.
David Nyssen, friend of Crispin Moor, 2012

My first visit to Lingfield was with Bacchy in those coupe-touring, pro-punting fuelled days chasing second rate jumpers around the country. My second visit was to witness some steeds with even less promise: my debut at the real live sand donkey racing.

I made the repeat Lingfield visit to meet up with a good friend of mine, Crispin who lived very near the track. And near the station. The juxtaposition of those two locations with his house meant there were often callers en route (in either direction) seeking various bits of crucial local information.

For instance, "Hello mate, where's the nearest curry house*/pub*/taxi* (*delete as appropriate). Crispin recalled an encounter in which a couple of likely lads knocked at the door and asked "Scuse me, have you got any playing cards?" In response to which, Crispin's daughter happily produced a pack and wished the travellers a safe journey. "No, no, no we can't just take them. Here, have this", said one and proffered a twenty spot. Despite all protests and refusals, these boys wouldn't take no for an answer and left to play snap with their very expensive cards on the train home, after - one would assume - a pretty successful day on the gee-gees!

I made the trip in part for some punting practice. As Dickie Bird used to say when he turned up at the Yorkshire nets in April, I just needed to get my eye in. Mrs A was part of a Berko Mums Gathering. They were a very organized crowd, with a kitty and everything. That Summer they decided to use the balance on the kitty as an investment opportunity. Why they don't just buy a half-decent bottle of plonk with it I don't really know. Instead, it was to become the stake on a horse that would win at sufficient odds to yield a return earmarked variously for spa weekends, retirement funds and sumptuous meals at the local gastro pub. Ambitious in the extreme.

And how would this horse be selected? Well, my name had mysteriously appeared in the frame. Apparently, my mate Dave is partly to blame for this. "Why don't you give the float to Mr A to put on a horse? Maximise your wedge… expand your wonga!" he said, or words loosely to that effect. This scheme was duly put out to consultation and the group responded with a resounding 'yes'. Motion carried. Particularly Sue's sister Jill whom, I gather, said "to win I hope. None of this each way nonsense!" Hmm. Bit of pressure here.

This happened once before when I became responsible for finding a winner to maximise the office lottery syndicate's loose change. On that occasion I turned £68 into £476 via a beautiful novice chaser out of the Paul Nicholl's yard, named appropriately enough, Tales of Bounty.

But delivering for the Berko Mums was a very different proposition, carrying a very different penalty structure. I was shortly off to Glorious Goodwood with the lads and we were eagerly anticipating the Sussex Stakes. This would be a grandstanding showdown, a proper duel in the sun on the high downs, between unbeaten wonder horse Frankel and the best miler of the older generation, Canford Cliffs. That day, it appeared, would also be the scene of a much lower-order of showdown: the day of the Mum's Horse.

So Lingfield was also a chance to refine those betting instincts in the heat of battle. But what chance did I have with my head in the Surrey sand?

Well, it was a top day. Crispin was in fine form and it was marvellous to catch up. A couple of pints of delicious Finchcocks from a Westerham Brewery barrel mounted on the bar counter helped to neutralise the drizzle outside. The racing was OK too, despite my damning summary at this chapter opening.

There were a couple of decent maidens crammed with prospects from all the top yards and I managed to land the winner of one of the more interesting handicaps on the card. Not quite the same luck for Crispin who was unable to urge 100-1 shot Barello into the frame, despite summoning up the spirit of his Italian-based brother, domiciled in the region of the famous wine. We left before the last race and I later found that I had landed the placepot too! Minimum stakes to a middling 20-1 return, but I'm not complaining.

So, the Ladies of Berkhamsted had no need to worry. The kitty-float-whip leftovers would be shrewdly invested by a punter whose eye was in and touch was sure. They could safely book up their spa days. On the other hand, maybe Spar daze would be wiser. The low-brow supermarket was running a good deal on Blue Nun…

The trip to Lingfield had another purpose. Crispin was a good friend of mine who had recently been diagnosed with a brain tumour. Achingly, he knew he didn't have long left. It was a chance for us to spend some time together. He died not long after our trip to the races.

I thought long and hard about whether to include this section in the book, just as I did when I posted some of this material in the original blog. It is too easy to bash out trite words and push them into the vastness of cyberspace, with no care for sensibilities. I don't want to do that. There is a danger of invading the space of a wonderful family and of friends and relatives who knew him better than me. I would hate to do that. There is also the risk of an overdose of sentimentality in a compendium that has already dealt with more death than enough, and certainly more than in the first volume. This fact is more a function of life-cycle than of misery-chasing.

Crispin was a man who touched so many lives in such a positive way, mine included. And for that reason I felt compelled to include my tribute here.

Crispin and I arrived at the Countryside Agency within a couple of years of each other. He became my colleague, my boss and my friend in quick succession. On my last day in the job, he gave me such an affectionate man-hug in the middle of the open plan that my ribs still ache to think of it...

At work, Crispin was a blend of idealistic visioning and pragmatic realism: he knew the battles that he wanted to fight and win. He held the bigger picture firmly in his sights, whilst acknowledging creeping myopia about 'interminable' budget processes and blurry 'detail' that could be resolved later. He also knew the value of a contented team and the balance between hard work and rewarding play. I remember waking up the morning after a drink with Crispin and Justin at the launch the State of the Countryside report in 2008 to find my laptop bag filled with the contents of my stomach (is this too much information?) and a two-week dose of conjunctivitis... I blamed them squarely for both!

My fondest memories remained those outside the direct line of duty, such as his brazen encouragement of my horse racing vice. When I booked time off for the Cheltenham Festival, he was more interested in my ante-post portfolio than my leave sheet. He was a regular commentator on my blog, offering hearty congratulations on those rare occasions of a successful tip, notably when Masked Marvel won the St Leger. And he remained supportively encouraging or mercifully silent about the pile of steaming junk that comprised the vast majority of those ramblings. The very fact that Crispin was reading them, let alone backing the horses displayed his typical loyalty, humour and mischief.

Crispin liked nothing better than a day at Lingfield races, at so it was fitting that our last encounter should be there. We had had a teary discussion about the indiscriminate, unjust illness that has now taken his life prematurely; and about his plans to make the most of the time that remained. He told me he was stopping short of a bucket list, but was taking and enjoying every day as it came. I saw how he was drawing such strength from his family, his friends and his faith. I was in awe of his humility, his fortitude and his positive outlook. I still am.

At his funeral, the tributes were uplifting. The readings were moving. None more so than a passage from a letter Crispin had written to his wife which, in parts, served as a goodbye to all of us. "Grieve and grieve well", he had said. The phrase was resonant and heartfelt. And it sliced through the carefully laid defences of the congregation like a rapier. This was raw emotion. I am not a good crier. Some dabbed delicately at moist eyes. Others blinked away a salty trickle. I convulsed with chesty heaves and a shoulder action more at home in a rugby scrum. It was not pretty.

And we did grieve well. We raised a glass to Crispin in The Star Inn. Such occasions are always bittersweet. This was mostly bitter, to be honest, but catching up with old friends and colleagues and meeting new ones was sweet enough. We read stories that had been collected by Crispin's wife as a keepsake for his children and published in a booklet for everyone to take away. This was a lovely touch. Vivid reflections of an inspiring, humorous, talented, eloquent, intelligent and passionate friend and colleague.

Fantastic stuff. Crispin Moor: A force for good.

20. DUEL ON THE DOWNS

*I went to bed and Shergar was rated 140
and when I woke up he was 136!*

Walter Swinburn, Shergar's Derby winning jockey, 2013

Glorious Goodwood swung into spectacular view. Probably the finest aspect in racing. By the time raceday arrived, the event had been predictably built up. 'The Duel on the Downs' splashed the Racing Post front page in 4-inch Times New Roman. The eagerly awaited clash between Frankel and Canford Cliffs got the full "so it comes to this…" fight them on the beaches treatment. Bacchy was a bit sniffy about Brough Scott's flowery prose. "There's no penetrative journalism in this rag any more." He was probably right.

All the same, I do love a bit of overblown drama and sentiment, building up the big day with hyperbolic superlative. Alastair Down is always the master. His piece the following day was anticipated with the slogan Down on the Duel. Ho ho!

Bacchy, Brynaldo, Ben and I were on a train crawling through ripening wheat fields, edging towards the 2nd day of Glorious Goodwood. The Sussex Stakes was indeed the jewel on the card. But the supporting races were taxing me more. The weight of finding two life-changing bets with the remnants of the kitty from Mrs A's Berko Mums drinking gang was bowing my back.

Not that I hadn't had some useful advice from some of the Mums. Only most of it came after I'd circulated the selections. Wisdom such as "I always back number 4 in the Grand National. It hasn't worked yet", "Would have been good to have something with 'red' in the name", and "I have a problem with all those colours" was all valuable in its own way.

So the plan was for two carefully honed assaults in a couple of handicaps which seemed to present the best chances of unearthing

Sunseeker-buying, pamper-purchasing, national-debt-clearing winners. The Goodwood Stakes featured a big field of 19 runners over a marathon trip of 2 miles and 5 furlongs. This race has traditionally been cleaned up by hurdlers. Two of them were ante-post favourites here, Spirit Of Adjisa and Liberate. So I shunned them both for Bowdlers Magic, a longer priced stayer from the Mark Johnston yard. Later on, we had course specialist Four Nations in the very hot UBS Stakes, a race smoking with improvers and unknown quantities.

But first we had to get to the track. The train was late and the shuttle bus was jammed in a queue snaking 6 miles back from Trundle Hill. The presence of Frankel had clearly put an extra 5000 extra punters at the gates and on the roads. Good for racing. Bad for us if we didn't get in for the first race.

We made it with few minutes to spare. We even got Ben in, somehow passing the stewards' smart-casual test despite his distressed jeans and 80's Harrington jacket combo, with, for God's Sake, a vest peeping out from under his shirt. A subversive in our midst.

Just enough time to grab placepot vouchers, make the losing selections and queue up at rammed Tote booths to strike the futile bets that would crash in the first. Perfect.

Goodwood looked splendid, packed to the rafters with scrubbed up punters (Ben excepted) set in a widescreen landscape of sweeping, sun dappled South Downs (is this enough Racing Post-inspired guff?) The track's marketing line is "The World's most beautiful racecourse". A lofty claim. Surely the delightful ICI factory vista from the track at Redcar runs it close? Or the concrete A1 flyovers filling the near-horizon at Wetherby? Disused mining spoil at Catterick not your thing? On balance, the Goodwood Estate possibly shades it.

We all drew a blank in the first, including the Berko ladies, I'm sad to say. I got one thing right. The race was won by a hurdler, but I didn't expect it to be Micky Hammond's Hollins at 20-1. Nothing in the formbook pointed to this. Their (my) luck didn't change in the next handicap either. Four Nations was prominent enough and came out of the pack down the hill, but without forcing his big frame into serious contention. I won't be able to show my face in The Lamb after 8pm on the 2nd Tuesday of every other month, not including school holidays, ever again…

The Berko bets bookended the best two races on the card. First, Bryn landed the odds in the Veuve Clicquot Vintage Stakes with Chandlery, who asserted pretty strongly from 2 furlongs out. Then we witnessed the duel that, in truth, became a tour de force. Frankel was masterly in the Sussex Stakes. Queally managed to hold himself together enough to give the horse the ride it deserved. The RP would say Frankel 'made all'. That didn't do justice to the pace and power of this consummate victory. The phrase "the term 'great' is overused" is overused. Frankel was great. Worth the admission price alone. Especially as we'd bagged a two-for-one deal, hey hey!

The beers began to flow steadily after that. This fact assuredly contributed to at least one winner getting away. Bacchy was munching on a chicken tikka pizza, nursing a beer and watching his unbacked fancy Rakasa cruise to a comfortable win. He'd forgotten to get his wedge down, distracted by our unearthing, or so we thought, of a proper old plot. We were convinced Dandy Nicholl's Scrooby Doo had been laid out for this one. Right idea, right trainer even. But wrong race. Dandy was cooking one up for sure, but it was in the last instead, where Aksaud bolted up. Mug's game is this.

One thing we thought we got right was to chill over a last pint in the boozer by the station. That way the crowds heading back to town would disperse on earlier trains.

Wrong. By the time we moseyed on to the up-platform, our train was already showing half an hour late. When it arrived, all those years of practice on the Cheltenham specials served us well as we ruthlessly bagged four seats at the expense of the sick, the frail and the jammy bastards who'd cleaned up in the handicaps. Joy was short-lived. One stop up the track and we had another 20 minute delay waiting for a driver. A driver! What happened to the one that got us that far?

There's always someone to jolly the troops along in situations like this. Here, it was an opinionated walking tour leader with an inescapable searing voice, penetrating through other conversations like a hammer drill.

"Southern Railways have no strategic approach when it comes to delays",

"They can't simply terminate this service at East Croydon! That's just not an acceptable solution to the situation that they have created! We should rebel!"

"I'm meant to be at a concert tonight and then get back to Brighton!"

It went on. He was nominally talking to a couple of his tour charges. They had rabbit-trapped-in- the-headlights eyes and, first chance they got, they bolted for a couple of seats at the back, turfing out another couple in the process.

It was, though, a painful, protracted journey home which took a little of the gloss from a top day out. Bryn and I kept our spirits up in the usual way – by debating which would be the best junk food option between the station and home. There's always solace in chicken curry and special fried rice. I clung to the hope that the Berko Ladies would feel the same way.

Sadly, they were not so charitable with their memories of the day. The Ladies have been much more careful since. They stay in the pub long enough to drink up the kitty now....

Frankel's ascendancy in that lovely Summer of 2011 reached the firmament the following season. Five straight group ones including, to my tired old eyes, his visually most impressive win in the Queen Anne at Royal Ascot when annihilating Excellebration. Greg Wood in The Guardian hailed this as "possibly the best single performance by any horse, on any track, since three Arabian stallions were imported into Britain to found the thoroughbred breed in the early years of the 18th century".

The Juddmonte International at York was special when he effortlessly stepped up in trip. After winning the Champion Stakes at Ascot to finish his career unbeaten, Cecil said "He's the best I've ever had, the best I've ever seen. I'd be very surprised if there's ever been a better".

Timeform raised their rating to 147, making Frankel the highest rated horse in their history. In an interesting aside, the World Thoroughbred rankings, using a slightly different scale, also put Frankel at the top of their list on 140. At the same time, the panel took used the emergence of a new 'greatest' to reappraise all the rankings since they were first issued in 1977. This recalibration put a few noses out of joint when Dancing Brave, Shergar, Alleged and El Gran Senor were all dropped a couple of points.

Walter Swinburn was particularly aggrieved. His caustic comment quoted at the top of this chapter made me chuckle. Swinburn ran the stables near me for a while and was a common site in the local shops and restaurants. I used to know his all-weather gallops maestro, Dave. He had worked with Swinburn and his Father-in-Law, Peter Harris for nigh on 30 years at the stables in Aldbury.

Talking to him at a party one night, he was full of great stories about Walter courting Arab Princes and hot shot financiers about investment in the stable. He wanted to move away from Peter's syndication philosophy and the small-time owners. Dave told me that Walter was an ambitious perfectionist. His mantra was:

'We don't want to be known as just an all-weather stable, do we guys?'

Dave shrugged his shoulders.

"Tell the truth," he said, "most small-time owners just want to see their horses run. I bet you'd be happy to turn up to Wolverhampton every day if you thought your horse would be turning out, wouldn't you mate?"

I grinned and glugged some more ale. If I was in horse ownership, I can't think of anything worse than cheering on the sand donkeys somewhere near Sandwell!

At the time, Church Farm had had a good season. Stable star Stotsfold had brought some precious Group class success. They had had over 50 winners in 2010 and picked up over £400,000 in prize money. Dave, a big bloke with an open face and more than his fair share of tombstone teeth, was optimistic about the future despite changes he was not entirely comfortable with. He clearly loved his job and the horses. And was very loyal to the Swinburn team.

"He's a genius. Just look at his record as a jockey".

It was to be short lived. Sadly, stable star Stotsfold died, 2011 was a less successful campaign and Swinburn quit the training ranks at the end of that season. It seems there was more to the local talk of disaffection and disharmony than at first sight. Peter Harris had remained the landlord at Church Farm stables and simply dispersed the racing stock and divested himself of the remaining assets. There remained a fully functioning state-of-the-art training establishment with no trainer and a bunch of talented and dedicated staff with no jobs. The finances of horse racing do not stack up for many.

I digress…not for the first time. The debate still ebbs and flows about whether Frankel is the greatest horse ever. In the context of the tendon injury that briefly threatened to retire him prematurely in the Spring of 2012, I'm grateful that he so brilliantly graced that season at all. The conservative nature of his campaign – mostly at a mile, and never outside the UK – surely means it is impossible to say he's the best of all time. It would be churlish to pick holes in the form (never set a track record, beat one horse four times and another twice in his last 10 starts), but it is a shame he didn't line up in the Arc, for instance. Or more wistfully, a 7f match against Black Caviar, whose owners I absolutely respect for their resolutely international campaigning of the wonder mare.

For my money, I can't help wondering what Sea The Stars might have achieved as a four-year-old. He didn't win races in the spectacular, dominating style that Frankel did. But the turn of foot he displayed to win the 2009 Arc is one of the most exhilarating spectacles I've seen in racing.

I know I'm swimming against the tide on this one. Frankel was massive box office wherever he went and it will be a very long time before we see his like again. And there's a human side to this story that probably helps to explain the campaign. Sir Henry Cecil visibly took strength from Frankel in his fight against stomach cancer. "I am so lucky to have been allocated Frankel to train. He has been an inspiration and challenge, which I really needed so badly", he said in October shortly before the horse's Champion Stakes appearance. Teddy Grimthorpe, racing manager to Frankel's owner, Prince Khaled Abdullah offered a different perspective on that oft repeated observation when he said "I always said that half of the horse was killing Henry – the worry and the strain of having to train him – but that the other half, the joy that he gave him, was keeping him alive".

Abdullah was one of the few owner-breeders to have stayed loyal to Cecil in his barren years during the early part of this century. He had named the horse after American training legend Bobby Frankel who passed away in 2009. Abdullah had been devastated by his death. The trainer had in large part been the reason why Abdullah's stateside operation became a success. He saddled 25 Group/Grade 1 winners in 2003 – a record that still stands. For Abdullah to name his most promising yearling after bobby Frankel - a streetwise, self-made man from the tough neighbourhood of Brooklyn and then send him to Cecil - laid back, aristocratic and from establishment stock was an irony that took on fairytale proportions.

My own fondest memory of Cecil's valedictory season is inevitably tinged with healthy northern bias. The touching and heartfelt reception he received from the knowledgeable racing folk at York after the International in August was as deserved as it was generous. The master of Warren House had been away from the races since early Summer before arriving on the Knavesmire to witness (arguably) Frankel's most devastating performance. This frail, hoarse, wracked and riddled gentleman had become a national institution by then and was given a standing ovation by a crowd who appreciated the effort it had taken for him to get there.

Cecil had many the qualities that endear him to the British public: a charming, polite and slightly aloof character with a whiff of roguishness and a hint of controversy (witness the high profile fallouts with owners over the years). An immensely likeable man who, latterly, was filled with oodles of humility. More than anything, an instinctive horseman who tenderly nurtured the talents of a staggering number of Classic and Group One performers.

Frankel, of course, outlived his master. Cecil died in June 2013. The racing world and many more besides mourned a great loss and shared fond memories. Frankel is having a right old time at stud. His fee in the first season of action was £125,000 a pop. He mated with 133 mares between February and June. A punishing schedule, no doubt! The first Frankel foal for sale was given the full superstar auction treatment in front of a specially convened crowd at Kensington Palace on the eve of Royal Ascot 2014. The foal fetched a cool £1,150,000.

21. NEWBURY AT THE DOUBLE

It was the year Valentina Tereshkova became the first woman in
space,
Britain was refused entry to the Common Market
and John F Kennedy was assassinated.
The Independent on the 1963 establishment of the then Schweppes
Hurdle, 1995

Déjà vu...all over again. In 2011 I pitched up at the rescheduled
Totesport Trophy meeting at Newbury after its electrocuting
abandonment the previous weekend. A year later I went to the same
rescheduled fixture, saved this time from more predictable frost and
snow.

But the fixture's consecutive rescheduling and my shifty appearance
at both are about the only similarities between the two years. Prior to
postponement, the 2012 card had already been augmented with the
Grade 1 Scilly Isles Chase, plucked from Sandown's earlier frosted-
off card. Betfair had supplanted Totesport as sponsor of the feature
handicap hurdle, for many years the Schweppes Gold Trophy. They
brought with them a hike in prize money and publicity that had been
rewarded with high quality, competitive fields right across the card.

Postponement usually means watered down fodder. The drop in the
funding pot is often the result of an unfathomable quadrilateral
equation between smaller TV audiences, fewer corporate jollies,
thinner crowds and busy-digited BHB calculator operatives. So a
hearty shout-out went to Betfair who overcame all four of those
elements in the rescheduled fixture. The free entry policy was a
major factor. Compared to the previous year, the place was jumping.

A quieter shout out went to Newbury, who did their bit and got the
fixture restaged, but failed to entice enough bars and food outlets to
open. Hungry punters queuing round the corner at overpriced (and
crap) 'gourmet' burger concessions is never a pretty sight.

The prospect of that Festival-standard card was enough to get Bacchy rolling the ball. "I'll probably be in Scotland, but with Betfair letting the punters in for free, just thought I'd mention the rescheduled Newbury gig this coming Friday" That was all Colin needed to bagsie a day's leave and he rounded up a mate to go as well. I deferred plans to travel to Yorkshire and Bacchy scooted back from north of the border. So four of us gathered at the Paddington Burger King ready for a day's punting. It was almost the Cheltenham routine.

We piled on to a four-car train that was plainly under capacity for the journey. But Col, bold as brass, strode into the 1st Class compartment and we plonked down at the table. "Col?' I muttered weakly. "They'll have to decommission 1st class. Too many people." he said confidently. I nervously looked round for the guard. The cab door opened. "Here we go", I thought. But the driver just looked at the shifting wall of people in front of him and went "Oh bloody hell!" "No-one told you there was a free race meeting today did they?' said Bacchy. "They bloody didn't" he chuckled and closed the door firmly. That's the last we saw of him. Boom!

It was good to chew the fat with Paddy, a mate of Colin's from way back when. He's into his racing and was soon signed up for the Fantasy Festival marathon later in the season. Come Friday 17th he would be joining our ever-expanding crowd of Barley Mow desperados, all reduced to feverishly searching for a last-roll-of-the-dice Grand Annual winner. (As it turned, Paddy found the 33-1 winner of the Triumph, Countrywide Flame and strolled off with the Fantasy festival trophy on debut, in a blizzard of double bourbons and mouthy taunts. Bastard!)

After placing the customary Placepot bookies benefit, we eventually found somewhere decent for a beer, overlooking the paddock from the 1st floor of the Berkshire Stand. Paddy was all for a double-round first up, though that was scratched when we realised we couldn't take drinks outside to watch the actual races. Come on Newbury. Sort it out.

Paddy claimed to be a novice at the races compared to Col. Well that apparent status didn't stop him accurately clocking the laboured efforts of my toiling bet Hold Fast in the first race. "That Nicholl's horse can't jump. He's knackered." Bloody right he was. Slewing out to the right at every obstacle and out the back for the whole trip. There went my Champion Chase ante-post token. It was always an ambitious bet, but I was hopeful of more than that. A bout of coughing was later diagnosed at Paul Nicholls' yard, after 31 entries over the weekend yielded just one winner. With three weeks to go before the festival, an outbreak of the lurgey was about as welcome as Japanese Knotweed at the Chelsea Flower Show.

Sprinter Sacre won the opening Game Spirit Chase as he pleased. Looking a bit of a handful in the early stages, he pulled himself to the front and then ran away with the race, even showing a little bit of canny jumping at a couple in the home straight. He joined Hurricane Fly and Big Buck's as nailed-on Official Festival Good Things. (The former bombed out and the latter won.) And Colin was off the mark with a place return on French Opera.

The Denman Chase was a much closer affair. Negatives could be made against most of the principals: Long Run's dodgy jumping; What A Friend's moody form; Burton Port's injury lay-off and arch enigma Tidal Bay's all-round flakiness. It was a cliché writers' dream and Pricewise had delved deep into time-worn racing phraseology in putting up 'old monkey' Tidal Bay 'who is a bit long in the tooth' as his selection. Love it. I am a confirmed supporter, if not plagiariser, of Tom Segal, Alastair Down and their analogising comrades!

In the end, we all remained unconvinced by Long Run's narrow win. My complaints were a slight tendency to run down the fences and not quickening sharply enough off the front. Both Bacchy and I were on Burton Port and he should have won really. Geraghty could be accused of tender riding tactics, albeit not helped by a moderate jump at the last. But a proper race, nevertheless, and a close finish had got the blood flowing.

Back to the balcony where Colin was describing his Working Man's Accumulator for the day, comprising a four-fold each-way acca struck to a stake of mere buttons. Mug punting in the extreme, but top entertainment. In fields of 8+, merely the place element was attractive. One day - one sweet day - every leg is going to come in. Surely. Colin was giving the template a full workout. "So what race is the final leg, Col"? inquired Bacchy. "Er, it's at Fakenham, Steve". Cue spumes of beer and cider spat out in mock derision….

Schweppes, Tote Gold Trophy, Betfair Hurdle. Call it what you will, that 2m handicap is one of the highlights of the season and boasts a rich pedigree (Persian War, Make A Stand, Spirit Leader). Zarkandar had been favourite since the weights came out with stable mate Brampour keeping the Champion Hurdle contender down at an attractive 11st 1lb. The field was strong and featured the usual mix of plot horses and progressive handicappers. Zarkandar duly came through to win under a very cool Ruby Walsh and completed the job without being fully extended. Nicholls later said he was one of the horses with a dirty nose, and thus argued that the win was worth more than the bare form.

However, in screaming my contender Sire De Grugy up the home straight, I'd missed just how easily Darlan was travelling when he came down; and that this had seriously hampered Get Me Out Of Here who eventually finished 2nd. So there were some question marks about exactly what Zarkandar had achieved. Nevertheless, that was his first run this season and I was pretty impressed.

Darlan went on to show he had the makings of a top class horse, finishing second in that seasons Supreme behind Cinders and Ashes before emerging as favourite for the 2013 Champion Hurdle. He came down at the last in his Festival prep when ready to show reigning champ Rock On Ruby a clean pair of heels. He never got up again. A bitter blow. Zarkandar managed 5th in Rock On Ruby's Champion Hurdle. Sire De Grugy went on to become horse of the year in 2013-14 when he swept all before him in the 2-mile division during Sprinter Sacre's absence. Get Me Out Of Here was runner up in two of the next three renewals of the ferociously competitive Coral Cup. On reflection it was a pretty good Betfair Hurdle!

So three races were down, three favourites had come home but we only had a couple of winning bits and pieces between us. I was checking out chasers in the making over by the parade ring when Col, Bacchy and Paddy broke in to unprovoked monologues from Billy Liar. Colin recited a startlingly effective Tom Courtenay piece, "It was a big day for us, we had won the war in Ambrosia. Democracy was back once more in our beloved country." It led to a surreal but welcome remembrance of classic '60's kitchen sink dramas, Alan Bates, John Osborne and Rita Tushingham. I don't know where it came from but the benefit was finished as quickly as it had begun. We were back to the serious business of Bacchy attempting to land the third leg of his crazy treble with Colour Squadron in the novice hurdle.

He might have done it too. The Hobbs horse came down at the second last. My bet, Montbazon, came home strongly. But on closer inspection, there was plenty of evidence to suggest Colour Squadron was going the better of the two. This was an informative race for a Class 4. The top four in the betting were all Cheltenham bound. Colin's working man's accumulator had bitten the dust also. No need now for us to crowd round the black and white portable telly in the corner, showing grainy images of some obscure East Anglian track.

The good races kept coming. Even the 3-mile handicap hurdle featured Grand National and Coral Cup plot horses (both from the same stable) and the Scilly Isles Novice Chase had a few more Cheltenham clues about it now that the Jewson Novice Chase had become an established feature of Festival Thursday. For Non Stop looked like a worthy winner.

The scenes had become very messy in the upstairs bar by then. A series of pints in quick succession between races had started to addle judgement and alter reality. We were determined to come out of the listed bumper, the concluding race on the card, well ahead of the bookies. I swear it was Paddy who suggested the combination exacta. Well, it sounded like a sure-fire winner to the rest of us. The strategy was simple: 'get' Gevrey Chambertin. Just like Barry

Dennis's long lamented Bismarks, we were taking on the favourite, over-hyped and too short in the market because of his relation to Grand Crus. Four horses made the perm. And apart from Village Vic, I can't remember a single one of them!

But that's largely academic, because we'd targeted the wrong horse anyway! As Bacchy later pointed out, the Pipe horse wasn't even the favourite. We were so mullered that we hadn't spotted the plunge on Shutthefrontdoor. This Jonjo O'Neill horse prevailed by a short head from Village Vic - who may have been backed separately by Paddy as well, though it was getting so blurry by that stage that I can't quite grasp all the elusive details.

Anyway, our plot was properly blown out of the water. Shutthefrontdoor's owner, JP McManus had earlier brushed past me on the terracing. So we concluded, fingers tapping wise noses, that this, all along, was the horse that he had made the journey from Ireland to see. Easily forgetting that Darlan and Get Me Out Of Here, both of whom he owned, very nearly won the massively more valuable Betfair Hurdle.

There was nothing for it but a last pint... And then a last round of double Johnny Walker Black Labels.

As we hit Paddington I was craving a curry. Colin had to be cajoled a tad as he had an ETA at home. But a quick curry wouldn't hurt, we said. We found a suitable establishment only after being turned away from another "because they weren't sure if they were open or not"!

Then reality kicked in. As I was poring over the surprisingly diverse Jalfrezi combinations, my fuzzy grey matter latched on to the fact that the family and I were heading up to my Dad's that night. I was due to be on the north-bound asphalt carpet in 20 minutes time.

"Shit lads, I've gotta go! Nice one, top day – absolute belter. Do it again soon. Catch you all later...."

I left with serious form questions to answer. As Colin said, "Poor judgement of pace, mate!" Too right. With that sort of performance, how was I ever going to find the winner of the Supreme?

Picking up the Sprinter Sacre thread from that stellar fixture, even then it was clear that he was something special. He won the Game Spirit as he pleased. Looking back at that meeting from the perspective of the 2015 close season, there is the sense that Sprinter Sacre will never achieve great things again. The heart trouble that first appeared in 2013 looks like it has cut short a spectacular career.

I've wittered on ceaselessly about my undiluted joy of the elite two-mile chase division. Within that discipline, Sprinter Sacre at his peak was the absolute pinnacle. I have been lucky enough to see him in the flesh many times. In the Champion Chase of 2013 he put in a brilliant display, never off the bridle. His cruising rate was so high that his jockey Geraghty was taking a pull. The horse just wanted to go faster. Ironically, his best performance came in the Melling Chase that year at Aintree. Stepped up to 2 ½ miles for the first time, there were some questions to answer in a stronger race than the Champion Chase. He put in a scintillating performance despite the field attempting to expose any stamina issues.

The Racing Post analysis had this to say: "however his response was fantastic and his jumping improved as he was allowed to go faster in closing them down. It was clear three out he was still cruising and he laughed at old rival Cue Card when easing to the front nearing the final fence."

The previous year's saved Newbury card had been an entirely different affair. For one, it was a spontaneous decision that I went; for two, there was nothing half so classy on view as the following year; and for three, the meeting had a strange, muted atmosphere hanging over it. The horrific electrocution of two horses in the paddock that caused the postponement of the original fixture the week before had left a mark. Fenix Two and Marching Song were due to feature in the day's opening novice hurdle. They collapsed in the paddock. Kid Cassidy went down too. Jonjo O'Neill, trainer of Fenix Two said later "We thought he was bucking and kicking and he went down on his knees. Then he seemed to be OK. Mine reared up and we couldn't get him back. It was like he was stuck to the ground. It was the weirdest thing I've ever seen in my life."

Disturbing scenes. A racecourse spokeswoman confirmed a cable had been found under the paddock. Southern Electricity then dug up a chunk of previously dormant cabling and then declared the site safe.

So off I set, eschewing the rubber soled wellies and instead trusting to the reassurances of the electricity company. As discussed earlier, the prize money had taken a battering, in anticipation of reduced revenue on the day, but the card was still very strong and packed with horses needing an outing before Cheltenham.

They weren't alone. I'd been off the track myself since the Oaks in the June of that year. An unprecedented absence. I needed a good blow to get me spot on for Cheltenham. I was feeling rusty and I knew I'd come on massively for a trot round Newbury's bookie pitches, Tote booths, bars and restaurants. A public schooling of my betting strategies would ensure my A game was ready for the Festival.

On the train over, I was sat next to a gaggle of journos, tipsters and media types. There was a bit of moaning about the early start.

"Paying peak rate fares not my cup of tea."

"Tried to get out of this one. Would have preferred Sandown. Didn't work. Bladdy hell".

I'd settle for a job covering the races, blimey! Miserable sods.

It was an early start though, that fact could not be denied. A crucial part of the restaging was securing telly coverage. Channel 4 came up trumps, but at the cost of an early finish so that Countdown didn't get knocked off its usual perch. Breakfast at Tiffany's had got the push from the afternoon schedule. No worries. I'd had Breakfast at Bagel Express.

It was battleship grey and low visibility at the track. And freezing cold. But the paddock had been repaired. Scarred but repaired. At the very least, I wanted to think that's how racing would be at the end of the day.

A decent handicap first up, won by 14-1 outsider, Stow. My selection was third, and hard on the steel two out, but ultimately well beaten. The winner was ridden by Aiden Coleman. Checking Twitter updates over a beer shortly afterwards, I noted his confident tweet "Job done at Newbury, now on way to Sandown". Not misplaced confidence either as he went on to ride a double there, including another 14-1 shot.

Just as an aside, I'd like to say that I do generally like Twitter. Like all media, social or otherwise, there is of course an awful lot of dull, self-serving and pointless crap to sieve through. However, the occasional nuggets make it worthwhile. Recently, I spotted some humorous material under the hashtag #ohgrowupnaughtytittermongers in relation to the French bay filly Tossof (by Slickly out of Tossup) when running at Maison Lafitte. Comments such as "beaten off", "was pulled" and "double handful" were enough to reassure me that the legacy of Derek and Clive is alive and well.

Back to Newbury. By the third race, the crowd had thickened a little, but to no more than a respectable and understated gathering of weekday greys and browns, rather than a frivolous and colourful exposition that decorates the weekend celebrations.

This all meant I had a perfect, uncluttered view of the beasts for the AON Chase in the parade ring. Odds-on favourite and potential Gold Cup combatant What A Friend looked a bit edgy, highly-strung and fractious. Does that make any difference? Dunno. He was part owned by Alex Ferguson, but there was no sign of the United manager amongst the suited and booted in the middle. I did see his trainer, Paul Nicholls and his able deputy, Dan Skelton though. Alice Plunkett from Channel 4 was interviewing the latter. He's a dashing lad and had our Alice was bucking and squealing behind the microphone like a two-year old racecourse maiden.

Fair Along caught my eye. From the Philip Hobbs yard, he was a little fella. Bit of a show-off too, tossing his head around and eye-balling everyone at close range. But he was tiny. How could he jump out of stodgy ground over those big fences for three miles? Then he had a big old turn out on his final circuit of the ring (I'm no expert, but they looked like healthy stools – definitely three weetabix for breakfast), so that might have made the take-offs easier. Dance Island was looking composed, compared to the other bunch. A big outsider too. So I fancied him to beat the non-stayers and make the frame. His trainer Ben Case helped jockey Daryl Jacob up into the plate. Immediately Daryl seemed more taken with the stable girl than with settling his charge. Worrying signs.

Good race, though. Noland made the pace fairly early on, jostling with Fair Along and the other outsider, Carronhills. My boy, Dance Island was nicely in touch for much of the race and I was fully expecting him to stay on past tired horses up the straight and chase home What A Friend.

That's what my Exacta predicted anyway. But the confirmed non-staying, ground-hating Noland galloped and jumped them all into submission. My lad clouted every fence down the back straight and was hung out to dry very early. Up the stretch, Noland out on his hooves. What A Friend began to get his act together, but was switched right by rookie jockey Harry Skelton and lost some valuable ground.

Meanwhile Fair Along had sprouted wings and was flying home too. He was relishing this tough test. Brave little horse ably demonstrating the value of a pre-race dump. What A Friend failed to get to Noland by a head, with Far Along ¾ length further back. Excellent finish, though, perhaps harshly, I'd say it has to go down as jockey error because of Skelton's move after the last. Those Skeltons eh? One flirting with the presenter, the other flirting with disaster. Hope Harry braced himself for the inevitable Fergie hairdryer. Dance Island lumbered in last.

Time to eat. The restaurants in the Dubai Duty Free Stand were completely deserted. I wasn't complaining. This meant I had good sightlines right across the pie counter and was able to choose my chicken, leak and mushroom pie, mushy peas and gravy with unhurried precision and demolish with unhindered relish. Who needs Breakfast at Tiffany's when you can have lunch at the Celtic Pie Co? (Am I overdoing this now?)

French Opera was a treat to watch in the Game Spirit Chase. This gluey ground wouldn't have been ideal for him, but he looked like poetry in motion to me. Bags of ability. Could he be a threat in the Queen Mother at festival? Better ground would suit and I swore he was still on the upgrade. I tried to get a photo on my poxy phone camera as they sailed over the water jump. Bloody shutter delay. Missed 'em. I tried later in the novice chase. This time I tried to anticipate the glorious leap of Aighteen Thirtythree who jumped his rivals legless. But no. Too early this time. I scowled at the screen. Bloke next to me grins and says, "Missed 'em didn't you?" "Bloody technology." I mutter.

Back in the Berkshire Stand, I was taking a leak in the well appointed gents. I came across a smug looking chap in a Ben Case Racing jacket. Well, I gave him both barrels for the lamentable performance of his horse Dance Island on the track today; and particularly the unprofessional attitude of his jockey. This lad might have been only eight years old, and possibly the son of Ben Case himself. But in my eyes he's got to take responsibility at some stage! This jumps game is no game you know.

The Totesport Trophy was the day's feature. Entries were down to 15 from Saturday's original 23, but it was still a very competitive affair. Nicky Henderson was mob-handed with top weight Solix, Swinton Hurdle winner Eradicate and Triumph hero Soldatino. Walk On was favourite, heading a market stuffed with more plots than a suburban housing redevelopment. I was on two of them: Irish raider (had to be) Sweet My Lord from Willie Mullins' yard and Bothy from arch-plotter Brian Ellison. The race was typical hell-for-leather. I was desperate for Solix to be given a bad ride so that I could say 'jockey David Bass looks like a fish out of water, flapping around in the saddle'. But he didn't, so I can't.

Bothy was up with the pace from early. Two separate incidents at the second last took out three or four contenders who were readying their challenges. Recession Proof came through to take it up at the last and seemed to have repelled Bothy. But he came back for more and they were both all-out to the line, with Recession Proof prevailing by a short head. Thrilling stuff though.

Upstairs in the Berkshire Stand lounge, munching on packet of overpriced hand cut (I just don't believe it!) kettle chips, I overheard connections of the winner toast "To the County Hurdle!" There was 8 or 10 in the group, all turned out in their refined finest, and they'd had a great day. I wished them luck at the festival.

I had a couple more close 2nds in the remaining races, but didn't trouser any wedge. Ericht looked the real deal in the bumper, as a watery sun fleetingly broke through the cloud. Trainer Nicky Henderson was later quoted on the horse's prospects in the Champion Bumper: "I hate the frigging race, but I suppose he'll have to run in it!" Yet another Festival clue (though this one proved fruitless) on a day of top quality action when racing began to throw off its gloomy mood.

Job done, as Aiden Coleman might have said.

22. BELLYACHING

Improbable, implausible, contrived.

Football Association Disciplinary Panel's verdict on John Terry's defence against claims he racially abused Anton Ferdinand (2012)

Summer 2012 was an eagerly anticipated marathon of sport that the weather almost drowned out. It became a heavy legged squelch through sodden conditions. Dreams of hot endless days of sport formed in a baking May almost rusted under the jet stream driven downpours of July.

The test series between the Windies and England was a poorly attended damp squib. The one-day series more so. Racing had never seen so many flat fixtures abandoned in the main turf season. The British Grand Prix was played out in front of empty seats because petrol heads couldn't get into flooded car parks. The build-up to The Open at Lytham St Anne's was dominated by observations on wind and climatic conditions. Andy Murray briefly lifted our spirits under a Centre Court roof that was pulled back and forth with the regularity of the shelf on a penny falls machine.

However, the tarnishing qualities of excessive rainfall were only partly responsible for the unsettled mood hanging over sport just then.

There were some disturbing revelations in a Westminster Magistrates Court that July that showed the extent of the dark place in which football resided. Rarely had the meaning and nuance of such vitriolic abuse been analysed as microscopically as it was in the John Terry/Anton Ferdinand racism case. The shoddy, degrading, offensive nature of football was exposed in the full glare of publicity. It was the culmination of long-standing ignorance, ineptitude and intransigence about recognising and dealing with corrosive racism in the game.

The mood I was in that Summer, I would have needed a barrow load of evidence to convince me that the game wasn't rotten to its very core at every level. And with the passing of time, how strange those events came to pass that illustrated that gut feeling more than ever.

Racism, violence and general offensiveness were not the only problems in football. Long-standing allegations of bungs, corruption and bribery at the very top of the world governing body had dogged the game for years. They rose again that Summer after the 2022 World Cup Finals had been awarded to Qatar. It made my nostrils itch with the smell of burning money. Film captured by undercover reporters showed FIFA's executive committee apparently offering to sell their votes in the hosting competition for the 2018 and 2022 World Cups. Later, FIFA buried the report by an American lawyer that investigating those allegations. Instead they published a brief summary claiming exoneration. Mr Garcia, the lawyer in question, disagreed, resigned and stated that FIFA's version contained "numerous materially incomplete and erroneous representations of facts and conclusions".

By 2015, finally, Blatter's power empire began to unravel. Tom Fordyce, BBC Chief Sports writer described it as the most immovable of dictatorships, a monopoly apparently immune to scandal, logic and precedent. "Blatter did not just control the most popular sport in the world, he acted as if he owned football itself."

The swift downfall came only four days after he had preposterously claimed a fifth term as FIFA's president by decreeing, "I am the president now, the president of everybody". That election followed a week when seven FIFA officials were arrested in Switzerland at the request of the US authorities who were investigating corruption of more than $150m; reports claiming FIFA general secretary Jerome Valcke was responsible for an alleged $10m payment of bribes over South Africa's bid to host the 2010 World Cup; and a separate criminal investigation by Swiss authorities into how the 2018 and 2022 World Cups were allocated.

Only a man of Blatter's supreme arrogance could think of standing for election again after presiding over that lot.

Fordyce picked up some of Blatter's observations about the game that reaffirmed his bloated isolation atop an ivory tower serviced by sycophants and acolytes:

- Racism in football was best cured by handshakes on the pitch;
- Women footballers should wear tighter shorts to bring a bigger audience to the game;
- Gay supporters attending the Qatar World Cup should refrain from sexual activity while in the country.

New allegations of dodgy dealings finally forced his resignation decision. In the end, it was a surprise. Given his blithe facing down of the charges against FIFA only a few days previously, we could be forgiven for thinking he would cling to power for another 17 years. The first real claims of massive back-handers at FIFA emerged in the book "How They Stole the Game" by David Yallop. The book laid bare evidence that delegates had accepted bribes totalling $1m to fix the result of that first presidential vote back in 1998.

Surely this is a chance for the game to drain the poison from the wound. The trouble is that such a level of greed is simply cascaded through tiers of the domestic game; agents creaming off vast profits, driving up fees; right through to aggression, interference and intimidation on the part of fathers at their sons' Sunday morning football. A picture emerges of a game in crisis, thinly veiled over by interested parties who point to TV money driving further greed.

One over-hyped Premier League season runs into another, dishing up more players diving, cheating and pressurising officials; managers coaching them to do so; ignorant tribal fans sending death threats (and in some cases letter bombs) willy-nilly to players, managers, board members or officials; owners running down and over-committing clubs for personal profit or ego-mania; and the media telling us this is the greatest game in the world.

There were some bright spots that Summer. I remember being cheered to see Scottish football club owners refusing to be intimidating by the SPL's threats of financial ruin and instead banishing newco Rangers to Scottish League 3. It was quite right that the management and resource atrocities committed at the former club should not have been swept away so easily. Rangers took their medicine and enjoyed the view from the corporate box at Glebe Park. Brechin City and every other League 3 club were welcoming hosts. A few capacity crowds at the lower league clubs wasn't the worst thing for the sustainability of Scottish football.

Accentuating the positive, I loved watching Spain's authoritative defence of the European Championships that Summer, sweeping away slights about a boring passing game with a gorgeous demolition of a pretty useful Italy outfit.

For all my bellyaching about football, it is only fit and proper to reserve a modicum of unvented spleen for the Olympics, too. The IOC in 2012 was only just emerging from the dingy place in which FIFA finds itself now. Jacques Rogge had done a lot to clean up the IOC since the monumental Salt Lake City bribery scandal in 2002 when 10 senior International Olympic Committee figures resigned. But so much controversy lingered on – remember the 27 Olympic officials and agents who were caught selling tickets for London 2012 on the black market before the games? Small beer compared to the seismic sums involved in the vote rigging scandals that both governing bodies have been involved in. Indicative, none the less, of the culture of corruption that riddles these bodies from top to bottom.

The rampant commercialism and image protection around the modern Games stuck in my craw: the "heavily branded corporate monster, devouring a city in which it is staged before moving on to the next" (Owen Gibson). Stories about police having to empty their crisps into unmarked plastic bags and a children's guard-of-honour being requested to wear adidas trainers were designed to wind me up in the same way that the reports of EU technocrats demanding straight bananas and the renaming of Cornish pasties are aimed directly at the bile of Little Englanders. And I rose to it every time.

Probably because I loathed being manipulated by corporate sponsorship more than I hated being manipulated by the press.

But I accepted that some of this was necessary to deliver an event that would not bankrupt the Country. I just wished we could have had lower ticket prices, more contracts for local companies and less kow-towing to big business. And less of the brand police tormenting independent bakers, for God's sake!

Despite these rants, I remained at heart a fan of the Olympics. As a family we had secured tickets for swimming finals, football semi-finals and handball group matches. We were properly looking forward to them. I anticipated becoming immersed in the action, developing an instant expertise in the tactics of, say BMX racing, modern pentathlon and taekwondo (though you could name any sport in which I was a novice viewer) that would allow me to scream advice and encouragement to any British competitors with an outside chance of making the rostrum.

So as I looked forward to the Olympics, to The Open, to England taking on the South Africans for top test team status and to a second half of an increasingly intriguing flat season, I noted that the jet stream was heading back north, where it belonged, heralding the chance of a break in the rainclouds. Golden light shining on a healthy dollop of spectacular sport would do wonders for my gloomy outlook. Though I reckoned it would take more than a few rays of the sun's glare to buff up football's tawdry image.

23. GAMES PEOPLE PLAY

BBC presenter: *Just tell me what you've been going through this past week.*

Beth Tweddle's Dad: *I've been laying a patio.*

An Olympics interview, 2012

Indeed, the 2012 Olympics were glorious. Like most of the nation I set aside griping about corruption, commercialism and corporate dominance to bask in a feast of well organised sporting achievement. I felt particularly privileged to have attended the first proper day of the Games. As a family, we were always looking forward to going, and the anticipation had grown steadily since we realised we had tickets for four finals on the first night of the swimming gold rush at the Aquatics Centre. That anticipation increased exponentially after the jaw-dropping opening ceremony the night before.

Danny Boyle served up an idiosyncratic take on the unveiling of the Games. His masterstroke was the perfect combination of drama, humour and relevance across three centuries of historical, social and cultural highlights. Daughter No 1, a confirmed Mr Bean fan, nearly split her sides when Rowan Atkinson turned up to guest his one-finger performance on Chariots of Fire. Granny was almost in tears at Emeli Sande's rendition of Abide With Me. She wasn't caught out by too many tunes in the tribute to great British pop and rock either. Perhaps only The Prodigy and Dizzy Rascal seemed genuinely beyond her… I loved the Olympic symbols coming together above the stadium, cast in the white heat of the industrial revolution. Fiery rings indeed.

When it came to the cauldron lighting, I was feeling quite smug. I'd already decided that Steve Redgrave was an absolute shoe-in for the gig. Who else has a CV like his? Five Golds at five consecutive Olympic Games. Awesome. And then a mate rang from the stadium where he was working with a film crew to say that he had heard from the production company that Redgrave had been practising the manoeuvre in rehearsals. At last! Decent, useable inside information.

I went off scouring online markets and High Street bookies to get some wedge down on Sir Steve. Many bookies had already closed their markets. Word was sneaking out, I wrongly concluded, about the identity of the firestarter. To me this was merely further confirmation that the bookies were running for cover. Possibly they knew that I was out and about with my fistfuls of fivers (and some supplementary two-pound coins, just in case).

So when Beckham's speedboat docked on the River Lee, I was not surprised (but possibly a little relieved) to see Sir Steve awaiting Becks' slightly awkward handover. I could look forward to counting my wedge. After the speeches, Redgrave duly trotted in to the stadium with the flame clasped in his fist. He received the appropriate recognition and I nodded my own tribute. Then something odd happened. He handed the flame over to a bunch of oiks in tracksuits. They jogged round fairly sedately and were introduced to the crowd. "Nice touch", I thought. "Give the youngsters a moment in the spotlight... Now give the torch back to Stevie, there's good lads and lasses".

But Redgrave was long gone. Nowhere to be seen. Torches were now being dolled out like it was a three-day-week. And then they turned to the cauldron, which we saw for the first time, at least in deconstructed form: 204 little copper petals on elongated poles, spread out in a huge circle on the ground. The game was up. It was the next generation who got the lighting honour. Legacy and all that. Leaving me nursing another catastrophic mug punt to rank with some of my finest. I felt a bit sick.

But only a bit. I was caught up in the moment. The ceremony was uplifting, flames dancing from one copper petal to the next, following by the slow rising of the steel pipes to form one giant canopy of flame. Pretty special.

On Saturday, we decided to make tracks for the Olympic Park early so we could have a good look round and soak up some of the much-touted atmosphere. But not before I'd summoned up courage to check the damage on my bookie accounts. Squinting at the screen with one eye closed, I was relieved to see that those nice people at Paddy Power and SkyBet had refunded my bets on Sir Steve. The markets had been voided because the result – the kids lighting the cauldron – was not in their list of possibilities. I'd almost got away with it. Only Coral played hardball when I pitched up at the shop with my voucher. In the end I had to e-mail them and explain that they should give me my money back because it was a void market. They did.

The Olympic Park was cool. Great architecture for a start. Daughter No 1 wanted to know what was the venue "that looked like a giant pringle" (it was the velodrome) and daughter No 2 thought that the water polo arena resembled "a giant mattress". There was a quite breathtaking view from the entrance to the Aquatic Centre back to the main stadium.

Nice landscaping too. We were very taken with the 'wild' flowers sown on every available patch of ground, the river walks and the big screen viewing areas, even if Mrs A did try to irrigate the floor with the contents of her wine bottle. Plenty of merchandising opportunities too. Of course. In one shop we bumped into a work colleague and her family. Can't go anywhere…

I've been to the park before. But it was a very long time ago and it looked a bit different, as Mug Punting observed in 2005:

>*…No regrets, then, about leaving behind the greyhounds of London Stadium. The track was a hole and resided in a run down part of East London in need of significant regeneration. The sun was out and was beginning to draw a heady stench from the urine soaked litter piled up in doorways and alleys around the perimeter of the track. It was a bizarre place. On one side was an expanse of open ground bordering the stadium, presumably once the site of a factory; and on the other was an array of traditional businesses: taxi cab firms,*

*kebab shops and junk emporia, as well as a smattering of
empty and derelict two-storey, flat-roofed shops and
terraced housing. The intimidating rubbish strewn urban
jungle on this side of the road provided a brief, surreal
counterpoint to the factory site on the other with its
savannah of tall grass waving lazily in balmy mid-day
sunshine.*

*No surprise to me that a few years later the dogs had
gone and the stadium closed; further rationalisation of
the sport in London. And then, a few years later still, I
read that the area has been chosen as the hub of
Britain's Olympic Bid for 2012. Hackney dog track will
be the site of an 80,000-seater flagship Olympic stadium.
Ironic indeed. There's a picture on the back of The
Independent showing the track littered with skips, sundry
ironmongery and rubble. And there is the rickety
enclosure we occupied with once proud letters
proclaiming 'LONDON STADIUM, HACKNEY '
emblazoned below the holed roof. Only some of the
letters have dropped away and HACKNEY is now*

_AC_NE_. Appropriate. "

We refuelled by the river and the water droplet fountain with snacks,
sugary drinks and alcohol. We needed them. The hike up to the seats
required oxygen masks and crampons. But the view from Block 412,
row 50 was awesome. Daughter No 2 thought so too, between her
nose bleeds and panic attacks of vertiginous origins, anyway. I was
psyching the girls up for the Ryan Lochte v Michael Phelps battle in
the 400m Individual Medley, which splashed off at 7.30pm. At
7.23pm, Daughter No 2 said, "Daddy, I need the loo". "What?" I
said, "Can't it wait?!" I could see from her squirming bum that she
couldn't. So we did the fastest stairs descent, wee and ascent the
stadium had yet seen. Possibly a new Olympic Record. As I laboured
up the last steeply inclined steps back to the seat, breathing heavily
and sweating freely, a bloke in the opposite aisle grinned at me and
said, "The other one wants to go now, ha ha!" Comedian, I thought,
as I poked him in the eye (mentally, of course).

The swimmers emerged on to poolside with the appropriate fanfare, though some of them looked faintly ridiculous. A Japanese competitor was replete in tight silver swim hat overlain with huge headphones and sporting reflective lens goggles. Had we stumbled into a Dr Who tribute? Was this the return of the cyber men?

Lochte was formidable, leaving Phelps struggling to come home in 4th. A major surprise that Phelps had performed so poorly. The second of my Olympic bets to fold.

We settled down for the Mens 400m Freestyle final. A chap in the row behind us tapped Mrs A on the shoulder and in a faltering voice, cracked with emotion said, "Would you mind staying quite still when the swimmers come out for this one? My son is competing in Lane 8 and I want to get a good photo." Oh wow! He was David Carry's Dad. Carry was competing in his third Olympics but this was his first final. What a special moment. We all wished him well and said how proud he must be. And he was, you could just tell. Carry competed with great credit, coming home in 7th. The race was won by Sun Yang from China in an Olympic Record time.

After a couple of semi-finals, we had a medal ceremony for the Lochte race. Daughter No 1 wasn't too impressed with the podium. "That's rubbish. It looks like a yoga mat!" She was not wrong! The medallist emerged to Chariots Of Fire blasting through the speakers. This just set her off again, chuckling uncontrollably and miming Mr Bean's one-finger virtuoso performance.

In the women's version of the 400m Individual Medley, Hannah Miley had realistic home team medal hopes. She was greeted to a deafening reception. The curious convex pool ceiling and steeply banked seating seemed to create a channel of sound. The atmosphere was palpable.

Smiley Miley was in contention for the first two disciplines, roared on by an ecstatic crowd, but she fell away over the final 200m. The 16 year-old Chinese girl Ye Shiwen took the race by the scruff of the neck at that point and smashed the World Record. I read later that she came home over the last 100m only 7/10ths of a second slower that Ryan Lochte in the earlier men's race. Third bet down.

The final medal event, the Womens 4x100m Freestyle Relay, was a complete bunfight. And that was just in the stands. The decibel level had cranked up a few extra notches. Everyone who had a flag, a banner or a poster was furiously waving it. As the swimmers began their merry-go-round of front crawl, we were shouting out the names of the red-hatted Team GBs swimmers like we had known them all our lives. "Go on Amy, go oooon…Come on Frankie, you can do it…" I looked at our two and they were screaming at the tops of their voices, red-faced with effort, loving every second. The Australians won, to the complete rapture of many nearby fans. The woman in front of me had the names of all the Team Aus swimmers neatly written out on a piece of A4 with the times of their races and personal bests written alongside. Dedication!

We hung around for the last medal ceremonies, then walked down the banking to get closer look at the pool and finally spilled out into the stunning park now illuminated in glorious Technicolor.

We had been incredibly fortunate with the tickets. It was all the luck of the draw of course. Initially I was disappointed to have missed out on a few events. The girls would have loved the tennis and gymnastics; and I was desperate for the athletics. But I quickly realised that this, in fact, was a top result.

The clamour for tickets had outstripped supply. More tickets were subsequently released at regular intervals, including for some of the showpiece events. But the row over empty seats that simmered away in the first part of the Games was entirely predictable. If tickets on general sale are in too short supply and massively expensive then of course there is going to be fury at evidence that venues that are not full.

I'm more than happy to point a cynical finger at the corporates and IOC affiliates for this, who scandalously don't use their freebies. Seb Coe's initial blithe comment that 'the venues are full to the gunnels' was wrong, insulting and glib on many levels. He backtracked from that pretty swiftly and belatedly moves were made to ensure people who actually wanted to see the competition used tickets. This kind of blatant manipulation always gets me chuntering.

But perspective, perspective. The Games overall were a massive success. By their finale, I was in serious cold turkey. To keep the adrenaline surging, I picked out some of my favourite mainstream and off-beat highlights.

1. FlyMo
An entirely predictable choice to head the list. And at the time, unashamedly so. Mo Farah, the brilliant Somaliland Londoner joined a small band of truly great British runners on an emotional final night of athletics when he brought home the 5,000m gold to add to his memorable 10,000m victory the week before.

On that first Super Saturday we had been in the Olympic Park and were still tripping on exhilaration by the time we got home to watch Mo's race. Something about being exposed to the highly charged atmosphere of the Games had turned Mrs A into a distance running tactical genius. After only a couple of laps, she was belting out considered advice to Farah about his track position and pace. "What are you doing back there? Get up amongst them!" It clearly worked.

For the 5,000m final, we were at Granny's. There is obviously something in the genes, because unbelievably, she too is a top level race analyst. From the gun, it was "Go on Mo, you need to be nearer. That's no good, don't let them get away. Are you really trying?" For my part, I was the doubting Thomas. Confidence dented by his lacklustre qualification and convinced this was too big an ask, I spent the final 600 metres predicting doom. "They're lining up behind him! He can't hang on! He can't shake them off" But his control was extraordinary. His confidence unshakeable. His pace judgement imperious. Mo wound the speed up by small increments and would not let anyone pass. At 200 out he turned both taps on and kept finding more. Only Gabremeskel from Ethiopia looked like a threat in the home straight. And then only briefly.

This was an awesome display. Brendan Foster gushed that it was the greatest single moment in British athletic history. I initially baulked at that. And then I thought; well, what else would be up there? Roger Bannister breaking the 4-minute barrier, maybe? But that wasn't in the Olympics. Coe and Ovett's mid-80's middle distance medal domination? Arguably they are devalued by being achieved in boycotted games. Thomson, Lewis and Ennis in multi-disciplinary Golds? Yes, but they weren't single moments. So in fact I'm happy to go along with Brendan on that.

Later, in the aftermath of a brilliantly a stage-managed medal ceremony climax, Farah could be seen doing The Bolt and Usain was Mo-Bot-ing like a natural. An informal touch of mutual respect.

Here we are three years later and the story has a different flavour. Allegations about Mo's coach Alberto Salazar at the start of the season were beginning to crowd in on Mo's achievements. He answered the critics in the only way he knew how. Another 5k and 10k double at the Beijing World Championships. Stunning. Though one suspects there is more to unfold on this one. Ho hum.

2. Angry Ben Ainslie

This pick was not so much about what he won, but how he won it. Off his game for much of the event and languishing somewhere claustrophobic in the Finn pack, three-time Gold medallist Ben Ainslie found some motivation at the expense of two of his competitors and channelled it ruthlessly to land a fourth. From the moment the series leader, Jonas Hogh-Christenson conspired with Dutchman Pieter-Jan Postma mid-race to allege a buoy infringement on the part of Ainslie, the Gold medal was in the bag. Ainslie immediately took a penalty turn – the standard price of such an infringement – rather than appeal after the race. He said of the incident, "They've made a big mistake. They've made me angry and you don't want to make me angry."

After his penalty turn, Ainslie fought back brilliantly, catching up 70 metres on the final downwind leg to overhaul Hogh-Christensen before crossing the finishing line and exploding in anger, pointing and shouting at the Dane.

He was still livid by the time he made it back to shore. He explained that he decided not to risk a protest post-race since he would have been outnumbered and might have been disqualified from the race.

The next day, the Briton hit back with a first and a third to narrow the gap to leader Jonas Hogh-Christensen to three points. In the Gold medal race two days later, Ainslie targeted his man and made sure he finished in front. Job done.

The clip of Ainslie's outburst was shown on Gabby Logan's evening highlights programme. John McEnroe and Michael Johnson, snuggled up on the couch that night, were both impressed. "Wow!" said Johnson. "That guy can talk trash!" said Mac, an expert in the field. I'll never forget the steely look in Ainslie's eyes. Wonderful stuff.

Ainslie now heads up his own yacht racing enterprise, which forms the basis for Britain's bid to win the America's Cup in 2017. Who says he's not the man to secure the oldest competitive trophy in sport for the first time since it's inauguration in 1851?

3. Bert le Clos
Chad le Clos did what had been unthinkable only a few weeks earlier and beat the great Michael Phelps in a dramatic final of the 200m butterfly. That was pretty remarkable. But this engaging, humble and respectful Olympian was completely upstaged by his father, Bert who was captured on camera in the midst of the packed banks of seating, gesticulating wildly, mouthing congratulations and waving flags.

Mark Foster was immediately dispatched to drag the exultant Bert le Clos to an interview with Clare Balding. He was brilliant. Talking whilst watching images of his pride and joy walking around the pool after the race, Bert kept shouting "unbelievable, unbelievable, unbelievable!" and "Look at him, he's beautiful, I love you". He noticeably jumped back and paused when he saw images of himself looking a touch on the large side on the BBC monitors. "Look at me", he said holding his belly, "I'm sorry…" And then to Clare, "Is this going out live!"

Wonderful scenes. Bert went on, at a million miles an hour in clipped, hoarse Afrikaans tones, "I have never been so happy in my life … It's like I have died and gone to heaven. Whatever happens in my life from now on, it is plain sailing."

Inspire a generation? Well the swimming has certainly had an impact on Mrs A. Her breast stroke at the regular 7.30am Aquaspace session has come on a bomb. She's adapted what she's seen in the pool to develop a new breathing/half-drowning technique and is currently half way round Guernsey. In bite sized chunks, of course. Thank you Bert le Clos.

4. Judo medals
There was a brilliant piece in the paper that described a women's judo bout thus: "to the uninitiated it is two very drunk women having a fight in a storm on the deck of a ferry." But for Gemma Gibbons, judo looked like everything in the world, for a few brief moments at least. Following her victory over Tcheumeo of France, the report carries on, "a tearful Gibbons falls to her knees, points the sky and mouths 'I love you, Mum'. A Disney director would cross out the scene on account of it being too corny". But this is real life. And not a dry eye in the house. For the judokas who only appear on the big stage once every four years, this is genuine sentiment.

Bronze for British judo journeywoman Karina Bryant was in some ways even sweeter. There were stories circulating that only two months before the competition she was asking strangers for cash so she could buy a car to get to training. Bryant is four-time European champion but has never won an Olympic medal. Her participation here was threatened by a neck injury that required surgery, but she chose to fight through it. At the fourth time of asking and at the mature age of 33, in front of her own passionate crowd, fighting an opponent four-stone heavier, coming back from two-scores down, she claimed an emotional bronze. Karina was absolutely overcome with unbridled joy and pride. This was her last chance of Olympic recognition. She got it and it was fully earned.

5. The Republic of Yorkshire

How could I ignore the sensational story of Yorkshire's stunning Olympic performance? God's Own County bobbed along at a high water mark of 7th in the Medals Table as the Games entered their 2nd week and finished with a cool dozen gongs. Reports of tykes out-medalling Australia had Ian Thorpe making those fluttery eyes at Gabby Logan and mouthing "Eh up" and "Nah then".

And it's not all exported talent or tenuous linkage either. Jess Ennis regularly turned out for her local Sheffield club and scared the living daylights out of opponents as she jumped out of the bus for regular season meets at the likes of Worksop and Retford. The awesome Brownlee brothers are based in West Yorkshire and train up and down Pennine slopes made of the same granite that forged their very sinews and determination. The story of their race can only grow more remarkable with time. Jonny had incurred a 15 second penalty for a cycling infringement. Alistair and he hatched a plan to go out severely hard in the final 10k to stretch out the field so that Jonny could complete his penalty and still have enough of a time buffer to land a medal. Alistair won and Jonny was third. The Guardian called it 'Tear-jerking brilliance'.

I'm not entirely sure where all the other Yorkie medals came from. There were some cyclists and rowers for sure. I'd like to think that the sphere of excellence is widespread. Who knows, maybe dressage Gold medallist Charlotte Dujardin can claim some Yorkshire heritage. I wouldn't be surprised if her middle name was Arkengarthdale or Smurthwaite, possibly...

6. Equestrianeous

Sticking with the gee-gees, I had to give a massive shout out to those barking mad show jumping course designers. What were they on? With every new competition, we were treated to increasingly outrageous symbols of Britain represented as jumping obstacles. Big Ben, the Cutty Sark, the Millennium Wheel... naval flags depicting letters of the alphabet in semaphore to spell out LONDON 2012. I even saw Stonehenge at one point, which brought shades of Spinal Tap firmly to mind. "Break Like The Wind, Zara".

And what were those mysterious letters around the dressage arena all about? According to the International Equestrian Federation, they just "appeared" for the first time in the 1920 Olympics held in Belgium. No-one has been able to establish the origins.

Greenwich was a fantastic venue for the horsey events. It was one of the more controversial choices, but in fact the cross-country course winding through the park with views over the Thames was stunning. The arena set against the backdrop of the Royal Naval College provided some appropriate gravitas, too. I'm less convinced that Horse Guards Parade did the same for beach volleyball, though maybe that wasn't the point...

7. Sitting down v standing up
One of the more humorous jibes to emerge at the Games was from the Aussies who, clearly piqued by their sub-standard medals haul, alleged that Britain was only any good at sitting down events. I quite like the implication of the sneer – old Colonial masters resting on their backsides to pick off easy achievements whilst the upstart nation has to grunt honestly and work harder for their rewards. It appears that the 2012 Games didn't absolutely give the lie to this taunt. By the close of the Games, of Britain's 65 medals, 35 were in sitting down sports – on bikes, in boats, on horses and the like, whilst 27 had been earned in athletics, gymnastics, swimming and other biped events. The 3 medals in triathlon and pentathlon involve a bit of both. So honours not quite even. What's wrong with a sitting down medal anyway?

8. Stephen Kiprotich
Kiprotich was at the time a 23-year-old from Kapchorwa in Uganda. He is from subsistence farming stock. Before the final Saturday of the Games, he was a big outsider for the marathon, the concluding athletics event. The race was dominated by heavyweights from Kenya and Ethiopia. And yet he managed to beat off the challenge of race favourite Wilson Kipsang and two-time world champion Abel Kirui in hot, humid conditions in the centre of the Capital. He became his nation's first gold medallist since 1972 and the first ever in the marathon. "I was unknown before today. Now I am known,"

he said. "I can say I am very happy to win a medal for my country. I love my people." He received his Gold medal in the midst of a full-production closing ceremony that otherwise paid scant regard to this particular piece of sporting endeavour.

This slot was a close run thing between Kiprotich and David Rudisha, so honourable mention goes to him. Rushida broke Seb Coe's long-standing 800m world record in 2010. In winning the Gold medal that August, he bettered his own standard, taking the time down to 1.40:91. The manner of his victory was breathtaking. Rushida led from the off and stormed down the back straight. No-one got near him. Coe said "he's the most impressive track and field athlete at these Games".

9. Redgrave the Mentor
It was obvious from the early heats on the water on that Steve Redgrave was fulfilling a dual role at Eton Dornay. His principal role was expert analyser to John Inverdale's rowing anchor. But the long embraces (not just with the women either), gushed thanks and words of respect showed Redgrave as a mentor, informal coach and all round inspiration to this generation of rowers. Katherine Grainger spelt out the value of Redgrave's support for, and belief in the nearly-boats of the women crews. Especially so from someone who had absolutely been-there-and-done it. The implication was that Redgrave had played a role in the emergence of Copeland, Hosking, Stanning, Glover and the others. And when Sir Chris Hoy surpassed Steve's GB record haul of Olympic medals, there was the man himself to offer up the first congratulations. Hoy had barely had chance to peel himself off his machine. Take a bow, Sir Steve. A true ambassador.

10. Wiggo
Fresh from a sublime victory in Le Tour barely 10 days earlier, and also from a typically unselfish attempt to set Cavendish up for the Road Race Gold on the first day of the Games, Bradley Wiggins' time trial Gold is one of my very favourite moments. As a spectacle, the time trial can't compete with the white heat of the velodrome. But in coming home 42 seconds clear of reigning world champion, Tony Martin of Germany, Wiggins delivered Britain's first Gold and

an emphatic statement of his stature in the sport. He would not celebrate until the final man had crossed the line and was prowling around on his bike whilst Martin was slumped against some railings. I like my heroes to be down to earth and approachable. On the podium in the Champs Elysee he turned away from the dignitaries to wave acknowledgement to the supporters. When handed the microphone he said "Right, we're just going to draw the raffle numbers." Here he celebrated his fourth Olympic gold medal by going out and getting drunk - and tweeting updates as he did so.

I was totally high on the Games and there were so many moments. It was hard to be so selective. There were a couple of near misses:

- My mate Bryn who had tickets for the rowing on the 2nd Saturday morning and tickets for the same Super Saturday in the Olympic Stadium. He returned there last Saturday to see Mo and the 4x100 World Record. In all he saw 5 GB Golds and one GB Silver. A Paralympic Silver medallist from Barcelona in 1992, he is only excluded from the main list because I am insanely jealous.

- Hungarian modern pentathlete Adam Marosi who has a tattoo of AC/DC's Angus Young on his calf. Cool.

Immediately after the Games closed, Britain was awash with a feelgood factor and high hopes that an Olympic Legacy would be preserved. There were early noises about investment decisions for school sports funding and many Olympic park venues were promised to be re-used. But feelgood factors don't last forever. The view from three years or so down the line is that the small window of opportunity to capitalise on those moments is closing quickly. Continued austerity measures that hit local authorities and agencies harder than any other sector are preventing real growth grassroots sport investment. Regeneration won't touch many of the East End estates that border the park.

Nevertheless, the venues have largely been preserved. Subsidised swimming at the Olympic pool is a wonderful thing. And the Queen

Elizabeth stadium will remain in active use, although as a football venue for a TV-monied Premier League club (involving millions in conversion costs). There will always be gripes, but I'd easily rather have had the Olympics to decorate that amazing Summer than not. Experiences are everything.

24. THE LANCE ARMSTRONG LIE

Probably the biggest cheat sport has ever known.
David Walsh, journalist and author, 2012

Like Sepp Blatter, the fall from grace of Lance Armstrong had been a long time coming. Allegations of drug misuse had dogged him for years. Critics had alluded to the use of his LiveStrong charity and furious fundraising as smokescreens and diversions. Finally the persistence and tenacity of the US Doping Agency caught up with him. Armstrong declined to defend in court the allegations of persistent EPO abuse. Not quite an admission of guilt, but enough to see him immediately stripped of his seven Tour de France titles.

Somehow the denouement came about very quickly. It wasn't so long ago that Daughter No 2 used Lance Armstrong as an example of a sporting hero because of the way he beat cancer and then went on to compete at the highest level. That much is still true. Armstrong's legacy is a complicated beast. For instance, Bradley Wiggins, the most strident of anti-drugs competitors, has remarked that Armstrong massively broadened the appeal of road racing and brought thousands out to watch the races. But of course, none of that justifies cheating.

I've developed late as a fan of road cycling. I registered the seven consecutive victories of Lance Armstrong in the Tour de France as notable feats in a gruelling competition. But doubts that clearly existed at the time about the validity of his first and subsequent achievements passed me by. Indeed, like many I bought entirely into the story of a supreme athlete who had overcome massive odds to beat cancer and then to land the tour titles. Superhuman, I thought. A genuine good news story. The Armstrong myth had taken flight and I wanted to ride it. It was me that suggested to Daughter No 2 that she should use Armstrong for that school topic. How duped I feel now.

Drug abuse has been a well known blight on the tour throughout his (now) discredited reign and since. I suppose I cynically thought that the whole road cycling game was so riddled with doping that Armstrong was no worse than the others. To the extent that I had given it any thought at all, I had concluded that EPO use, blood transfusions, cortisone injections and the like were so widespread there was a hideously warped but bizarrely level playing field.

So thank God for the campaigners, the doubters and the whistle-blowers. In the early days, there were very few. The Sunday Times journalist, David Walsh was amongst the first and the most vociferous. He waged a tenacious 13 year battle to expose Lance Armstrong's cheating, lying and systematic abuse. His story is remarkable because of the intimidation and manipulation he suffered at the hands of Armstong and his organisation. And also because of the link to a personal tragedy when his son was killed in a cycling accident at the age of 12.

Walsh was everywhere after the pantomime of Big Tex's Oprah Winfrey confession in late 2012. He was seen and heard refusing any inclinations to triumphalism and yet calmly pointing out the limitations and omissions of the Winfrey charade. He also said he would accept an apology from Armstrong though he felt it had been "hesitantly offered" during the show. Walsh often talked frankly about how the obsessive nature of the investigation almost consumed him. In well-known interview with the World Service News Hour in the wake of the Winfrey show, Walsh became very emotional at the personal nature of Armstrong's vilification, finally uttering the words "probably the biggest cheat sport has ever known".

I shared in the widespread reaction to the Winfrey interview as a shallow and stage-managed stunt. A mate commented in the pub afterwards, it was "more Alan Carr than Jeremy Paxman". I still felt as though I was being manipulated by the myth: here was a calculated show of contrition, a shaky foothold on redemption, a tentative brand relaunch. Does he still retain political ambitions? It wouldn't surprise me.

I saw an amusing pic on Twitter of a neatly typed sign in an Australian library declaring "All non-fiction Lance Armstrong books, including 'Lance Armstrong: Images of a Champion', 'The

Lance Armstrong Performance Program' and 'Lance Armstrong: World's Greatest Champion' will soon be moved to the fiction section." The library denied having placed the sign.

Ironically, the profile of road cycling had never been higher in the UK at the time of Armstrong's demise. Wiggins had won the tour in 2012 and Froome currently dominates. Their Team Sky had adopted a zero tolerance approach to doping which quickly led to the departure of two of the management team. It will take many more such deep cleaning operations before the spectre of doping is convincingly dismantled in cycling.

25. THE DARK, THE FOG AND THE FLUKE

I'm not just in it for the gore.
James Herbert, author, 1993

In the aftermath of Cheltenham Festival 2013 I noticed one piece of non-racing news that caused a little pause for thought. The author James Herbert had died. Like most blokes of my vintage, Herbert's dark, often psychological horror was required reading during the early eighties. As a teenager with a healthy, inquiring mind, Herbert hit the spot for both suspense filled fear and the best naughty bits going.

Facebook posts paid glowing tribute to that very duality in the wake of his death. It was with some regret that I realised you could not find the high class filth in a well thumbed electronic copy of, say, Creed by shaking the spine of a Kindle to see which pages were bent back the furthest. Where did today's teenage boys get their cheap thrills? That's a rhetorical question. I don't really want to know.

The Facebook discussion about Herbert's demise also led to the title of this chapter. As I listed my favourites from his oeuvre, Brynaldo suggested this would be a good title for my Cheltenham Festival post mortem. A doomed strategy conceived in the Fog, delivered in the Dark and supplying just one Fluke winner. I might add that my selections acted as a Jonah for many horses, but that was a crap book, so doesn't get a mention.

A more straight-forward title might have been "Where did it all go wrong" but there is a risk of confusion with the Manic Street Preachers' 2010 track "Golden Platitudes". That track expresses a frustration with the retreat of radical politics, rather the puncturing of a punting strategy. It's hard to see Nicky Wire penning anything for the Racing Post.

The stats offered no platitudes, golden or otherwise. Nowhere to hide: 42 bets, 1 win, 4 places, points staked 382, net loss 229. ROI - 60%.

My worst festival ever. It took me over a week to come to terms with it. I even ploughed back through my records to seek a sliver of comfort. There was none. I had a bad year in 2005 when many ante-posts went astray. I had Black Jack Ketchum at fancy prices for the (then) Sun Alliance Hurdle, but his 'canny' trainer mischievously rerouted him to the new 3m Brit Novice Hurdle. He won at a canter. I lost a wad. But not as much as this year.

I also discovered that I had made a profit – some very healthy ones too – at eight of the previous 12 festivals. However, 2011 was scrawny black type at only £15, and 2012 earned me a small loss. These were worrying signs pointing to a well-set downward trend. It gets harder every year with more races, moving targets, deeper plots, bigger fields and tougher competition.

Those challenges reflected the increasing prominence and domination of the Festival over the rest of the season. Indeed, to the utter neglect of the rest of the season. I moan (too often) about insultingly small fields for novice and intermediate chases, as well as graded hurdles and chases offering good prize money. It remains a pathetically valid point. Before that Festival there had been 23 grade one events, 16 of which were won by the favourite, and 6 by the second favourite. How competitive were those fields? Not at all is the answer.

Another issue that burned me was the pointlessness of leading stables who would rather give their best Festival prospects a track gallop in front of a few hardy punters at the end of racing rather than a test in a real race. Vacuous arguments about too few appropriate races and losing valuable work time due to bad weather just did not wash. It absolutely undermines the game. Bob's Worth, Grandouet, Binocular and Riverside Theatre all raced just once before the Festival; Dynaste and Simonsig hadn't been spotted since Christmas. (And yes, I was jabbing an accusatory finger firmly in Henderson's direction, but he was not alone). Add to this the relentless concentration of big talent in a small number of yards and resulting reluctance to run stable stars, or horses in the same ownership against each other and we are left with plenty of evidence of the pitifully weak top class action outside Spring. Thank God for the handicaps.

On the question of the overall quality of the Festival itself, I tended to agree with my mate Bacchy who observed that:

…with the principal Grade 1 winners lining up in the 4-miler and the Jewson, the RSA was an anticlimax. This is not what we come here to see - especially when Back In Focus and Dynaste are allowed to contest those lesser events without a Grade 1 penalty. That's what they mean when they talk about diluting the Festival...

All this rustling bluster could easily be seen as an attempt to obfuscate the direness of my punting week at, despite these rants, the greatest week of racing on the planet. Time to man up.

So. Where had it all gone wrong?

Bad judgement and poor research: I got too many of the big calls wrong. For instance, Silviniaco Conti was always going to be outstayed by Bob's Worth, and despite my attempts to rationalise his suitability for the track before the event, SC patently didn't warm to Prestbury Park. Even had he stood up, it was hard to see him coming up the hill like BW did or even Sir Des Champs.

Another example: one of the few things I got right was the ground call. It was pretty much good to soft until Friday that year. So how did that square with one of my main bets on Taquin Du Seuil whose knee action betrays a liking for mud flying up by his ears? Missed that one.

And, hands up, I got Cue Card all wrong. Concerns raised by his win over 2 ½ miles at Ascot and the proximity of Captain Chris before his final flight blunder were banished here. Cue Card sluiced home with confidence and stamina after making his own running at a pace too sharp for First Lieutenant.

Bad performances: Alongside the rank bad selections, I'd argue that too many of my selections did not run to anything like their marks. In the big ones, Arvika Ligeonniere (Arkle) failed to settle or jump with fluency; and Unioniste (RSA) was entitled to run much better on all known form. Elsewhere, She Ranks Me (Mares Hurdle) barely travelled a step; Loch Ba (JLT Specialty) was being rousted disturbingly early and eventually unseated; and Cotton Mill (County) and Kashmir Peak (Triumph) both disappeared without a trace. Dodging Bullets' run in the Supreme fell into the same category, and just look what he has done since.

Bad luck: Not too many moans here, given that we are talking about 27 races. That said, a triple whammy on Friday just about put the tin lid on my Festival. Cousin Vinnie brought down in the Albert Bartlett before the race had got serious, Siviniaco Conti falling before the hill and Tetlami crashing through the wings whilst leading the Grand Annual just about summed up my week.

I didn't mean this chapter to turn into spleen-venting about the Festival. For all the concerns about the dominance of these four days and its impact on the rest of the season, and indeed the shape and quality of the four day bonanza itself, I would not be anywhere else on earth. For just a few days, my world revolves around those gleaming acres of turf sitting beneath Cleeve Hill where the most intense kind of equine theatre is played out for an audience of screaming, laughing, weeping emotional and financial wrecks. Bonds forged there in the white heat and heady atmosphere of Festival competition are never broken, whether that is man-to-man or man-to-beast.

That year, the highlights came hurtling at us from the very first moments:

- Champagne Fever's gutsy win from the front in a brilliant finish to the Supreme.

- Ruby Walsh in very different mode getting Hurricane Fly back on the bridle to then win the Champion Hurdle as Mike Cattermole was desperately trying to call his race over.
- Sprinter Sacre causing the biggest intake of breath in the Champion Chase since Master Minded sprinted clear in less anticipated circumstances back in 08.
- The New One already setting pulses racing for a tilt at the following year's Champion Hurdle.
- Bob's Worth equalling Flying Bolt's 47 year old record of winning three different Festival races.
- Quevega matching Golden Miler's achievement of five consecutive wins.
- Cue Card shutting up all the doubters in the Ryanair.
- Our Conor dropping jaws in the Triumph.

I could go on.

On the human side, thoughts were immediately with JT McNamara. He remained in an induced coma for many months after the Festival following a horrific tumble from Galaxy Rock in the Kim Muir. My mate Chris was walking the path outside the perimeter fence at the time, showing his young son some of the action. He witnessed the incident and heard a crack as rider and horse came down. His relief at the sight of the horse getting up was immediately replaced by concern that the jockey had not moved. The green screens were erected to shield the view from the stands – but curiously not from the perimeter fence – and as Chris saw medical staff and ambulances arrive, he realised it was time to move on. Disturbing scenes.

I have always had a soft spot for JT. He rode Rith Dubh to a beautifully crafted victory in the 2002 Four Miler. That was my only winner at that year's festival. I celebrated like I had screamed home the trifecta. In 2013, 11 years on, my only winner at the Festival was also in the Four Miler.

The Festival can be a dangerous place in many ways. Col, Nev and I had formed the Cheltenham posse that year. Nev was the life and soul on Tuesday and Wednesday where he smashed up a series of improbable forecasts and then blew a chunky part of his stash on the Coral Cup. He wouldn't be the first to do that. On Gold Cup day, back in the Barley Mow, Nev left early, clutching his sides. We later discovered that he had been diagnosed with acute diabetes and spent the next week in hospital.

Things were different for Nev for a good while. New diet, new fitness regime, new drinking limits. Seeing him quaff small glasses of chardonnay in the boozer instead of jugs of Fullers Red Fox was a jarring experience.

But to conjure up another of James Herbert's images, Nev was a cast-iron Survivor and we knew he'd be back.

26. FIELDS OF ATHENRY

When I am an old woman I shall wear purple
With a red hat which doesn't go, and doesn't suit me.
And I shall spend my pension on brandy and summer gloves
And satin sandals, and say we've no money for butter.

Jenny Joseph, from the poem 'Warning', 1987.

It is worth taking a moment here to pay a little tribute to Granny Milner. There's no specific racing or sporting link to be plundered in this chapter. Granny loved the Grand National as much as anyone ("…Is there one wearing green, or an Irish one? I'll go for that.") Her sister Mona, of course, hosted Bacchy and I over many memorable Cheltenham Festival excursions. Instead, this is a moment to stand back and recognise the individuality of a woman who never fully recognised the impact she had on those around her. She passed away in 2013.

I'm picking up the tale at the point Granny celebrated her 80th birthday.

The madness had begun with Auntie Sue's arrival from Tenerife at about 2am on a Thursday morning before the celebrations. It didn't subside until I scrabbled back home, dazed and confused, at 6.30pm the following Sunday. And even then I knew it was only an ebb tide in an on-going torrent of insanity.

Auntie Sue had a plan. It involved whisking away the children on a secret mission to Berko, Hemel and all points in between to empty pound stores and gift shops of their party poppers, bunting, balloons and stocks of assorted celebration-fare. Then she moved on to the children themselves: party dresses, footwear, haircuts, and French manicures. It was a blizzard of activity. I'd never seen anything like it. Not since the last party anyway. The girls loved it.

In amongst this whirlwind, Mrs A, Auntie Sue and the girls had made two trips to the airport to collect Auntie Betty from Florida. On the first occasion they lost her. Or, more precisely, Delta airlines did. They cancelled her flight from Boston and would give Mrs A no information (or they had none, I'm not sure which) about which flight she had been moved to. Eventually, after much pressing, they learnt that Auntie Betty was on an American Airlines flight arriving about 24 hours later. 0/10 Delta, you scumbags.

At least she was on that one and the welcoming committee was there for her. She'd had a good flight and had been put up in a decent hotel. By the time I arrived home, Betty was lying out full stretch on the garden bench, wearing wrap around sunglasses and supported by cushions, pillows and blankets. She was resting, aided by a second gallon of hot, sweet, milky tea.

"Dave! How're ye doing? I just got here. They cancelled my foolish flight. I like your new office – it's not a doghouse anymore is it? Wow, it's a palace, right! And what about this garden. Jeez, it's like the botanical gardens, right? The girls are so lovely. I can't believe how they've grown! I'm having a little rest now. I didn't sleep for two nights. They put me in a bootiful hotel room though. A bathroom the size of your house."

I hadn't uttered a single word yet. There were stories emanating via friends in the States that Betty was quieter these days, after some treatment had improved her hearing. I'm pleased to be able to scotch those dirty rumours. Betty's astonishing Irish-Floridian accent is still up at 11 on the Spinal Tap-scale, utterly belying her tiny, frail 4' 10" frame.

She was to be the surprise guest at her sister's 80th birthday bash. Trying to keep this a secret was a nightmare. Every time Granny rang we had to get Betty out of earshot of the phone. Not easy, given her larynx was impersonating an F16 fighter on full transatlantic afterburn.

But eventually, party time arrived. Presents, guests, luggage, bedding and music were all rammed into the charabanc. No room for me though. I was packed off to the railway station. Nor the bedding, either. A hasty phone call from the car on route from Daughter No 2 said simply 'sleeping bags'!

To maintain the cloak of secrecy, we had all arrived at Granny's together, minus Betty who had been dropped off at Bruv-in-Law, Chris's. They would then bring her to the party once it was underway. Meanwhile a gang of us decorated the hall under Auntie Sue's expert direction. Daughter-in-law Sharon had expertly procured from her work over 100 A4 and A3 photos of Granny spanning her full, packed, 80 years, which we gummed up on the walls. At the end of the night, friends and relatives were peeling them off and taking them home as souvenirs.

They were a keen bunch in Old Stratford. We'd barely finished blowing up balloons and sound checking the singer ("two-two-two, scream for me Milton Keynes…") when the guests turned up and starting necking the fizz. The room was soon filled. Marcel, Rita, Paul and Clare and families – Granny's nieces and nephews from Gloucester - had come up for the party and there were people dropping in from all over the place.

I was in the side room ordering a few drinks when Betty arrived. I knew because I heard the screams. Infact I saw the screams when the sound waves ricocheted around the corner and popped the three glasses I was holding. Almost. The surprise worked a treat. Eyewitnesses describe Granny spinning in a circular jig "like a dog chasing its tail", beaming like the North Wall lighthouse! Granny really did not know her sister was coming. She spent the next hour touring Betty round all the tables introducing her to every guest. Even those who already knew her. Fantastic scenes: the two remaining Moffit girls in harness again at 82 and 80.

Hardly worth stating the bleeding obvious, but that was one good night. Highlights? Well, almost too many to record…Granny opening her 'This Is Your Life' photo album and passing it round the guests for them to sign, with Fiona doing a top marshalling job to get it moving around the tables……… the birthday cakes moment –

there were two – where blowing out the candles took a full 5 minutes (where was she aiming?)…

And then the inevitable singing later on as Peter the Turn was forced to share the mic with a succession of entertainers from within the family. First, bruv-in-law Chris marched up to the front and held together a surprisingly tuneful Dirty Old Town; then the birthday girl and Auntie Betty started a very cheery version of Sisters that went something like "Sisters, Sisters, There were never such devoted Sisters" "I'm here to keep an eye on her." "No, that's not the right line Chrissie what are you singing" "Well that's the way I've been singing it for 50 years" It was quickly aborted in favour of Betty ripping out a stunning version of the Irish Rover. Finally, Chris, Granny, Betty, Frank and Peter did as much justice as it's possible to do to the tortuous, lengthy and dirge-like Fields of Athenry. It's always there isn't it….

Back at the house, people were spilling out of bathrooms, bedrooms, in the garden, under the gazebo. I spotted Peter the Turn over in the corner at one stage, holding a cup of tea and being talked at by half a dozen revellers. He needed to get back to London that night for a gig the next day and was wondering how he would ever get out of the room.

By about 2am the singing started again. Maybe it had never stopped and I'd just been stuck outside with that big-eared bloke talking rubbish about Leeds Utd for longer than I thought. I had also considered it my Uncle-ly duty to check over my niece Robyn's new fellah. He's seemed pretty cool to me. Not exactly sure what Uncle-ly tools I had in the box if I didn't like him, mind….

Back to the singing…I'd muscled my way past a couple of septuagenarians to assume control of the ipod flight deck. I found what we were looking for. Neil Diamond Song Sung Blue (everybody here knew one) and Sweet Caroline. Sue gave me such a hard time about that. "I hate this one," she mouthed through the crowd, " 'touching hands'…urggh, creepy!". I could barely hear her for the noise of the "bah-bah-bah" bouncing round the room. There was a bit of ole blue eyes too, My Way and New York, New York.

Chris (no, a different one - keep up!) and John had become good friends of Sue and Granny whilst in Tenerife. It was great to see them here. John was sat in the corner belting out New York, New York with gusto. I swear he was louder than all the rest, rumbustuously cranking out all the wrong words at the wrong time and in the wrong key. Fantastic! I thought it was just me.

My kids had also been chucking their heads back and screaming "I did it miiiiyyyyy waaaaayyyyy" at full tilt. Great to these classics being murdered right across the generations. There was a bit of Presley, a bit of Cliff's 'Congratulations' and then a raucous round of Happy Birthday To You with Chrissie in the middle of the room.

At one point Joe, our 20 year-old nephew, elbowed me out of the way and scrolled through the ipod menu. Oh no I thought. If he finds the girls' Olly Murs or JLS on there we are doomed. But no. Out of the speakers snaked a lithe and dangerous 'Walk The Line' and Mr Johnny Cash. It's OK folks, the future is safe.

Later still, we had the ska revival. Chris's moves to One Step Beyond were mind-boggling. Still later still, everything had gone properly pear-shaped. Someone had found the Val Doonican CD that I thought I'd hidden in the locked filing cabinet down the cellar behind the door marked 'beware of the tiger' (apols to Douglas Adams). The three Milner children, Granny and Betty and assorted others were rattling out the convoluted lyrical concepts of Paddy McGinty's Goat, O'Rafferty's Car and Father O'Flaherty's Irritating Bowel Syndrome. Might have misheard the last one.

By 5am, things had wound down. Most people had left and those that remained grabbed whatever berths they could find.

I surfaced about 10.30am next morning. Granny and Betty were already up and had gone to mass on about 4 hours' sleep. Where they got the stamina from I never knew. I'll be happy if I'm half as fit (but maybe twice as sane) as that at 80.

Apparently Bruv-in-law, Chris had called earlier to see if I fancied a round of golf. Another with an iron constitution. Unbelievable. It was only a few short hours since he was giving the finest air-saxophone solo to 'Ghostown' that I've ever seen. He'd had a bit of kip, apparently and woken with a raging thirst. He couldn't find any cold soft drinks in the fridge and so resorted to another Strongbow! He'd turned up at the course with an inevitable massive hangover. "I couldn't see the ball", he said. "I took 24 shots on the first hole. I've had another couple of cans though and I feel fine now!"

Mrs A had been up a while and had brought all the presents back from the hall. The lounge was suddenly claustrophobic with gifts that were roughly themed around flowers and plants, chocolate and alcohol. Only the alcohol would have been a surprise to the casual observer. Granny had never drunk much. (Heaven forbid. She really didn't need to!) But it had become common knowledge lately that she liked a splash of Baileys Irish Cream on her porridge of a morning. "Smoothes it up!" she says. So this fact accounted for the five bottles in three different sizes of the stuff parked on the coffee table.

Granny and Betty opening the presents was a scream. But trying to work out who had given which gifts became a convoluted, repeating saga worthy of any Laurel and Hardy sketch. Daughter No 2 was attempting to write the presents on the cards as they were opened so Granny wouldn't forget. It should have been that simple. It wasn't.

"I've got Clare's card here. Where's Clare's present?" Granny looked confused.

"We haven't got to it yet Auntie Chrissie", helps Marcel.

"Is that Joan's there. Well, see, maybe that's Clare's. What did you write on the card Catherine?"

"Pendant and chocolate, Granny."

"On Joan's card?"

"Yes, Granny."

"Well where's Clare's then?"

"I don't think we've got to it yet Auntie Chrissie." Marcel again.

"Is that Clare's then?"

"No that Joan's. Still."

"What's this?" Granny finds a nice Cath Kidston-inspired bag. " 'To Auntie Chrissie love from Clare and the gang'. There it is! We hadn't got to it yet!"

Mrs A and I went out to return the crockery to the caterer. On the way we took a detour and stopped a while to ponder quantum physics and count ants. This was preferable to returning back to the chaotic system in the house too quickly. On our prolonged return, Daughter No 1 had taken over card annotation duties from No 2 who was now gibbering in the corner with a wet towel around her head.

"Now, where did I put…"

"It's over there Granny"

"Is that the…"

The rubbish pile is here Granny"

"Did you…"

"That's the bag pile Granny"

Daughter No 1 had already perfected the eye-rolling and head shaking that many a grown-up would struggle to master.

One barbecue cooked in the rain later (a Summer tradition…), we heard the ice cream van turn into Mounthill Avenue. Auntie Sue and Daughter No 2 popped out to grab one each.

"Do you need some money?" said Granny.

"No, we're fine", replied Sue.

"They're a pound each."

Sue was grinning when they come back.

"Mine was £1.60 and Catherine's was £1.40."

"Oh!" chuckled Granny. "I always give him a pound. He never asks for any more!"

"Brilliant!" we exclaimed. "Great approach. Does it work everywhere? How much did you pay for the telly? Tenner?"

The madness continued. The following week, we all took Granny and Betty ten-pin bowling for the first time. Those lanes really took a battering. We shuddered every time Betty delivered one of her over-under-arm launches. Then they went to Ireland and raised mayhem around Killestre, Swords and Howth. Next it was on to the Gloucester crowd for a few days. The British Isles, merely pin-pricked by the riots of that year and the bad weather, was cowering and licking her wounds by the time Betty left in early September.

Granny fell ill a couple of years later. The diagnosis was terminal. However as befits her amazing spirit, she didn't slow down until forced to. Her will remained ferociously unbroken. Auntie Betty came back from Florida to spend as much time with her sister as possible.

We dropped in to see the sisters on the way oop north one afternoon. Auntie Betty was in predictably fine form. She liked my trainers and I said she could borrow them.

"What size are you, Betty?"

"Well, you know, I'm a five over here, but a seven in the States. Yeah. My feet don't change sizes. They just have a different number here!"

Classic Betty. Daughter No 1 was in physical pain, bobbing up and down with mirth. Betty had been in fine form since she got there a fortnight before. The first time we visited, she opened Granny's door to us and with no fanfare whatsoever, shoed us inside.

"Come in, come in", she said and flicked thumb in the direction of the lounge. It was only when we were inside and she recognised me that she stopped.

"Oh my god it's the Eya-atkinsons! I thought you were more nurses! It's been like Grand Central in here with doctors and nurses coming and going!"

She clasped the girls' faces between her hands in turn and said, "You've changed so much. Gorgeous girls. I'm sick of looking at old people…"

When Granny sadly succumbed to the vile disease last year, the funeral was an epic of its kind. As befits a life full of love, friendship, selflessness and good humour, Granny's final appearance at the Church she adored was played out before a packed house. Her religion was at the very core of her being and she had nominated the full Requiem Mass long ago, and even selected some of the hymns. She rightly got the send off she wanted.

We were grateful to the Priest who carefully indicated to the non-Catholics our precise location in the marathon service; and for which bits we should sit, stand, kneel, pray, sing and recite. Uncle Chris was particularly pleased and thanked him afterwards.

"Those prompts were handy. It's all changed since my day."

His newly interned Mother would already be spinning in her fresh grave, had she known of her son's confession.

In fairness, the Priest played a blinder. He delivered the touching eulogy that Mrs A and the family had written with warmth, humour and the insight that his relationship with Granny brought. Though to announce his own support for Chelsea as well as Granny's was rather unnecessary, in my view. He also nearly burnt the baggy sleeves of his vestments on the candles that were crowded too closely around the coffin. Cousin Fiona, berthed in the outside stall, rescued him and averted fiery disaster on a number of occasions.

The candles and their ornate sticks remained a problem throughout the proceedings. Belligerent Auntie Betty paid them, and anyone else in her way, scant regard as she took her communion and bulldozed back to her seat, leaving a trail of hot wax and bruised toes in her tracks.

The potential for disaster was everywhere. As the service was getting underway amongst smoky incense and doomy organ, the Priest collared Mrs A and Auntie Sue, asking them if they would bring down the wine and the water at the appropriate moment from the back of the Church to the front for said Communion.

The vision of Mrs A inching her way down the aisle, visibly shaking with nervous mirth (despite the solemnity), clutching a jittery tray laden with silver cups and vessels of wine will stay with me for a very long time. As Sue said afterwards, it was all a little bit Mrs Overall. "One...soup? One...soup? Two soups?"

Fiona contributed in other ways too. It takes reserves of steely nerve to stand up and deliver a eulogy to your Grandmother at her funeral. That she did so with such controlled emotion and genuine feeling pays her a tremendous compliment. She hit so many evocative notes when recalling the limitless generosity with time for anyone and everyone, unfailing good humour – right to the end - and unplumbed wells of stories and songs. Not a dry eye in the house.

We followed the coffin back outside where the congregation was able to mingle for the first time properly. This is always my worst moment. More tears, group hugs and tender words with people who have often travelled miles, countries and continents to pay respects.

It was, though, nearly a double burial. Up at the cemetery, Auntie Sue had a bit of a moment with the holy water sprinkler. The immediate family all had a sober shake over the coffin to bless it. When Sue took her turn, she thought the aspergillum was coming apart and tried to grab it with her other hand. She was worried about it dropping into the grave. I was more worried about her following it in. She was perilously close to the edge…and Fiona wasn't near enough to rescue anyone this time. But Sue recovered her poise in time, chucked in her rose and restored the air of decorum in the nick of time.

The wake was held in The Plough, a pub where Granny had enjoyed many a vibrant Paddy's night. Mourners spilled outside where tables were piled with drinks in every size and colour, plates of pastries and buffet food, and boxes of assorted tea towels. Granny had been a life long collector and had amassed over 500. She had indicated to Mrs A that this would be the cornerstone of estate. Mrs A was not so impressed.

"Tell you what, I'll give them away at your funeral", she had laughed.

"OK then, I like that idea", Granny had replied.

So that's what happened. Everyone rummaged through the boxes and took away a tea towel to remember her by. It worked on so many levels. Some took souvenirs of places they had visited together; others claimed rhymes, humorous verses or religious proclamations. My Bruv took one that advertised double cream to mark the many stand-offs he and Granny had endured over the last scoop of trifle left in the bowl.

The gang began to break up. Liam and Eileen roared off down the road aiming to catch the 8pm sailing back to Dublin. Eileen hadn't told her Mother she was coming over on the back of Liam's bike. She'd only have worried. Bruv, Dad and I left the rest of the family to their remembrances as Uncle Chris was cranking yet out another shaky rendition of 'Fields of Athenry'…

Call it sentiment, for that's what it is, but I backed Aiden O'Brien's horse of the same name every outing in the Summer of 2015. His third in the St Leger promises much for next season. Legacies and all that.

27. RACING ENGLAND

Backing horses is, taking it by and large, a mug's game.
Patrick R Chalmers, from the book Racing England, 1939.

I was put on the trail of author Patrick R Chalmers' curiosity, Racing England when stumbling across a reproduction of the front cover in one of those nostalgia heavy, romanticised visions of Britain that the National Trust do so lavishly. Flicking distractedly through its pages in the gift shop of the Rothschild's neo-Renaissance pile at Waddeson Manor, I stopped immediately at Brian Cook's block coloured representation of Ascot Gold Cup Day from the early 20th century. It was a thing of simple beauty.

Brian Caldwell Cook, was born in the leafy lanes of Gerrards Cross in 1910. He created the lithograph that would become the cover to Racing England in 1937 and Batsfords, the old-established London publishing company of which his Mother was a member, eventually published the book in 1939. Cook would go on to produce many covers for the company in this series, with titles such as Hunting England, Farming England and Villages of England.

Tracking down copies of the book online wasn't difficult. But finding one with an intact dust cover of the lithograph proved harder. I don't think the book or the cover are particularly collectable, but I was prepared to part with a few quid to get a reasonably presentable one. So when a copy turned up through a second hand specialist requiring the investment of a whole £6 it seemed like decent value. The transaction was made.

I was pleased with my purchase. Opening up the packaging, the mustiness of the volume hit me immediately. The 145 pages of text were stiff, a little mottled and almost coarse to the touch. The thickness of the age-beiged paper had absorbed 64 years of atmosphere on shelves, in boxes, under beds…who knows. They almost crackled as I turned over the leaves. The text was bold and large. If it had been printed today, it would be squeezed into a flimsy-paged, small-scripted book of half the size and presence. It's a pre-loved book, too. Still in good condition, despite the mottling, and has a charming inscription on the flyleaf: "To Mary, with love from Mother."

Cook's art is still wrapped right around the book from front to back and the condition is pretty good, given its likely exposure to the years. The colours have faded a little compared to the copy I saw in the National Trust book. But not much. The spine is darker than the rest of the image. I guess it has attracted dirt through grubby fingers and pawing thumbs.

What engrosses me about this piece of graphic art is the style as much as the subject. The 'blatant and strident' colours (in the words of the artist) used liberally to create a vibrant, uplifting scene. They must have been stunning on the original. It echoes many of the optimistic, bucolic art-deco designs used to advertise the inter-war golden age of steam like LNER's 'East Coast Joys' (Tom Purvis) and the expanding public transport network, 'Box Hill by Motor Bus' (F Gregory Brown). I know now that the Jean Berté process, which used rubber plates and water-based inks, achieves this effect.

That said, the subject is equally engaging. It depicts the finish to the Ascot Stakes handicap at Royal Ascot viewed from within the betting ring on the heath. Three closely matched horses are bearing down on the finish line framed by a ramshackle collection of packed stands.

This Ascot is unrecognizable from the current course. A corporate-friendly building styled more like an airport terminal with the atmosphere of a doctor's waiting room now occupies the approximate site of those tiny, cramped stands. The wrought iron three column race information indicator – fore-runner of the tote boards - is also long gone. In fact the heath side of the track has not hosted bookies or punters for many years. Even the track itself has been realigned.

The jockey's looked almost comical. Long legged, upright positions, which seems to push them half way round the horses' necks.

As much as anything else in the image, this dated the scene to sometime just after the turn of the century. But that's not quite precise enough. Cook created the image from a photo that appears in the book. The photo is captioned, 'Royal Ascot on Gold Cup Day', alongside others from the turn of the century. So the cover was not necessarily of a contemporary scene. I can see from the results board that the race in progress is the Ascot Stakes, but none of the runners' or riders' names are clear enough to make out and research. I still don't know the exact date or the horses involved.

Patrick Chalmers was an Irish writer, biographer and poet. A lot of his output seems to be related to field sports. 'The Angler's England' and 'The Shooting Man's England' for instance, alongside this volume. However, I was mildly interested to note the etymology behind the phrase 'its all swings and roundabouts', not inappropriate to a book about gambling. It derives from one of his poems:

"But lookin' at it broad, an' while it ain't no merchant king's,
What's lost upon the roundabouts we pulls up on the swings!"

The linguistic style of Racing England is very much of its day. The book is a loose account of the development of racing in the country and Chalmers employs a charming, if ramblingly anecdotal, approach to the story. It is dominated by discussion, in the circuitous and opaque language of the time, almost entirely of flat racing. The jumps game hardly gets a look in. Prefacing a chapter on 'Some English racecourses', Chalmers says,

"Twenty three meeting-places in all. For we cannot include here the many steeplechasing courses and simple days of good sport, good sportsmanship and open air."

That said, the Grand National, held at an Aintree that in those days predominantly hosted flat meetings, is described in lavish terms:

To the spring meeting, the 'national' draws all that is
best in sport from all parts of the Empire. On no English
course do so many Irishmen foregather, in no paddock,
not even that of Ascot, may you see fifty masters of
foxhounds at once, and at no other fixture will you find
the leading cross-country owners and jockeys rubbing
shoulders with their flat-racing kind.

Some of the earlier chapters deal with formative events and early luminaries of the game. Admiral Rous, Bunbury and lineage of the thoroughbred racehorse get some laboured, rather prosaic coverage. Much more interesting is the sections devoted to horses, jockeys and owners. Alongside the profiles of better known riders such as Sir Gordon Richards and Steve Donoghue is an interesting piece profiling the American rider Tod Sloan:

Sloan was the pioneer, and possibly the greatest
exponent of the new style – the monkey-on-a-stick style,
the style that rides 'short', the knees tucked up, the chin
upon the horse's withers.

Fred Archer's career is also examined in depth. Chalmers describes the devastating wasting (10 stone out of season down to 8 ½ stone when riding) and tragic suicide at the age of 29 in typically thorough, though surprisingly matter of fact terms, given the predilection towards flabby yarns about trifling incidents elsewhere in the book.

He also describes Archer's ride aboard Melton to win the 1885 Derby as his greatest ever ride. Paradox was favourite for the race and was regarded as "infinitely the better horse". Archer rode a spectacular 'finish', employing what we would term exaggerated hold up tactics in today's game, to steal the race by stealth:

Melton drew up to Paradox 150 yards from home and
thenceforward to the winning post the two horses were
engaged in a tremendous struggle for the mastery.
Paradox had a shade the better of it when fifty yards
from home; three strides from the post he looked like

winning by a neck. Archer seemed to wrap his legs round Melton's girth and up went his whip. He hit Melton a terrific one-two. Those two mighty welts, delivered almost simultaneously and smacking out like pistol shots, achieved their object. Melton leapt convulsively forward and, in the last second of time, his head was in front. It seemed to the spectators that Archer had, literally, lifted him past the post.

As entertaining (for most part) as Chalmers' stories are, I found the illustrations, plates, engravings and photos equally and some times more compelling. Of course the stunning cover by Cook is the reason I tracked down the book. That powerful image and the photos dating from the late 19th century up to the verge of World War II captured a phase of the sport long gone. Defunct racecourses, outmoded betting practices, changed fashions, rebuilt architecture and infrastructure.

But above all, the vast, vast crowds. There were fewer meetings at each course back then, and, by and large, sport did not have so many rival distractions as now. Attendances at football matches and greyhound meetings were similarly huge. Every image in the book seemed to feature people wedged into terraces, platforms and stands, rows of bookies five deep at mid-week fixtures, or punters lining both sides of the running rail for furlongs up the track. The queue for a pint and a pie does not bear thinking about.

This book hardly gets a mention in the top rank of racing literature. That's probably about right, given the overall scope of the material. But it's a fascinating period piece at worst and will take high order in my own library, spine displayed proudly to attract another generation's grubbiness.

28. THE ETHICAL BOOKMAKER

Bookies are a blight on the High Street.
Harriet Harman, Shadow Culture Secretary, 2011

The link between racing and betting is of course inextricable. Without the latter, the former would be unrecognizable. Bookies, along with the courses are accused of buttoning up the game for their own ends. However, the wider interests of bookmakers frequently come under attack, and often from political circles.

In the early days of the last Coalition Government, there were calls for a crackdown on high-stakes gambling machines in betting shops, known as FOBTs, amid warnings about their addictive nature. Harriet Harman in particular had the humble bookie in her sights. Labour's then Deputy Leader described betting shops as"blight" on London's high streets.

A report by NatCen, the Government-funded centre for independent research, together with the Responsible Gambling Fund, concluded that slot machine arcades were taking over vacant shopping centre and leisure outlets in places that have been worst hit by the recession.

This research was asserting that the gambling industry had been fast off the mark in plugging the gap in the high street entertainment business, targeting depressed areas. In so doing the industry was roundly accused of exploiting the inactivity associated with high unemployment in places like the Welsh Valleys, Barnsley, Halifax and parts of Glasgow.

Harriet Harman Ms Harman has a long history of vilifying the betting industry for preying on the most vulnerable in society. She argued that in her own constituency of Camberwell and Peckham, betting firms were deliberately opening branches in poor areas, pushing families further into poverty and creating a link between benefit dependence and gambling. Labour wanted new powers to enable councils and local people to stop betting shops opening. Interestingly, betting shops are classified as financial services, meaning that if a bank closes a betting shop can open in the property unchallenged.

There were 1,773 betting shops in London in 2012, according to the Campaign for Fairer Gambling. But it is what goes on in them that was the subject of a debate called by Ms Harman. FOBTs can accept stakes of up to £100 and offer prizes of £500.

Research by the Campaign estimated that FOBTs in the 50 parliamentary constituencies with the highest unemployment rates saw a turnover of £5bn in 2012, generating a profit of £173m. However, in the 50 constituencies with the greatest employment levels, the bookies made only £44m. This led to accusations by Dianne Abbott of the industry targeting the poor, saying: 'It's a business model which sucks money from the poorest communities.' The Daily Mail, never one to miss a trick, got its teeth into this as well, bandying about puritanical headlines pointing to 'the crack cocaine of gambling'.

The Government was not for turning on that occasion. Culture Minister Hugh Robertson blithely commented that there was little evidence they caused serious problems. Really?

Instead, an amendment to the 2005 Gambling Act now requires those who stake above £50 a spin on FOBTs to seek permission from staff or sign up to a loyalty card. Newham Council recently led 93 Councils in a bid to cap the maximum stake of FOBTs at £2 a spin - a significant reduction from the £100 currently permitted. The proposals were made in attempt to prevent clustering of betting shops, particularly in deprived areas. Newham's proposal was rejected.

This debate gave me a chance to dust off my social enterprise hobby-horse: the potential role of the ethical bookmaker. For my part, I would like to see bookmakers that can contribute to the regeneration of the deprived areas they are accused of exploiting and to be more proactive in identifying and tackling addictive behaviour.

Surely there is a role for an ethical bookmaker. A bookie that is run as a social enterprise and re-invests profits into the local community where it is based and from where the customers come. Even better, those communities could run the bookies.

It's not that far-fetched. In my day job, I work with many community organisations who are refining their entrepreneurial flair to develop enterprises that can help to regenerate areas and offer tailored services to local people. An ethical bookmaker can have role in this world.

As Ms Harman observed, bookies have a deep reach into many of the most deprived areas in the country. Half an hour in any bookie off the Holloway Road would confirm that. A social enterprise makeover for the humble bookmaker could provide investment in local infrastructure and services. They might also act as a gateway to other advice and support services, perhaps including help with gambling and other addictive behaviour. Profits would be harvested from responsible gambling and re-invested in community projects.

There would be barriers to such an approach, of course. Moralistic arguments, amongst others. Prospective investors in the model – likely to be public sector in reality – might be squeamish about basing a community policy that relied on encouraging gambling. On the other hand, we seem to have got over that problem when it comes to the National Lottery, often perceived as a tax on the poor. And now we have a Health Lottery that has been criticized for creaming off too many profits for its operators. So what's the difference?

I'm not the only one to have a similar idea. Keeping with the NHS angle, my good friend Crispin - subject of an earlier chapter in this book - whilst undergoing some pretty serious treatment at Kings College hospital said via Facebook "Thinking as a patient, one of many things the NHS 'needs' is a betting shop in each hospital. Why not an 'NHS Tote', the 'People's Bookie'?!"

"Absolutely right," I said, "Crispin, you've read my mind. For years I've been touting the concept of the socially-motivated, community re-investment bookmaker as a tool to resource urban and rural regeneration. Can't find a funder to back me though!"

He continued, "but it's definitely a good idea…I have now posted this approach/suggestion - i.e. an NHS Tote - to the Dept Health 'consultation' whilst the Government 'pauses' to reflect on any changes to their NHS reforms...."

Needless to say, neither of us have had any success in turning this half-baked idea into reality. I once suggested this approach in a 'Dragon's Den'-type competition held in advance of a conference promoted by my former employer. Sadly the conference was cancelled and my idea never saw the light of day.

I got as far as writing to Harriet Harman about it. I didn't get a reply. I made the mistake of providing a link to my blog. Her office probably deduced, after a quick shuftie of the nonsense on there, that I was some kind of self-publicist chancer! Nevertheless, I think its time I put my head above the parapet again. I still think it's a winner. Just don't put your mortgage on it.

29. BUTTS MOTT

Greyhounds he hadde as swift as fowel in flight
Of prickyng and of hunting the hare
Was al his lust, for no cost wolde he spare
William Chaucer, Canterbury Tales, 1215

The Monk in Canterbury Tales owned a greyhound. So did Bacchy's mates in an online gambling forum. This proved to be a much more profitable experience for them, and us, than for Chaucer's monk.

Across the short days and small fields of the winter jumps season, the lads accumulated a very decent sum just shy of three hundred knicker by punting a beautiful little greyhound bitch called Butts Mott. We intended to use the pot to power an assault on the Cheltenham Festival. Things don't always go to plan though, do they?

The journey began with the whip. Or more correctly, it all started with beer. Like it always does. After the last knockings of the pre-season fantasy cricket curry night, we scooped up the kitty left over from the boozer and as usual we decided to have a bet with it.

We once had a decent run in the Rugby World Cup by reinvesting whip remains in Argentina's group games. We had built up a tidy enough amount as the physically tough and arbitrarily dirty Pumas surprised many in the early stages of the competition. We got greedy and took fancy prices about their quarter-final with the All Blacks. Our loyalty towards the Pumas went scandalously unrewarded and the All Blacks predictably smashed them up at Eden Park, 33-10.

After most Cheltenhams we lumped various kitty dregs on rags in the Grand National that usually declined to even show up.

So whilst blowing out the whip was familiar territory, no-one had any hesitation in following through on a tip from Bacchy. A greyhound. A 'kin greyhound! I probably looked aghast. It's my standard reaction when anyone talks about punting up the dogs.

The mut was called Butts Mott. It hosed up first time in a pup's race at 7-2. The whip nosed smoothly from mere coppers to a smidge over twenty quid. Apparently the bitch was something of a decent prospect. Bacchy circulated some commentary from the syndicate that owned her:

> *The plan is to go for the Angel of the North, the northern oaks at Newcastle in about 4 to 5 weeks. She has now won 8 on the trot. The good news is we should get a price ante post. The final is on Sky so lets hope we get through so we can all have a good night's viewing.*

We caught up again at the post-season curry night and watched her easy progress in the Angel of the North trials via Nev's smart phone. A couple of days later, Bacchy took 5-1 ante-post for the big one.

Connections again:

> *Hope a few of you have got a few nice ante-post vouchers in your hands and hopefully Tuesday Butts does the biz again. She has won the last 9 now. 10 would be memorable.*

And then a day or so later:

> *Right guys tomorrow is D-Day as they say. We've been discussing the draw and have both come to the conclusion that Butts will have to be on her very best game to get herself in a good position out of the 4-box. We really could not have had a worse draw. The worry is that the 1-dog, Bridge Ruth, might move over to the right as she comes out of the box as she is generally a middle runner.........*
>
> *In my opinion there is going to be trouble at the first bend and someone is going to suffer, hopefully Butts*

might trap a bit faster, the 3 pings out, goes over to the rail and does the 1 and 2, leaving us a bit of racing room. The dog with the best draw of all is the 6-dog. And the 5 might be in front of us at the bend as well. One thing is for sure - Butts has developed great track craft and if there is a gap and a way of winning she will take it. Hopefully we don't get squeezed and lose the race at the first bend.

This analysis proved to be more accurate than a mouthful of Ben Stokes sledging. The first bend produced the absolute carnage predicted by connections, in exactly the consequential order speculated. These boys knew their onions. Somehow - maybe that track craft they had seen - the beautiful Butts avoided the worst of it, slammed round the dirt and held on by a breathless, thrilling 100th of a second.

Bacchy on e-mail the next day:

The lovely BUTTS has served us up a 26/1 double, so a whip that wouldn't have bought a brace of Doom Bar now stands at £135.

This prompted an interminable e-mail thread that debated what to do with the winnings. Tortuous and argumentative, but very amusing. Only Nick remained consistent in his approach. "Drink it", he implored every time options were aired.

Some ridiculous split-stake doubles and savers on England's Autumn World Cup qualifiers were mercifully avoided. Eventually we settled on the Tingle Creek Chase. Most of us would be there at the track and Colin, who couldn't make the trip, put up Sire De Grugy as the bearer of our whip. Good shout.

The Tingle Creek meeting has been one of our regular events for years. I met Tim at Watford Junction. He was nestling over the Racing Post. "Real racing starts at 7.20 tonight", he remarked, looking at the Wolverhampton pages. He wasn't joking.

None of us had much luck. The first loser of the day was Ben, whom we found at the station-side entrance to the track, forking out for a South West Trains penalty fare. And Bryn had his Grandstand ticket but was already inside, prompting some logistics-texting action.

Not a great start. Although Nev got the forecast up in the first. How does he do that?

I had a winner at Chepstow, Sausalito Sunrise, which I'd just about glimpsed on the Ladbrokes screen in between bobbing heads and pints of Hogsback T.E.A. I was busy celebrating enthusiastically before I clocked the long odds-on price. That took the wind out a little.

The magnefique Sire De Grugy didn't let us down though. Bacchy had scoured the rails bookies and found a bit of 2-1 for a significant slice of the Butts whip. Jamie Moore had the horse in a fraction too close to a couple of the railway fences and the horse had looked plenty more fluent round here on other occasions. It didn't matter. The class kicked in and just before the last he reeled in Captain Conan and came up the home straight tidily enough. That was a special moment.

Nick did the honours of collecting the hard cash from Cecil Howells, Bookmaker. I was acting the fool, taking photos and generally whooping it up. The bloke behind Nick was grinning at me. "We don't win very often!" I excused and then took his photo as well.

Racing is finished by mid-afternoon in early December. This means the drinking starts dangerously early too. Pre-race beers before the first at 12.20 through to a post meeting session kicking in from about 4pm in the Wheatsheaf on the green. Such things take their toll. On the way home, Si, Pete and I were able to give convincing accounts of how we were vigorously and persistently chatted up by the attractive, merry, female remnants of a pub Christmas party.

Whether or not the rest of the boys bought our hazy recollections, what is beyond unsubstantiated claim was that Bacchy found a quid on his way out, which he donated to the whip. Thus the fighting fund nudged the £300 mark.

Long after we had disbursed the winnings from this successful series, Butts Mott reappeared. She had been given a long, well earned rest after her Angel of the North heroics. The industry had voted her 'Bitch of the Year 2013' and the dog enjoyed some down time at the Elderberry Racing stables in Monmore. She was trained by Patricia Cowdrill, whose late husband Pat Ryan had established the kennels. Many had considered Pat to be one of the shrewdest judges in the game and from the same mould as the legendary dog trainer Charlie Lister.

Butts was set to work again the following Summer. She was entered in the Brighton Belle, a series almost as prestigious as the previous year's. After a couple of sluggish runs, she once more hit top gear, attacking the bends with relish in the semi and cruising in to the final. The lovely bitch was saddled with the remnants of another of the lads' whip by this stage, though more modest than the previous outing. We had availed ourselves of 8-1 after the first qualifier.

A week before the final, the camp had this to say:

> *Well tonight's the night Lads. We got a great draw in the semis and a bastard of a draw in the final - got the 4 box with the fav in 5. I am not bothered about anything else to be honest. The 5-dog has gone 20 spots faster than us last week but we will find the 20 spots next week no bother. Spoke to Pete and he thinks we will lead the 5 into the bend, then we will see if she still has the old sparkle. If she has she will win........ Fingers crossed. She has won out of the 4 trap before and it is a nice long run up to the first bend at Hove.*

And on the night of the race:

> *Just spoke to Pete who is just giving her the final walk before they set of for Hove. He has got her as well as can be expected in the time we have had. She's beginning to*

come into her own again now, muscles becoming more predominate through her coat. It's in the lap of the gods now.... We will know by 9-25 tonight...

Again the syndicate was spot on its analysis. The Butts slammed home. The Racing Post, at its incisive, alliterative best declared that "Blistering Butts blasts Brighton Belle babes" Fantastic! I could write this stuff! Jim Cremin went on to report "The bitches' feature, worth £2,500 to the winner, fell to Patricia Cowdrill's Monmore raider as she cut across her rivals on her inside, and then resisted a surge from favourite Roxholme Dream who found crowding on the opening bends. It was Butts Mott's 18th win from 23 starts. Her record makes her one of the most formidable bitches of recent years."

The success of Butts meant a lot to connections. Patricia posted a comment on her website to say, "Sometimes dreams do come true and with Butts Mott we live that dream every day."

The story ends there really. She ran a couple more times that Winter, but her form was a little below par and this wonderful hound was gracefully retired without further ado. I haven't backed a dog since.

30. RASPBERRIES

I can't believe it. I was never on the bridle. I was never in the race.
The whole field was in front of me for the whole race.
I had to sit and suffer the whole way.
Davey Russell, Gold Cup winning jockey aboard Lord Windermere,
2014

The comedown. I was laid at the bottom of the stairs like an uncoiled slinky dog, limp and tension-free. All latent energy consumed and potential dissipated after a headlong, blinkered rush.

Back to life, back to reality, as Soul II Soul accurately recorded. Crumpled there in the shadow of the bottom step, I found a moment for reflection and gathered together a few indicators of the pleasure and pain, joy and grief, stimulation and banality that comprised Festival 2014:

Feeling the quality

It was interesting to see the ratings published for Lord Windermere's Gold Cup. Both Bob's Worth and Silviniaco Conti ran at about a stone below their best. The quickish ground a contributing factor, no doubt, but the way Conti struggled up the hill was alarming. Not a high class renewal, but quite a spectacle.

Many judges, both sound and otherwise, questioned the form of the Champion Hurdle too. The New One being the recipient of favourable analyses because of the ground he lost avoiding the ill-fated Our Conor. To the naked eye, I wasn't so sure. He conceded a few lengths after the third flight but was back on the heels of the leading group at the top of the hill. He then seemed to get outpaced, something he has a tendency to do in his races. Twiston Davies galvanised him eye-catchingly well up the hill, of course, to prompt the unlucky epithets.

No doubts about the World Hurdle as the race of the meeting for me. More Of That storming away from Annie Power after a right old ding-dong in a deep renewal of the race was a defining moment of the Festival. And happy retirement Big Buck's.

Mullins was all about quality. His brace of high class novices confirmed their early season promise: Vautour stylishly crushed my Supreme dreams (again) and Faugheen dismissed rivals and hurdles alike in a brutal Neptune victory. Quevega probably put in her most unconvincing performance in landing a record-breaking 6th Festival win.

Jockeys in focus

Injuries took high profile, encapsulated by Daryl Jacob's crazy week. Despair when nosed out of the Pertemps Final to elation winning the County Hurdle, swiftly followed by smashing bones and a hospital bed. His fall from Port Melon was a freak. Jockeys are used to landing on turf. Catapulted into the concrete via a camera crew is a different matter. Ruby's broken arm, suffered in the Triumph was also a horrible fall. Bryan Cooper and Paul Townend suffered other injuries. McCoy typically rode through his injury and stood himself down after the Festival had closed.

Ruby Walsh found plenty of telly and press coverage. Not all of it as sympathetic as his Channel 4 three-part cosy chat with Mick FitzGerald. Walsh's remarks about Our Conor were seized upon with frenzy by certain sections of the media peddling an ill thought through line from PETA. Walsh said, "It's sad, but horses are animals, outside your back door. Humans are humans. They are inside your back door. You can replace a horse. You can't replace a human being". Far from a callous, ruthless dismissal of the beasts he bonds with day-in, day-out, this was simply a reasonable, if clumsily expressed, reminder that people matter most.

Redemption for Davey Russell. Having lost the top job at Gigginstown to Cooper, Russell claimed the ultimate compensation with a short-headed, steward-queried victory on 20-1 shot Gold Cup winner Lord Windermere. "For Davy Russell this has been a redemptive week and he wouldn't have expected more personal miracles if they had transferred the Cheltenham Festival to Lourdes." Alastair Down in the Racing Post.

Textual torment

Whilst sinking a Guinness or two in the Desert Orchid Bar with Bacchy, Mrs A texted to say RMT union leader, Bob Crowe had died. The same moment, Nev texted to say he and Si were nearly there and to get double rounds in. "Jesus", I replied. "What a shock". And then, "Sorry Nev – meant that for my wife. Bob Crowe has died." Nev didn't bat an eyelid. Back he came with "Yeah. Charlton's Chris Powell has just been sacked as well." Bacchy remarked it was fortuitous that I cocked up the response that way round. A "piss off and get your own drinks" text to Mrs A would have bordered on inappropriateness.

After Western Warhorse nicked the Arkle at 33-1 by no more than a curled lip, my Bruv texted "Well that makes the 40 to follow interesting, doesn't it?" I had been storming the tri-lateral competition by a good 25 points. Western Warhorse was on his list and this did indeed change things. My instantaneous response, 'Pies off', was the result of a sanctimonious spellchecker intervention. A correctly syntaxed 'Piss Off' followed a good two minutes later.

That didn't help my mood. I had descended into grumpy bastard mode after a complete blow out in the Supreme and then the Arkle. After Jezki landed the Champion Hurdle for me by the smallest margin (how many desperately close finishes at this festival?), Bacchy texted, 'Happy Now? Guinness Bar'. But sent it to the wrong Dave. Dave Briscoe, a million miles away, replied 'Trust you are at the Festival! Go girl!'

War horses

I was desperately sorry to see the demise of Raya Star in the Grand Annual. A high class horse and one I had followed for a couple of years. Our Conor, stunning Triumph winner only the year before, was of course a big loss.

Briar Hill broke his cheekbone after a crunching smackdown. It looked like he may have fared worse but will in fact live to fight another day.

Last Instalment was retired after injuring a tendon for a third time. He'd already done two and had recovered magnificently. At least this way he avoids the full house. Sensible decision.

Big day for Gigginstown

£1 risked on their eventual 82,653-1 final day four-timer would have seen a satisfying return. Apparently this is just what happened to someone in O'Leary's box. Tiger Roll 10-1, Very Wood 33-1, Don Poli 10-1 and Savello 16-1. Four different trainers and three different jockeys.

False steps

"Two false starts in the Gold Cup. It isn't only the Grand National whose starts can make us look silly to the watching world." From Twittersphere.

The bottom line

A hard cash profit of £147 and a return on investment of 35%. Solid enough. The portfolio whimpered a little on days 3 & 4 after roaring magnificently in the first half of this epic punting marathon. But I'm certainly happy with that. Jezki was an early, magnificent highlight. Once again, Day 2 proved to be my most profitable. Sire De Grugy, already a firm favourite with the boys, filled the coffers a little more with an emotional win. And ante-posts were most definitely back in favour. O'Faolains Boy won the RSA Chase at 16-1 after I'd backed him before the Reynoldstown at 33-1.

Fantasy Festival

Always an absolute scream. This year the lead changed hands about 10 times over the four days, including three on the final day. After

Adam somehow found the winner of the Gold Cup he overtook Bryn to occupy the box seat at the start of the last leg. I tried to reassure Ad that the compo was very rarely won on the back of the murky lottery that is the Grand Annual – knowing that's exactly what had happened to me a few years before. (If I ever hear the words 'Tiger' and 'Cry' in the same sentence, I come out in hives.) Yet it happened again. Much respect to Paddy. Backing outsiders had been his hard-and-fast strategy all week. So it was fitting that Savello was produced like an ace from the massing pack and won comfortably at 16-1. Top competition once again.

The Barley Mow

Scene of betting bedlam and beery bullshit from noon until midnight. A glorious, raggedy, indulgent celebration.

Nev was back at the scene of his diabetes break down last year. His regime after a prolonged hospital stay last year had initially been rigorous. He lost weight, cut down on the drinking and ate healthily. The sight of him supping Pinot Grigio in the Mow was enough to mess with your head. The new order didn't last too long. Before this Festival, the weight had gone back on and the Guinness was flowing. He was carrying condition.

The Butts Mott whip, so carefully cultivated over the winter was ready to be harvested at the Festival. We had big dreams. And yet… Doesn't it always go this way? Somehow, carefully studied form lines and strategic analysis disappeared in a wave of unsatisfactory punting by committee. We recklessly backed a cross-section of animals with variable chances, including some wretched sentimental cash on Hurricane Fly. Famous dreams of Cheltenham doubles and value thievery later in the Festival slid away with those day 1 & 2 bets.

In the end, there was no appetite left to punt any more of the hard earned Butts Mott pool on Gold Cup day; only for more beer. Nick got his long argued way. In that sublime afternoon, we drank the substantial remainder of the Butts Mott whip right through to a glorious, but ultimately dusty and dry emptiness, richly toasting the slippery greyhound's good health as we went.

Highlights of the day became hazy to capture crisply after that. Later, much, much later, Colin was down on his knees at the feet of grown men, blowing… dirty big raspberries on anybody's belly he could access. Bryn was one reluctant recipient. Paddy, another, though touched by this endearing act, decided enough was enough and took Col home.

And then there was the arm wrestling. Well why not? Si contrived to let me win one bout and when I asked him why he had capitulated he beamed "Cos I love you, man!" Otherwise, Si and Steve seemed to sweep all before them.

It was a fine night. Some of the less obvious wreckage emerged over the next few days in texts and tweets. I found on my phone a pissed, sentimental, 'I-really-love-you-guys' text from Bryn tottering around a suburban station somewhere, extolling the camaraderie of the gang. Then it emerged Si got stranded in London after the pub shut and had to whistle up the accommodation services of an ex-girlfriend. Steve it transpired also missed trains and buses. He was left to taxi-it all the way home from Upminster.

Rinsed. The lot of us.

And finally

I love David Ashworth. His – these days, rare – pieces for the Racing Post are a scream. He has a wry take on life and on racing. I tittered at a couple of choice pieces from his insanely brilliant column after the Festival closed, entitled 'Your Cheltenham questions answered…'

> *Dear Sir*
> *On Tuesday I backed Champagne Fever, My Tent Or*
> *Yours and Shotgun Paddy. On Wednesday I backed*
> *Smad Place, Get Me Out Of Here and Any Currency. On*

Thursday it was Southfield Theatre. I am thinking of killing myself. What can I do?

Dear Ernest
Your own suggestion seems a reasonable one. Did you back them each way?

Dear Sir
Would you believe it? I'm from Rochdale and in 1996 I went to their home game against Cardiff City. Cardiff's in south Wales and Fingal Bay's in New South Wales but I didn't think of it until after Fingal Bay won the Pertemps final. How unlucky can you be? I hate racing.

Dear Stephen
I sympathise with you because, only last week, I commented on how many hawks you see nowadays and, lo and behold, Hawk High wins the Fred Winter Juvenile Hurdle at 33-1. So you don't need to tell me about bad luck.

Time to recoil the spring.

31. GROUP C

I lost my balance, making my body unstable and falling on top of my
opponent.
At that moment I hit my face against the player,
leaving a small bruise on my cheek and a strong pain in my teeth.
Louis Suarez, 2014

Summertime Rolls, as Jane's Addiction sharply observed back in 1988. I don't think they were talking about bread-based picnic provisions.

The fireworks had barely expired at the glittering World Cup 2014 in Brazil and yet the papers reverted to transfer gossip and manager mind-game-mongering with unseemly haste. Back to their bread-and-butter rumour-milling. The domestic season always seems to kick on with fever, leaving moments, events and experiences struggling for attention in its dusty Summer trail.

In football terms, the tournament is remembered as a success. We enjoyed more goals scored than in any of the previous Finals; witnessed some electrifying skill (Van Persie's arched back header will live long in the memory); confirmed a new generation of talent (Rodriguez looked sublime) and marvelled at vibrant, emotional, spine tingling support from the home nation. And the best team won.

Brazil's problems won't go away because of that hosting success. The controversial investment in the World Cup and 2016's Olympic Games at the perceived expense of local jobs, facilities, housing and transport will continue to spark fervent protests. Even Daughter No 2 boycotted the matches as a mark of solidarity with the locals who were 'developed' out of their homes. Then again, she hates football, so the real value of her sacrifice is difficult to calculate… At least there was some opportunity to raise the profile of these issues. Amongst them, I thought the Rio in Rio programme was excellent. If inevitably more about the player than the slums. The sections with the kids in the favelas were really well put together.

Shame England's brief contribution didn't match the overall panache of the event. For the Costa Rica game, Nick had sensibly reserved a couple of tables in The Barley Mow. We reasoned that it might be a cliffhanger. Sadly, England's tenuous grip on the chalk face had long since eroded. Their chances lay crumpled and forgotten at the bottom of the sheer slope, battered by wind and wave. By the time the game came around, only half of us half-heartedly turned up.

Whilst our beers flowed with unaffected regularity, it was curious to observe only distracted viewing of the game by those present, together with the higher level of background banter. The evening's defining moment came after the dreadful 0-0 draw had concluded and the remaining punters got the telly turned over to watch Jimmy Anderson and Mo Ali almost bat out a heroic draw against the Sri Lankans. Every ball that Jimmy survived in the final few overs was greeted by a louder cheer than anything we had seen for the football. And when he capitulated to a fierce rising delivery, the match's penultimate ball, we were crushed. At least it was a genuine moment. Something real for the indifferent crowd to get behind.

England's footballing travails registered barely a perceptible blot on the tournament. By contrast the 2010 World Cup in South Africa as a whole was more blot than tournament. As a football spectacle most commentators agreed that the quality of the action was low. This merely continued a declining trend that began four years previously in Germany. Whilst South Africa saw (arguably) less blatant diving, air-card waving and general referee pressurising, there was a desperate rise in the level of well organised defences, negative tactics and cynical play.

Technically proficient European coaches bringing about massive improvements to the defensive qualities of uninspiring African, Asian and Australasian teams are certainly part of the explanation. It is far easier to coach organisation, discipline and tactical awareness than it is to produce brilliance, creativity and invention in a squad of average footballers. Alchemy would be easier.

So it was interesting to catch up with my friend Karen who is a bona-fide globe-trotting England footie fan. She and her brother had recently returned from Rio and Brasilia, having watched four group-stage games and one quarter final. That quarter-final had been Germany's spectacular 7-1 demolition of Germany in Belo Horizonte: Brazil's first competitive home defeat in 39 years.

The game had been the highlight of the trip, naturally. She recounted the two clearest incidents that stood out. First the tear-filled passion and pride with which the home fans threw themselves into singing their national anthem. That came across on the telly loud enough. Being there sounded incredible. Secondly, the real physical pain and wretchedness that those same fans felt after the brutal manner of the defeat. The old epithet about football being more than a religion to Brazilian fans hardly does the strength of feeling justice. Karen made it sound like the game was the very fabric of life and death, irrespective of gender and generation.

In waxing lyrical about the tournament, I was surprised to learn that as an all round experience she had enjoyed her trip to the World Cup hosted in South Africa much more. There had been something about the magnificence of the landscape and the journey of the people that stood out. At the time, South Africa's reputation for tourist-focused crime was through the roof, and yet, football aside, Karen's highlights were trips to the Soweto township. Amongst the squalor and painful contrasts with the rich suburbs across Johannesburg, the spirit of ubuntu was alive and well, 'I am, because we are'. She saw the unity, togetherness and the emotional connection that thrives in the townships. Conditions were improving, too. New housing and facilities were slowly replacing the worst excesses of apartheid control.

I tried to get the girls interested in the World Cup that year. At 12 and 10 I thought they were ready. So it was that Daughter No 2 and I were poring over the pull-out from The Observer in early June.

"Who will you be supporting then Cathy?" I inquired, rather hopefully.

She looked at the double spread before her. Pondered the fixtures. Glanced at the team names and then uttered quite convincingly,

"Group C."

I can see that I still have some way to go....

32. BACK TO CATTERICK

To Redcar on the Costa Del Teesside for the inaugural running of the Alastair Down Gravestone Selling Stakes for which the first prize is £1,706.
Almost the exact sum that it costs in petrol to drive there.
Alastair Down, Racing Post 2011.

Down's acerbic, tongue-in-cheek feeling about Redcar, matched my own about Catterick Bridge. I hadn't been to that particular outpost for about 25 years. My previous experiences weren't very positive.

Ramshackle grandstands, fizzy beer and crap racing, as this chunk of Mug Punting makes clear, scarred my formative punting years:

> *....Catterick was worse. The track was surrounded by towering piles of unwanted spoil from the adjacent quarries carved disrespectfully out of prime Yorkshire moorland. An ugly, crusty and polluted lake covered much of the inside of the track which served to encourage the feeling of dereliction. It was a hole of a course with no facilities to speak of. I stumbled across a gem of a book called 'Cope's Racegoers Encyclopaedia 1962'. Leafing through its mottled pages I discovered that 'in January 1961 Catterick Bridge opened a £30,000 new stand which provides facilities previously undreamed off at this small Yorkshire course'. That must have been the twisted pile of rusty iron and crumbling grey brick that I could see across the track. The intervening 27 years had not been kind.*

> *We used to populate a brick outhouse construction in the silver ring where we partook of fizzy keg bitter, traditional for the time (long before widgets had been thought of) from a dirty pump dispensing beer and Legionnaires Disease in equal measure. The only food to be had was a hot dog/burger van outside the bogs. I had*

had enough of burgers one desperate Friday afternoon so I asked the bored 'sales assistant' for a cheese sandwich as advertised. The guy took one of his burger buns, slapped in a sliver of plastic unmelted dairylea and charged me £1.50 of my hard-granted wedge! I was appalled.

There was no way of seeing the horses all the way round the track from where we were herded. The quality of racing was always as miserable as the course. At least there was the outside chance of a decent race every so often at Redcar. I never, ever had a winner at either Catterick or Redcar and I never, ever want to go back there.

Dad and Bruv began to frequent the track regularly about five years ago and I never missed a chance to scoff and taunt about gaff tracks. Bruv would with rejoin with "So why does McCain send his best novices there then? Why did Grand National winner Ballabrigs have his prep run there? Eh? Why did Jonjo send up Holywell last year? He's favourite for the Gold Cup now y'know." Bollocks. "Well they wouldn't have risked them if they knew how good the horses were. Obviously a trainer mistake."

Despite my grumpy response, it was clear that the track had come to be held in fair regard by local trainers at least, and evidently by yards further afield as well. The time had arrived for a grudging repeat visit.

We picked the track's first jumps meeting of the season and I steeled myself for Class 6 three-runner novice chases viewed from broken plastic chairs.

3rd December dawned crisply clear and frosty. I was at King's Cross by the time weak daylight hit the northbound rails and at that point I did have a quick shufty at the Racing Post site to confirm that the cold night hadn't jeopardised the fixture.

The RP also showed me that the races were pretty healthy fields of between 9 and 16 (apart form a 7 runner novice event) across a mixed card of hurdles, chases, bumpers and handicaps. Not much wrong with that. And I also spied that Nicky Henderson had sent up an expeditionary force of three novices to wick away some modest Yorkshire prize money.

I texted Bruv to make sure we were all still on track. That I got a reply represents progress. Text speak is not his forte. When Dad and Bruv looked after the girls recently, he texted them to say what time they would be arriving. He signed off with a 'U.P.' as in 'Uncle Paul'. The girls thought this attempt at txt spk was spectacularly funny and marvellously off-point. Clearly Bruv is not down with the kids (in the way that his older sibling is, obviously). Daughter No 2 was so tickled that she took a photo of the text for posterity. I think it was the grammatically correct use of the full stops that sent them over the edge.

Last year, Daughter No 2 was at home when she received a text from Grandad's mobile phone. Except there was no text. Just a blank message. She found Mrs A and said,
"Mummy, I think Grandad just tried to text me".

Mrs A looked and thought she's better phone my Bruv.

"Just checking everything's OK, Paul. Catherine received an empty message from your Dad."

"Oh, I see" said Paul. "I think that means he's ready to be picked up after his haircut. I told him to text me when he was done. Better go, thanks, byee". Modern communication is a marvellous thing.

Northallerton Station was largely deserted as I stepped down from the train, save for a stout fellow blocking out the low sun and casting a weak, wintry shadow down the platform. It turned out to be my Bruv. Everything was going to plan. Dad was already in the motor and we were navigating the narrow lanes to Catterick in an instant, glibly exchanging exaggerated opinions about the quality of the track. "Hope they've tidied away the discarded quarry gear from the

2 mile start", was my concluding hope, "really messes up the action of those juveniles."

Having blatantly set myself up for the inevitable climb down, I'm secretly delighted to report that first impressions of the track were considerably more favourable than on my last visit. I blame the sunshine. It flooded the venue with spirited rays and threw the surrounding northern fells into glorious sharp relief. The old grandstands may not have had any structural investment for many a long year, but at least they had had a lick of paint that gleamed and reflected back the light for all it was worth. The bright weather had bestowed a cheery disposition on the ticketing manager too. She supplied my outstanding-value punters package from her snug office with a smile and fine welcome: 22 quid for a grandstand ticket, the dish of the day in the café, a pint, a Tote bet and a racecard. Dad and Bruv eyed my stash enviously.

Inside, the stands had been dragged into the 21st century. Comfy chairs, bench seats and carpets replaced Formica tables and broken bucket seats. The beer was a passable pint of Tetley's and the dish of the day was chilli and rice. I was happy. Until I saw the pies. We had noticed people obviously queuing by the bar, but not buying anything. Then surly Sandra (she needed to get out into the sunshine) brought in a tray piled high with crusty fare. "Pies are here now!" she announced and began fulfilling the orders of those in the well-behaved procession. We all looked longingly at the firm, round meat and potato, beef and onion and chicken offerings. Though perhaps less longingly at the puce-coloured accompaniment of indeterminate state somewhere between mushy peas and East End liquor, ladled on top of the pies. The green gunge didn't particularly appeal but I really wish I'd saved my token for one of the stout looking pieces of pastry perfection underneath.

It wasn't all about pies though. The racing offered morsels of nourishment too. We watched most of the heats from the top of the steppings, squinting in to low sun, as horses lapped the compact, undulating track. Decent viewing - a nine furlong circuit meant the beasts passed the stands three times in a 3 mile event. The addition of a large screen was welcome progress from my previous visits. It was sited in the silver ring, adjacent to the stand that I had berated as inhospitable in those student days. The building still didn't look much. I'm sure it was lovely inside though…

We all had winners. Sue Smith, whose horses "always improve for a fence" according to Bruv had a good day with her novice chasers. I was on the right side of Oorayvic in the 2nd race. She also had Grate Fella later who won powerfully at a staggering 10-1. The market was made by Henderson's Cocktails At Dawn, who went off odds-on, fell and then ran through the running rail after the line. He bucked and kicked a bit but seemed fine when the stable staff collared him. Hendo's other two runners were also well backed but neither made the frame.

Dad and Bruv both struck in the lucky last: After Tonight looked good in the bumper. We all took away this improver from the mercurial David O'Meara as one to watch. But probably only around the northern circuit.

None of us were as fortunate as a Scottish guy sat next to us in the bar though. Cooking Fat, a flashy chestnut, had won the juvenile novice hurdle in much better style than his odds of 66-1 suggested. Medicine Hat, at the same price, followed him home. This bloke had contrived to combine them in a minimum stakes exacta, paying out at 701-1. He was more shocked than jubilant. The good ladies in the Tote booth had to fleece all the other Tote windows at the track, empty the manager's safe and rummage around the stashes in their knickers to settle his bet.

The chat in the bar was good natured, clique free and indiscriminate. Just before the Scottish exacta sting, we were debating whom to back in that very juvenile event. We were looking at Scrafton. "Aye. Quinny's got a good record here", muttered someone. An old lag piped up "Aye. He's here as well!" Dad picked up on that. "Quinny's here is he?" It was echoed by a couple on the next table. Soon, "Quinny's here" was murmuring its way round the bar. We all looked at Scrafton's figures a bit more closely. The old lag again: "Mind you, he's got two in this race…"

I reflected on a top day as I stood on the southbound platform back at Northallerton, watching the sun dissolve out of an orange sky above the goods line. Catterick has come far. My opinion of this well-appointed, comfortable track with entertaining, competitive racing had risen immeasurably, as it was always destined to do. The over-riding feeling was of a friendly, informal venue. Emblematic was David O'Meara, welcoming back horse and rider into the winner's enclosure and yet having time to acknowledge the genuine greetings and well-wishes from departing racegoers.

And as I climbed aboard the Euston express, I recognised the sentiments, if not the reality, of a crusty farmer sat on the terracing of that 1961 grandstand, belly hanging over his worn cords like Kilnsey Crag. He could have been there since its construction. He said to an accomplice, "Well, I've never left Yorkshire meself. Not in all maa born days. Never seen t'need to, to be honest with 'e".

Three days later I was at the other end of the scale for the boys' annual Sandown Tingle Creek trip. The fixture was blessed with the same winter sunshine as Catterick, but otherwise the venues inhabit different universes. This fixture is a perennial seasonal highlight, even if it was lacking in the depth of quality seen in previous years. I'm not sure what my crusty farmer would have made of the hen parties, mulled wine and lairiness, but thank heaven there is room for both worlds in the fixture list.

33. BETTER THAN CHRISTMAS

A pal of mine sent me a text this morning, saying 'I'm wishing you the worst day
in bookmaking history', which I thought was quite good.
Willie Mullins after Douvan won the Supreme, 2015

It seems only right that one of the closing chapters in this ten-year stock take should focus on Cheltenham. The festival itself occupies such a central position in my year, with the agitation of virtual notebooks and ante-post markets starting ridiculously early in the season.

For the 2015 renewal, my anxious, studious but heartily misinformed prep had taken its customary knocks. Not that this stopped me from pontificating confidently to anyone who would listen, and many who wouldn't, about the chances of various runners. A shiny, sharp-quiffed young fella-me-lad had started work at my Camden base. Top bloke. Sports development was his business. He liked a punt too, mostly on the football, though he'd had a few decent days out at the races too.

Well it didn't take me long to start calling the odds with enough bravado to sow insidious seeds in his untarnished mind. Classic badinage that might suggest to the uninitiated that I knew what I was talking about. If that really was the case, why did I promulgate a first-day four-timer constructed entirely around Willie Mullins' barn? Douvan, Un De Sceaux, Faugheen, Annie Power. Ridiculous.

A couple of days later, at the very moment that quiff-chap was asking if his acca was still safe and I was saying that the weak link was probably Douvan, Bacchy was sowing some mischief of his own. We were in the middle of a protracted e-mail transfer window for our 12 Horses To Follow stables. "Douvan doesn't go in the Supreme", wound Steve and cheekily sent us scuttling to Twitter and various racing fora. Nothing. "Wind up", I eventually said to my young colleague. Bacchy had achieved his objective all the same.

Earlier in the week, Bacchy, Si, Nev and I had met up in the Willow Walk to talk proper racing and put the final touches to the logistical operation. Si and I planned to stay with some friends in Cheltenham who would be shipping out their children to make room. Nev would be berthed in the chocolate box Bourton-on-the-Water. And Bacchy… well, Bacchy, it transpired, would be staying at home. He confessed over a few beers that he would not, after all, be joining us. As in other years, his school commitments during term time were a problem. A precedent had been set in 2014 when he snuck away for Champion Hurdle Day. It seemed, however, that a repeat was not on the cards now that Bacchy's missus and head teacher had resumed her steely grip on direct line management duties.

It was a long and drunken night. Again. On the way home, Bacchy and I paid a visit to the rather fine kebab house on Vauxhall Bridge Road. I was still stuffing it in my face whilst stood on the tube. Bad form, I know. Needs must.

I became aware of this gorgeous young woman who had sidled up to me. She asked for a bite of my kebab. I chuckled and asked what was she offering in return. I realised she was with two conspirational chaps sat opposite who were egging her on mercilessly. So she started fondling her left breast. I value my kebabs pretty highly, so I pointed to the other one as well. Too bad the tube lurched into Euston at just that point.

Bacchy apparently had no such luck. He agreed that his kebab was indeed very good, but found that his body rejected it rather violently the next morning, during morning assembly. And then again at break time.

Si fared the worst of all. Claiming that the fresh air assassin assaulted him, he missed his train and ended up in the Victoria Wetherspoons with another pint. The last train home was delayed, then diverted and he needed a cab home. His phone had died by that point. When he awoke the next morning he found that his boiler was broken.

Staying in the town itself, at the very epicentre of the Festival fiesta was a long held ambition. It is the natural aspiration of any regular Festival stalwart. However it is harder to pull off than you might imagine. Securing a berth in the hallowed heart of this Regency gem is either an exorbitantly expensive or frustratingly booked-up undertaking. Had Mary & Joseph pitched up here for the virgin birth, the only way they would have found a stable would have been to part-own the favourite for the Supreme. In which case any Irish landlady would have willingly thrown open her doors.

There is another way. What you need are some very good mates who are happy to convert their splendid abode into a 5-star b&b for the duration. Best result of the week. Chris and Laura, impeccable hosts, looked after us wonderfully. And it was not without some risk on their part. Yes, they knew me. And I could vouch for Si. But they had never met Nev before… Still, the behaviour benchmark was fractionally lower than we had anticipated. "Have they been sick on the carpet yet?" had asked Laura's Mum.

Nev only joined us at Chris and Laura's on Wednesday morning. He had booked into a tidy spot in Bourton-on the-Water before the Cheltenham opportunity became available. He made his mark though. Within half an hour, he was hammering away at our hosts' generously lent laptop, trying to find and then print his Wednesday ticket. Because he'd lost it. Honestly, what sort of total prat would do such an idiotic thing?

Well, me for one. A few years ago I spilled out of the first day, exhausted and winner-free, saying to Bacchy that I'd avoid any confusing ticketing issues by ripping up that day's expired voucher and chucking it away. I realised the next morning that I had, nervelessly, trashed the 2nd day ticket by mistake. That was an expensive tout-job to get in.

And Bryn for another. After leaving our Tewksbury base for the track at our very first three-day adventure, he realised he'd left all our tickets back at the ranch.

Nev was unable to recover the e-mail with the all important pdf attachment. Neither could he wring any support from the Jockey Club. After getting a runaround from their sales team that would make the Cross Country course look like a straight five furlong sprint, he gave up. Laura had already done so, having dashed out of the front door some minutes earlier with a yoga mat tucked under her arm. Peace for body and mind. Si and I thought about joining her.

Approaching the collection booth up at the track was a lot more fruitful. Nev decided on a tête à tête with the ticket lady. Literally. He stuck his head so far through the half-window that he was on tip-toes with his builder's backside in the air. "Go and do something funny with Nev", said Si, priming his phone camera. I demurred. There are enough of those kinds of photos of me in circulation already…

This in-yer-face approach worked. Nev got his ticket re-emailed, which he then downloaded to his phone so the man could scan it with the magic machine at the turnstiles.

Faugheen was the highlight of Ruby Tuesday. We were stood by the rail in glorious sunshine watching the tactics unfold on the big screen. It was hard to judge the pace but when The New One and then Jezki came almost alongside to lay down a proper challenge, the excitement was palpable. And then, easy as you like, at top of the home straight, Ruby let out a little bit of Faugheen's tight reign and whispered "go". Did he go! The roar from the stands opposite, in all my 16 festivals, was the loudest, most spine-tingling sensation I've ever experienced. I'll probably say the same next year.

This was the third leg of the famous bookie-busting four-timer that never was. The opening leg was my first Supreme win ever, Douvan. However, that status remains in some doubt because the wager was struck with William Hill as a qualifier for a free bet in their massive Supreme give-away. "Does it count?" I texted Bacchy. "Does it fuck", came the reply about three seconds later. Fair enough.

By the fourth leg, Nev had found himself in a deep (but fairly one-sided) conversation with a broad scouser, made more unintelligible still by his level of intoxication. Nev was trying to explain that his three-timer rested on Annie Power winning the mares race. Scouser dribbled something back that involved a fair amount of "eerrrraaaarrrffkkkknnncchhhhhhhhhh" running into "fffkkkkkcccccchhhhhhhuuuaaarrcchhhh". I've never seen Nev silenced. He couldn't understand a word. His jaw was hanging loose. Si always has a canny ear for an accent and translated. Between them they informed Scouser that it was "a mares race…lady horses". Scouser looked askance and then responded (after translation) "I don't want a fucking education! I want a fucking winner!"

When Annie Power overreached at the last flight and triggered a ticker-tape storm of spent fourfold slips, there were immediate cries of bookie collusion and thrown-race allegations around us. Punters always want someone to blame. The fantasy could not have been better scripted if Fleet Street hacks had authored it themselves. News stories later in the day about bookie share prices falling sharply and then rising again just added to the drama. Great stuff.

Sharp-quiffed young fellah-me-lad had a bit of good natured grief for me when I returned to the office. He'd shown his four-timer slip to a few mates and they had followed him in. To be honest, I think he had rather enjoyed the ride and the sense of being part of something big.

Si is the handicap king. No question. Coming in to the festival he'd punted Ebony Express (33-1) in the Imperial Cup and Violet Dancer (20-1) in the Betfair Hurdle. Across those four tumultuous Festival days, he went on to find The Druid's Nephew in the 3 mile chase on Tuesday, Killultagh Vic in the Martin Pipe on Friday and a good few placed horses besides. He also had Quantitativeasing bustled out of the way by Toutancarmont in the Cross Country when being wound up by Nina Carberry for a decisive thrust.

For my handicap contribution, I found Call The Cops in Thursday's Pertemps Final after being impressed with his easy win two weeks before at Doncaster. Bacchy, in his fantasy festival update to the lads saw it another way:

"Three years ago Davoski collected a stack when Call The Police finished a remote third in Bobs Worth's RSA Chase. So naturally he backed Call The Cops today. Finding easy winners like that - it's what life's all about."

Cheeky bastard. So much for blood, tears, toil and sweat.

It wasn't just the handicaps that fell prey to Si's voracious appetite. He was feasting everywhere: Windsor Park in the Neptune; Vautour in the JLT; Martello Tower in the Albert Bartlett. He also had Moon Racer in the Bumper. But I didn't mind that because I was on myself at a reasonably good ante-post price. My biggest winner of the Festival. I celebrated by smashing my half pint of Guinness into the ground in front of the big screen and taking a bow. A bloke in a fluffy-hooded parka came up and wrapped his arms round me. "Did you win or lose?" he shouted. Really?

All that winning took some serious celebrating. This is where our exquisite pad in Cheltenham came into its own. And where Nev's in Bourton didn't. Fed up with paying £40 taxi fares, he headed home after racing on the last bus. Conversely, with the knowledge of only a short stagger home smugly tucked in our exit plans, Si and I picked up the craic in town. A few beers and a tasty curry were on the agenda.

We smashed the former and utterly bombed on the latter. The highlight of the boozers was the Bath Arms at the end of the night. The stars of the show in this intimate local were not the assorted festival goers, but a revelling birthday party crowd who took turns to dance on the chairs and tables. One of the lads trying to elicit the affection of birthday girl slapped down some eye-popping moves reminiscent of the helicopter dance by the beanpole in the Ladbrokes' advert. Si thought we could do better, but thankfully, we decided against putting that assertion to the test.

Finding a curry proved to be a challenge too far. The first restaurant was full of loud xenophobes; the second turned out to be a basement bar; and the third was rather too fine dining in price. The greasy chicken kebab and cardboard chips we ended up with from a takeaway joint was a total fail.

Nev was with us the next night when we celebrated our winners in the Queens Hotel, the legendary, almost mythical base of JP McManus and venue of the finest party in town: witness the gentleman on dance floor who could have passed for John Gosden in his heavyweight cashmere overcoat, navy Italian suit, silk tie, flapping members' badge and flashing black brogues, giving the Kaiser Chiefs large and punching the air with each Ruby, Ruby, Ruby, Ruby belted out by the band; or the group of young guys in front of us who had quite clearly clubbed together to buy the company of a couple of escorts for the evening and were awkwardly groping their way around their trophies who discreetly wagged fingers and whispered the rules of engagement when the lads went too far. All human life…

We shipped out early on Thursday morning. My call. Si was well up for another day at the track, but the bookies were laying evens that my liver would pack up fractionally before my wallet, well ahead of the Kim Muir amateurs' race.

Chris gave us a lift to the rail station. Above and beyond. If they had put their gaff on Trip Advisor, we would all have given it the full five blobs. There was further ticket trouble for Nev. This time the return rail ticket. He had to upgrade to an off-peak ticket from a super saver just to get through the barriers.

Uxizandre was my biggest winner on the Thursday, though it should have been bigger. The Alan King inmate was in my 40 to follow for the season, but I had lost confidence in this exuberant jumper and had only backed him to small stakes. I thought he had lost form. It was good ground he was waiting for. And a galvanising ride helped. McCoy at his brilliant best aboard his last ever Festival winner.

The star of that electric Thursday was not Uxizandre though, but Vautour in the JLT. Ruby was buzzing after he climbed down from one of the cleanest, boldest most exhilarating rounds of jumping seen at the track by a novice in a good few years. A dream Gold Cup renewal in 2016 is already being plotted by commentators that involves a triple-handed Mullins with Vautour, RSA winner Don Poli and this year's blue ribband runner up Djakadam taking on stunning all-the-way novice winner Coneygree.

All-the-way winners were a real feature of that classic Festival. Eight or so horses made all or nearly all to win big Grade 1s and handicaps alike. The usual win-strike rate for front runners is two or three across the entire piece. It's probably not a new trend, rather a mark of the quality of horses we've been treated to this year in a high-class exhibition.

£9.58. That was my total profit after 27 races and months of agonising. Head above water. Barely. There were some near misses though. The big one that got away was Road To Riches in the Gold Cup. My most confident bet. Landing that would have been a game changer. Whilst better ground would have been ideal, there are no complaints. He ran his race and was beaten by a tremendous horse on the day, who did not put a foot wrong.

I'm not sure that is how the Ladies of The Lamb saw it though. Earlier in the week, a certain Ms Johnson had e-mailed the good ladies and said:

"With a combination of the Cheltenham Festival and a boozy lunch at the Atkinsons in the offing, you should really know better than to leave me with the kitty. Let's just say, after a few beers and glasses of wine it again seemed to be a good idea to get Mr Atkinson to put the tenner to good use by turning it into lots of tenners using his enormous skill and judgement.

"Dave – please would you let us know which 'sure thing' we should cheer for on Friday as, I hope you realise, the hopes and dreams of the Ladies of the Lamb are resting on this."

Sadly, Road To Riches proved to be more like a cul-de-sac for the ladies' ambitions as well as my own. That was the second time I had let them down and I suspect a third chance will not come calling.

Fantasy Festival was an epic this year. Played out once again in the pressure cooker of the Barley Mow. Doubles had been landed all week to set up a dramatic final day. Running up to the Gold Cup, my Bruv was holding a slender advantage over Bryn. For some inexplicable reason, he decided to go all in on Silviniaco Conti, rather than playing a canny hand going in to the final competition race, the Grand Annual. Shedding his usual cloak of caution, Bruv predictably went down in a glorious ball of flame, handing the trophy and £170 notes to Bryn.

Many beers and then whiskies were consumed and yet it was probably a more restrained affair than last year. Certainly in the sense that we didn't descend into arm-wrestling competitions; most people got back to their actual homes as opposed to other peoples'; and Col didn't blow raspberries on the exposed bellies of variously assembled punters. Col remains the most enthusiastic and committed cheerleader (minus pom-pom) of our involvement in this monster Festival and its associated competitions. He landed a spectacular acca on that final day and strolled out of the pub declaring the week to be "better than Christmas".

I posted this account on the blog and there was some post-script electronic banter from the boys:

> *Bryn: Great blog, Davoski. However, a point of order if I may. Colin did in fact blow a raspberry on my belly.*
> *Colin: I shall have to take your word for this new information, Bryn. What I will say is that I would more than likely have left within five minutes of my signature greeting/ farewell.*
> *Bryn: It only came back to me when I read the blog. I think you did it when I mentioned that you hadn't done it to anyone yet. It was very tickly.*
> *Colin: That's fine, mate. It was a teasing invitation I could not resist.*
> *Nev: Just another week to forget - had to pay yet another taxi to get home on Saturday morning as I awoke late somewhere. It might have been Canning Town. Only twenty notes this time...*

And later,

> *Nev: And another addendum for the blog. I lost my oyster card on that faithful (sic) Friday 13th and only found out when I tried to embark on another trip to London a week later.*

After the week he had endured, it just had to be Nev to bring down the curtain.

34. LADIES DAY

Dress shabbily and they remember the dress;
dress impeccably and they remember the woman
Coco Chanel, designer, 1956

And so to Aintree. Second only to the magical Cheltenham in quality and importance at the top of the national hunt hierarchy. This season there was an extra week between the two equine festivals, courtesy of a religious one. This meant there was precious extra recovery time for trainers looking to send Cheltenham horses to Liverpool. Others bypassed Prestbury Park altogether in favour of competing fresh on the flatter, tighter track. And all-conquering Willie Mullins looked like sending more of his stars to Aintree than usual as well.

It was not just horses that welcomed the extra break. After a frenetic Cheltenham Festival, I was delighted to report that I had some welcome box rest, had eaten up and was looking forward to making my debut at the Grand National Festival.

We had taken a well-earned rest in Whitstable. Charming town, amazing sunsets, good friends. My only complaint was the lack of internet access. Yes, I'm all for low-fi-get-away-from-it-all breaks. Any time at all. Except when I need to make crucial, possibly life changing transfers in the jumps' season 12-to-follow competition. Going in to Aintree I was leading a ravenous pack snapping at my heels, and feeling confident about holding them at bay. It turned out that my inability to do any intensive web-based research into the stats, entries, forums, and general e-banter about the forthcoming Aintree meeting lost me the prize. Right there. Only I didn't know it at the time.

Packing up for home, I was doing a last sweep for dirty socks and hidden glasses upstairs when I missed out a step between the loft bedrooms. I went down like Latalomne at the second last and smashed my head in to the door. I could feel the sinews in the back of my neck crackle as my head was thrust back. It really hurt.

I had only two thoughts. The first, as I looked at the blood smeared door panel was, 'I hope we get our damage deposit back'; and the second was, 'I hope I don't get concussion that stops me going to Aintree'. On the way home the girls were told to keep poking me in case I fell asleep.

I was due to be there for Ladies Day the following Friday and I couldn't wait to finally get a sight of the famous track.

Bacchy and Debs swung by our place on the Thursday afternoon, first day of the meeting. Bacchy's finely crafted plan involved me joining them for a departure just before the Foxhunters so the three of us could hook up with their friends in Altrincham. From there to the races the next day.

The trip had its roots in a drunken conversation in the Mow during a Christmas drink. How many similar aspirations never even make it out of the pub door? So there was cause for smugness as we sat in our back garden, lapping up the Spring rays and contemplating a decent opening day card. My lumpy forehead, courtesy of that losing altercation with an intransigent Whitstable door, was no more than a last minute scare. The tennis ball on my left temple was receding by the hour.

We caught the majority of the action between the bookies and the telly, whilst Debs and Mrs A hit the hostelries.

Silviniaco Conti was brave in the Betfred Bowl, confirming, if further proof was needed, that Cheltenham is not his track. The Aintree Hurdle was disappointing. Arctic Fire looked booked for a comfortable win before Ruby took a tumble at the last, a la Annie Power. It denied us one last battle between this generation's pre-eminent jockeys. McCoy aboard Jezki was left to coast home unopposed.

The Foxhunters rolled around and no sign of the girls. We watched Nina Carberry complete an impressive Cheltenham-Aintree foxhunters double aboard On The Fringe. She may only have one way of riding, but it is very effective. She went on to bag the Punchestown equivalent too.

We bombed up to Altrincham in Bacchy's new, low-slung saloon, accompanied by The The and Neil Young. The late departure was very squarely blamed on the ladies' overdue return from the pub. I was only marginally maudlin about the fate of my day's race selections. Three of them hit the bar, the last of which, I learned as we circumvented Bicester, was chinned in the big handicap of the day. Call The Cops owes me nowt, though.

There was time at Bacchy and Deb's mates for a couple of beers before heading out for some grub. Jules and Mark took us to a restaurant where The Real Wives of Cheshire is filmed. Finally, credibility with my teenage daughters! The jokes were that this part of Cheshire is known as Orange County, such is the demand for spray-tan studios.

Mark informed me that we were in Hale, not Altrincham. One of the richest and most desirable areas in Manchester. Mark had been in advertising. He told me that he didn't know Pickering, my home town, but knew Malton down the road because it had a billboard-sized advertising hoarding on the A64. "I know 'em all mate. I know 'em all." I didn't doubt it. He knew his stuff, talked a million miles an hour and repeated everything. Everything.

Wayne Rooney is an occasional visitor to The Railway for a game of darts. This excellent boozer where we rounded off the evening has a traditional local feel and, rather pleasingly, sits awkwardly with the swish wine bars, double fronted antiques shops and million-pound estate agents down the high street. Refreshing.

Bacchy had been toying with the idea of driving to the track until Mark set him straight. "No, you gotta see the sights on the train up to Aintree. Top entertainment. Top entertainment." The public transport plan sounded convoluted but workable. Either side some studious web-based punting, there was even time for a rather fine bacon and tomato flaky pastry wrap from the superior bakers on Hale High Street. You don't get quality like that in Altrincham.

Mark's scheduling was spot on. We were at Liverpool Central in bags of time. The platform was crammed with eye-popping distractions. Aintree executives had discouraged the press from taking unflattering photos of Ladies Day scenes out of 'respect for all our racegoers'. Snappers have had a field day over the years posting pics of brassy Scouse lasses in skimpy dresses, tottering on mega-heels and engaging in unrestrained behaviour. The racecourse was keen to claw back some integrity and had issued a new style guide based on the Coco Chanel maxim, 'Dress shabbily and they remember the dress; dress impeccably and they remember the woman'. Coco was a fan of the races, apparently.

Up at the track, the sights and sounds were even more diverting. We nearly got derailed before the turnstiles by a stream of women alighting a coach each wearing golden sashes identifying them as Cheryl's Hen Party. I flinched at the rasping cry at my left ear: "Mam! Have ya gorra drink, yeah?"

The Radio Mersey stand was belting out some furious dance beats and the DJ was giving away free flip-flops from giant piles in front of the speakers. "Ladies. Never mind those heels. Try our flip flops! Come to the races and save your souls!" That's what I call a pitch.

We hooked up with Mark's crowd in the KFC. They'd got a minibus up from Lancaster that morning and had already made a steady start on the ale. This was an annual fixture for Mark's squad and we left them in their usual berth by the two-furlong pole to recce the track for ourselves.

Navigating the Cheltenham Festival logistics is all well and good with 15-odd years' experience to draw on, but Aintree was a whole other ball game. Finding somewhere to watch the racing and grab a pint was a challenge.

40,000 punters were squeezed in to a strip from the turn after the winning post back passed Mark's gang to temporary stands way up by the three-furlong pin. Three new grandstands clustered around the bend. We gazed enviously up to galleried lounges filled with smart-suited types taking in great views through floor-to-ceiling windows over the parade ring.

Checking out the runners for the first, we overheard a Burberry-clad Southerner mutter, "It's not like Cheltenham is it?" Spot on. Though everything we saw was honest, good natured and well meant. Loud, yes. In yer face, yes. But as far as lairy behaviour goes, nothing tops my only experience of Royal Ascot one hot Summer before the redevelopment, where the scenes were a lot more like Geordie Shore meets Ex On The Beach than Made In Chelsea. Binky wouldn't have known where to look.

As the races unfolded, we found the best place to stand was at the top of the concrete embankment about half a furlong out, next to the parties and picnickers who hadn't seen a horse in the flesh all afternoon.

My only winner of the day was a good one: Malcolm Jefferson's Cyrus Darius pulled well away in the Top Novice Hurdle. Quite how strong a renewal this was is open to question with the unconvincing Vago Collonges back in 2nd. But Cyrus will be chasing next year and went straight on my list.

I had half an eye on the 12-to-follow all day and when Saphir Du Rheu won the novice chase in commanding style, I was back in front and feeling confident.

The showpiece of the day was a competitive looking Melling Chase with a host of multiple Grade 1 winners stacking the card. Don Cossack made a mockery of all that with some big jumping and ran away from the toiling pack. Both my fancies fell. Sire De Grugy had not been the same horse all season and came to grief at the ditch. Balder Succes, tragically, had to be put down the following day, unable to recover from the damage in his shoulder sustained in his tumble. Steve Ayres, the horse's lad was distraught. "I really do feel I've lost my best friend", he said after he shared his grief on Twitter. Desperate stuff.

That might have put my 12-to-follow grief in to a more sober context, had I known. As it was, Don Cossack's impressive win had put Bryn in charge. The game was up. Both selections I'd made for the two bonus races that day had been declared non- runners. Pesky Whitstable Wi-Fi. The consumption of a foot long, luke warm, gritty hot dog with watery onions in a dissolving bread roll did nothing to lift my mood.

On the other hand, watching the Topham Chase from in front of The Chair was a proper thrill. Its reputation as the most spectacular obstacle on the course meant that there were cameras and booms of every description lodged in precarious positions, all aiming to capture the drama. The rail was packed too. The lads next to us in three-piece suits and slicked haircuts were rehearsing a barrage of Aston Villa-taunting songs in advance of their clash with Liverpool in the FA Cup semi the following week: "They're here. They're there. They're every fuckin' where. Empty seats! Empty seats!" Villa fans had the last laugh in that particular encounter, though.

Sam Whaley-Cohen steered Rajdhani Express to a victory that meant he became the winning-most jockey over the National fences. Not bad for an erudite amateur.

Bacchy was still winless. We both fancied Alpha Des Obeaux in the Sefton Novices Hurdle, and headed back to Mark's pavilion to watch it. Turned out a couple of the other lads had fancied the big price about this Irish raider too. He was running a stonking race when headed by Thistlecrack coming to the last.

Dickie Johnson aboard Alpha had galvanised his charge, as he so often does, and fired the horse into the final hurdle. And also as he so often does, he couldn't get the horse back up again. When Alpha hit the deck in a heap, the air instantly turned blue with murderous expletives directed Johnson's way. The horse was probably beaten, but our well-practised glower over pints of Crabbies (…yes, it had come to alcoholic ginger beer by then…) told you we would have liked to see him try.

Barter Hill won the bumper well for small-time trainer Ben Pauling. Bellshill rolled up in second, I'm pleased to say. A steaming Dubliner in a pub toilet in Cheltenham had tipped him to Si and me and I'd let him go off unbacked here.

At that point I made a hasty retreat to catch my connection home via Chester. Bacchy and Debs were spending another night on Merseyside and coming back the next day. Passing the Radio Mersey stand, I noted the piles of flip-flops had been decimated. Nearly every woman near me was wearing a pair, saving their souls, and taking their heels home slung around the straps of tiny handbags.

The schedule was fairly tight but I made my transfer with a few minutes to spare. "On the Chester train. Cheers for organising a top day", I texted Bacchy. His reply a few hours later suggested he had just crawled out of the pavilion after a few more sherberts with the Lancaster boys and was heading for a night in town.

He posted a photo on facebook of the wreckage, captioned "Still life - Ladies Day: broken heels, bookies pens and drinks." Before the ink on the post was dry, an animal lib friend of mine commented "and dead horses." I unfriended her immediately. No need for that misdirected abuse.

35. THE WRAP

*So the great ship Racing continues to scrabble sideways like a
disoriented crab.
It remains underfinanced and misdirected.
Unless someone grabs the tiller with a firm hand,
the great ship looks to be heading for the rocks.*
Julian Wilson, writer and broadcaster in 'Back to Basics', 1994

Julian Wilson was the face of establishment, old school racing
broadcasting for over 30 years at the BBC. In this book, I've
admittedly given over one or two tart paragraphs to air concerns,
criticisms and a couple of condemnations about racing and sport
more generally. Wilson, though, puts me firmly in the shade.
Everything I've read about this acerbic character merely emphasises
his reactionary, traditionalist and elitist views. He campaigned
vigorously against Sunday racing, detested the all-weather variant
and lamented the "incessant battery of commercial opportunists" in
the game.

He held a long-term grudge against Sir Peter O'Sullevan. Barely
credible, is it? Wilson had turned down the vacant mic job at rival
ITV because he supposed that the more prestigious BBC role was
destined to be his. He believed O'Sullevan had said he would retire
in 1983. In fact O'Sullevan had been talking of retiring from
journalism, not commentating.

Wilson's spleen-venting about pandering to fashion and populist
culture in the Beeb's coverage of Royal Ascot eventually led to his
resignation in 1997. Clare Balding took over the position full time.
The old curmudgeon didn't get on with her either. "She was
beginning to get on my nerves" he remarked.

So why begin this concluding chapter with one of his frontal assaults
on racing? Because, whilst the old bastard was right to air his
grievances, he was wrong about the inevitable downward spiral of
the game. His comments serve to illustrate that racing has been here

before. Racing will endure. There will be changes – some unpalatable, and some choppy waters ahead for the 'great ship Racing'. I am certain that the sport will sustain and thrive. That doesn't mean there are not legitimate reasons to be concerned.

My heart lies with the jumps game. Deeper still, it beats with a loyal passion for the northern tracks where I cut my teeth as a nipper. That heart bleeds dry to see the state of jumps racing back home right now.

But I'm an optimist. The soon-to-be-completed BHA Comprehensive Review of Jump Racing can't deliver solutions soon enough. The review got underway in April 2015 and has a remit to "assess the health of the sport, identify challenges and deliver recommendations to safeguard the future of the code and deliver growth." No small task then. The BHA comes in for a fair amount of stick in an average season, but I applaud the review, or at least aspects of it.

The jumps race programme, prize money and field sizes have long been a problem. The dominance of Cheltenham and its impact on the rest of the season is part of this. It is a structural issue that a bit of extra prize money won't be enough to fix. Though increasing it would help. The panel will also have a particular focus on grass roots and the middle tiers of racing. To my ears that last element includes the declining racing centres and ownership patterns in the north.

The recently constituted Horseracing Bettors Forum may also provide a valuable channel to feed the concerns of punters directly in to the BHA. Bookie bashing, of course, is a popular pastime amongst any punters worth their salt.

A cause that has gained real traction over the last decade is the practice of bookies closing or limiting the accounts of profitable punters. I touched on this in the chapter about the end of Bacchy's pro-punting experiment. This will be something for the new Forum to really sink its teeth into. If it has any.

Whilst it is unlikely that my low-level staking is ever likely to attract the interest of Victor Chandler's accountant-hatchet men (though if it did that would indeed prove the complete regression of the industry to narrow-minded risk-free bookkeeping), I loved the intervention made by former First Minister of Scotland and well-known punter Alex Salmond. He said, "It is not acceptable for bookmakers to refuse to take a reasonable-sized bet because the client has a record of winning.

"There is a difference between bookmaking, an entirely respectable profession, and fleecing people, which isn't. Maybe it is time that the distinction was made harder in terms of the law. An unreasonable refusal to accept bets should, in my estimation, be a reason for disqualification from a bookmaker's licence."

And now the big mergers: Coral/Ladbrokes and Paddy Power/Betfair. The landscape looks to be shifting again, together with protracted discussions about the bookies 'levy' and the strategic funding of the game. Julian Wilson would have found plenty to occupy his sharpened nib.

Perhaps I'm most concerned that racing too often takes its collective eye off the animal welfare ball. With a steadily gathering voice, those who are opposed to horse racing on the grounds of alleged cruelty present the biggest threat. There is a lot of ignorance and distrust amongst the wider public about how animals within the sport are treated. Racing can do more to regulate, demonstrate, innovate, argue and publicize than is currently the case to pre-empt criticism rather than react to it.

I am only a fan. An advocate. A punter. And these are my views looking from the outside in. Allied to that, my ability to predict the future is as consistent as my chances of picking the winner of a two horse race. Always backing the outsider. In the final pages of Mug Punting, wrapped up in the heady summer of 2005, I was forecasting more horse ownership for me and a professional punting career for Bacchy. If that had come to pass, maybe I would have been on the inside looking out.

I'll settle for being a fan, though. Here at the end of book two, not so very much has changed. Maybe I can detect the emergence of reflection and attitude elbowing their way in to these pages, wedged in amongst the irreverence and cheek like a mature student at the Union bar. Worrying signs of grumpy bastardness and wistful sentimentality that only Victor Meldrew could whole-heartedly endorse. Life happens, I suppose.

Most of the themes explored in those earlier recollections have continued to unfold along a similar trajectory. Whilst Bacchy, the only serious punter amongst us, didn't make the transition to sustainable pro-gambling, the mug punting gang has happily carried on drinking and losing sportingly. And occasionally winning gloriously. That still matters.

It's true, we meet up less often these days. Fatherhood, responsibility and divergent career paths have all had their various impacts. The cast has changed a lot along the way. But there are some new, younger faces to keep the rest on our toes. Some of us are slowing down and it takes longer to recuperate from the excesses these days, of whatever nature.

However, the much abused roller coaster analogy remains intact. The top speed may be down, maintenance levels up and the gradients flatter. But we are all still clinging on for the ride. Here's to the next decade.

16397569R00150

Printed in Great Britain
by Amazon